# ARTIFICIAL
# NEURAL SYSTEMS

# NEURAL NETWORKS: Research and Applications

## SERIES EDITORS

**Shun-ichi Amari,** University of Tokyo

**James Anderson,** Brown University

**Gail A. Carpenter,** Center for Adaptive Systems, Boston University

**Rolf Eckmiller,** University of Düsseldorf, FRG

**Stephen Grossberg,** Center for Adaptive Systems, Boston University

**Eric Schwartz,** New York University

**Allen S. Selverston,** University of California, San Diego

**Bernard Soffer,** Hughes Research Labs, Malibu, CA

## Pergamon Title of Related Interest

**Grossberg/Kuperstein** NEURAL DYNAMICS OF ADAPTIVE
SENSORY-MOTOR CONTROL, Expanded Edition

## Pergamon Journal of Related Interest
**(Free sample copies available upon request)**

NEURAL NETWORKS

# ARTIFICIAL
# NEURAL SYSTEMS
## Foundations, Paradigms, Applications, and Implementations

**Patrick K. Simpson**

General Dynamics Electronics Division,
San Diego

**PERGAMON PRESS**
Member of Maxwell Macmillan Pergamon Publishing Corporation
New York • Oxford • Beijing • Frankfurt • São Paulo • Sydney • Tokyo • Toronto

Pergamon Press Offices:

**U.S.A.** Pergamon Press, Inc., Maxwell House, Fairview Park, Elmsford, New York 10523, U.S.A.

**U.K.** Pergamon Press plc, Headington Hill Hall, Oxford OX3 0BW, England

**PEOPLE'S REPUBLIC OF CHINA** Pergamon Press, Room 4037, Qianmen Hotel, Beijing, People's Republic of China

**FEDERAL REPUBLIC OF GERMANY** Pergamon Press GmbH, Hammerweg 6, D-6242 Kronberg, Federal Republic of Germany

**BRAZIL** Pergamon Editora Ltda, Rua Eça de Queiros, 346, CEP 04011, Paraiso, São Paulo, Brazil

**AUSTRALIA** Pergamon Press Australia Pty Ltd., P.O. Box 544, Potts Point, NSW 2011, Australia

**JAPAN** Pergamon Press, 8th Floor, Matsuoka Central Building, 1-7-1 Nishishinjuku, Shinjuku-ku, Tokyo 160, Japan

**CANADA** Pergamon Press Canada Ltd., Suite 271, 253 College Street, Toronto, Ontario M5T 1R5, Canada

First edition 1990

**Library of Congress Cataloging in Publication Data**

Simpson, Patrick K.
    Artificial neural systems : foundations, paradigms, applications, and implementations / Patrick K. Simpson.
        p.   cm. -- (Neural networks, research and applications)
    Bibliography: p.
    Includes index.
    ISBN 0-08-037895-1 -- ISBN 0-08-037894-3 (pbk.)
    1. Artificial intelligence. 2. Neural computers. I. Title.
    II. Series.
    Q335.S545   1989
    006.3--dc20                                             89-33899
                                                              CIP

*Printed in the United States of America*

⊚™

The paper used in this publication meets the minimum requirements of American National Standard for Information Sciences -- Permanence of Paper for Printed Library Materials, ANSI Z39.48-1984

# Dedication

To Christalyn and
my parents, Ken and Verna

# Contents

# Preface

I was attending the University of California at San Diego (1983–1986) when I first became involved with artificial neural systems. My first exposure was a very frightening and frustrating experience. There was math on almost every page of every paper I found on the subject and every paper seemed to introduce a completely new set of terminology. What I really wanted, but could not find, was a book that described the fundamentals of artificial neural systems and outlined most of the primary paradigms. Quickly I discovered that no such text existed. In lieu of this deficit, I worked through several mathematical texts on topics that included differential equations, linear algebra, dynamical systems theory, probability and estimation theory, and calculus. Also, during this time, I read everything I could get my hands on that even remotely dealt with artificial neural systems.

Eventually these early efforts led to a technical document entitled, "A Survey of Artificial Neural Systems." I was working at Naval Ocean Systems Center (NOSC) at the time (1986–1987). NOSC was interested in learning more about artificial neural systems; so the group I was working for (Code 441) supported my efforts and allowed me to write a technical document on the subject.

The technical document was advertised on the ARPA-net's Neuron Digest and several hundred copies were distributed. One of these copies was read by Prof. Bourne at Vanderbilt University. Prof. Bourne liked the paper and invited me to expand it into a critical review for a new journal that he and Prof. Sztipanovits were editing for CRC Press entitled, *CRC Critical Reviews in Artificial Intelligence*. I eagerly accepted the professors' invitation and began to expand the NOSC technical document. Nine months and 270 pages later I had finished a two-part paper entitled, "A Review of Artificial Neural Systems." After the submission to CRC Press, I distributed copies of the paper at a conference and to other interested parties via the mail. One of these copies was sent to Prof. Gail Carpenter.

On the last day of August, 1988, I received a letter from CRC Press explaining that the journal was cancelled. Almost miraculously, during the same time period, Prof. Gail Carpenter contacted me and explained that she was one of the editors for Pergamon Press' *Neural Networks: Research and Applications* book series, and asked me if I would submit a prospectus. Of course I did, and the rest of the story is now self-evident.

The intention of this book is two-fold: (1) to provide the reader with a rapid introduction to the concepts and terminology of artificial neural systems, and (2) to provide a valuable reference guide to most of the primary artificial neural systems and the associated analyses, applications and implementations. In essence, I wrote the book I would have liked to have written when I started out in this field.

I have made a very diligent effort to give credit to the originator(s) of each paradigm. I have also tried to present the simplest form of each artificial neural system and provide references to the literature where the more complex versions can be found.

P.K.S.
San Diego, CA
April 30, 1989

# Acknowledgments

There are many that have helped me to write this book in many different ways. I would like to thank General Dynamics Electronics Division for the use of their equipment and facilities to produce this book. I would like to thank J. Harold McBeth for his unwaivering support and his exceptional advice. I would like to thank Bruce Edson, Russell Deich, Richard McDuff, Karen Haines, and Stephen Luse for many hours of delightful and stimulating discussion. I would like to thank Steve Biafore for his able assistance in preparing the cover art. I would like to thank Prof. Bart Kosko for his invaluable advice, his unparalleled tutelage, and his supporting comments during all phases of this book's development. I would like to thank Prof. Gail Carpenter, my editor, for suggesting this book to Pergamon and working hard to see that it got equitable consideration. I would like to thank my son, Zachary, for helping me to unwind in those moments when the book was weighing heavily upon my mind. Most importantly, I would like to thank my wife, Christalyn, whose support, love, patience and advice truly made this book possible.

# CHAPTER 1

# Introduction

It has been a goal of science and engineering to develop intelligent machines for many decades. These machines were envisioned to perform all cumbersome and tedious tasks so that we might enjoy a more fruitful and enriched life. The technologies that have emerged to meet this challenge include cybernetics (Ashby, 1957; Weiner, 1948), machine learning (Nilsson, 1965), automata (Shannon & McCarthy, 1956; Tsetlin, 1973), bionics (WADD, 1960; Gawronski, 1971), mathematical biophysics (Rashevsky, 1948), general systems theory (Bertalanffy, 1968), self-organizing systems (Yovitz & Cameron, 1960; Yovitz, Jacobi & Goldstein, 1962), artificial intelligence (Minksy, 1961; Barr & Feigenbaum, 1981), cognitive science (Rumelhart & McClelland, 1986), and artificial neural systems.

Artificial neural systems (ANSs) are mathematical models of theorized mind and brain activity. ANSs are also referred to as neural networks, connectionism, adaptive systems, adaptive networks, artificial neural networks, neurocomputers, and parallel distribution processors. ANSs exploit the massively parallel local processing and distributed representation properties that are believed to exist in the brain. The primary intent of ANSs is to explore and reproduce human information processing tasks such as speech, vision, olfaction, touch, knowledge processing and motor-control. In addition, ANSs are used for data compression, near-optimal solutions to combinatorial optimization problems, pattern matching, system modeling, and function approximation.

The attempt to mechanize human information processing tasks highlights the classic comparison between the information processing capabilities of the human and the computer. The computer can multiply huge numbers at blinding speed, yet it cannot understand unconstrained speaker-independent speech. Human abilities complement those of the computer in that we can understand speech (even when heavily slurred in an extremely noisy environment), yet lack the ability to compute the square root of a prime number without the aide of pencil and paper—or a computer. The differences between the two can be traced to the processing methods each employs. Conventional computers rely on algorithm-based programs that operate serially, are controlled by a complex central processing unit, and store information at addressed locations in memory. The brain relies on highly distributed representations and transformations that operate in parallel, have distributed control through billions of highly interconnected neurons—or processing elements (PEs)—and appear to store their information in variable strength connections called synapses.

ANS theory is derived from many disciplines, including psychology, mathematics, neuroscience, physics, engineering, computer science, philosophy, biology, and linguistics. It is evident from this diverse listing that ANS technology represents a "universalization" among the sciences working toward a common goal—building intelligent systems. It is equally evident from the listing that an accurate and complete description of the work in all the listed disciplines is an impossible task. In light of this, we will focus upon ANS paradigms that have applications, application potential, or infrastructural significance. Hence, this book will not fully discuss the significant work in biology (Kandel, 1979; Kandel & Schwartz, 1985), philosophy (Churchland, 1986), linguistics (Arbib & Caplan, 1979), or psychology (Grossberg, 1982a; Rumelhart & McClelland, 1986).

This book contains an explanation of the relationship between real neural systems and artificial neural systems, an overview of the foundational concepts, constructs, and termi-

1

nology used to describe ANS models, descriptions of 27 ANS paradigms organized into a coherent taxonomy, and a brief history of the field from the early 1900's to the present. Each ANS paradigm includes a mathematical, and sometimes an algorithmic, characterization; a discussion of its strengths and limitations; and a brief description of its current and potential applications and implementations.

The goal of this book is to provide an overview of ANS technology and several of its key paradigms. We have reserved judgment and opinion concerning each model's overall comparative worth, choosing instead to focus upon its mathematical and algorithmic principles, its applications, and its implementations.

We would be remiss not to mention previous surveys of this field. Each review varies in its emphasis and completeness. The list includes Arbib (1964, 1972), Barto (1984), Grossberg (1988a), Feldman & Ballard (1982), Levine (1983), Lippman (1987), Miller (1987), and Rumelhart & McClelland (1986).

# CHAPTER 2

# Comparing Real and Artificial Neural Systems

## 2.1. SIMPLIFIED NEURON

The human information processing system consists of the biological brain. The basic building block of the nervous system is the neuron, the cell that communicates information to and from the various parts of the body. Figure 2-1 shows a simplified representation of a neuron. The neuron consists of a cell body called a soma, several spine-like extensions of the cell body called dendrites, and a single nerve fiber called the axon that branches out from the soma and connects to many other neurons. Inside and around the soma are ions including sodium ($Na^+$), calcium ($Ca^{++}$), potassium ($K^+$), and chloride ($Cl^-$). The $K^+$ concentrates inside the neuron and the $Na^+$ concentrates outside. When the soma's membrane is electrically stimulated—usually by a voltage drop—its membrane allows the $Na^+$ and other ions such as $Ca^{++}$ to pass across its membrane and change the soma's internal state. The connections between neurons occur either on the cell body or on the dendrites at junctions called synapses. A helpful analogy is to view the axons and dendrites as insulated conductors of various impedance that transmit electrical signals to the neuron (Arbib, 1964; Churchland, 1986; Kandel & Schwartz, 1985; Lindsay & Norman, 1977). The nervous system is constructed of billions of neurons with the axon from one neuron branching out and connecting to as many as 10,000 other neurons. All the neurons—interconnected by axons and dendrites that carry signals regulated by synapses—create a neural network.

The model neuron in its simplest form, shown in Figure 2-2, can be considered a threshold unit—a processing element that collects inputs and produces an output only if the sum of the input exceeds an internal threshold value. As a threshold unit, the neuron collects signals at its synapses and adds them together. If the collected signal strength is great enough to exceed the threshold, a signal is sent down the axon which abuts other neurons and dendrites. The soma adds all the signals, gated by the synapses from the impinging dendrites. The total signal is then compared to an internal threshold value of the neuron, and propagates a signal to the axon if the threshold is exceeded. Artificial neural systems are created by interconnecting many of these simple "neurons" into a network.

## 2.2. FORMAL ARTIFICIAL NEURAL SYSTEM DEFINITION

ANSs are neurally inspired models of brain and behavior (Arbib, 1964; Grossberg, 1982a & 1986a). Hecht-Nielsen (1988b) offers the following as a general, yet rigorous, definition of an artificial neural system:

> A neural network [ANS] is a parallel, distributed information processing structure consisting of processing elements (which can possess a local memory and carry out localized information processing operations) interconnected together with unidirectional signal channels called connections. Each processing element has a single output connection which branches ("fans out") into as many collateral connections as desired (each carrying the same signal—the processing element output signal). The processing element output signal can be of any mathematical type desired. All of the processing that goes on within each processing element must be completely local; i.e., it must depend only upon the current

3

values of the input signal arriving at the processing element via impinging connections and upon values stored in the processing element's local memory.

A simpler, but less rigorous, definition of an ANS is a nonlinear directed graph with weighted edges that is able to store patterns by changing the edge weights and is able to recall patterns from incomplete and unknown inputs (Simpson, 1987). The key elements of most ANS descriptions are the distributed representation, the local operations, and nonlinear processing. These attributes emphasize two of the primary applications of ANSs — *situations where only a few decisions are required from a massive amount of data* and *situations where a complex nonlinear mapping must be learned.*

It becomes obvious from these definitions that mathematics is the backbone of ANS theory, an idea perhaps best expressed by Arbib (1964, p. ii) in the following passage:

> We apply mathematics to derive far-reaching conclusions from clearly stated premises. We can test the adequacy of a model of the brain by expressing it in mathematical form and using our mathematical tools to prove general theorems. In the light of any discrepancies we find between these theorems and experiments, we may return to our premises and reformulate them, thus gaining a deeper understanding of the workings of the brain. Further, such theories can guide us in building more useful and sophisticated machines.

The mathematics most often used in ANS technology includes differential equations, dynamical systems, linear algebra, probability and statistics. Two excellent sources that cover the majority of these areas are texts by Hirsch & Smale (1974) and Papoulis (1965).

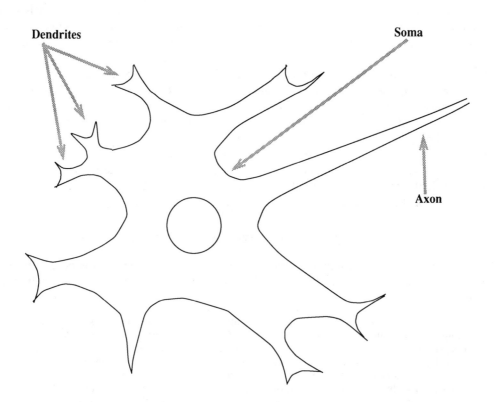

FIGURE 2-1. Simplified representation of a neuron. The neuron has a cell body with a nucleus, called the soma, an axon that carries the signal away from the neuron, and dendrites that receive the signal from other neurons.

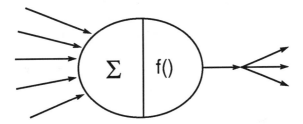

FIGURE 2-2. A neuron as a simple threshold unit. The incoming lines represent dendrites. Each line carries a signal that is added, $\Sigma$, together. After the addition, the signal is processed through a threshold function f(), which produces the output signal.

## 2.3. BRAIN VERSUS COMPUTER PROCESSING

Neural models are based on how the brain might process information. In reference to human information processing problems, the processes performed in the mind and in a conventional digital computer will now be compared to gain an understanding of why the mind is so adaptive and resilient and the computer is so rigid and precise. The reasons for using ANS models to solve human information processing and constraint optimization problems are highlighted by discussing these restrictions and assumptions of brain-style processing.

### 2.3.1. Processing Speed

Cycle time is the time taken to process a single piece of information from input to output. The cycle time of the most advanced computers, corresponding to processing one step of a program in the CPU during one clock cycle, occurs in the nanosecond range ($\sim$4.2 nanoseconds for a Cray 3). The cycle time for a neuron in the brain, corresponding to a neuronal event prompted by an external stimulus, occurs in the millisecond range (Cottrell & Small, 1984; Crick, 1979). The difference in speed is $10^6$—the computer processes an element of information as much as a million times faster.

### 2.3.2. Processing Order

If the most advanced computers are able to process information one million times faster than the brain, why is the brain so superior for human information processing problems? The difference between the two can be traced to the processing order. The brain processes information in parallel and the computer processes information serially. Feldman (1985) has extended a constraint from this distinction called the 100-step program: "If the mind reacts in approximately half a second (500 milliseconds) to a given stimulus (i.e. answering a true-false question or naming a picture) and the cycle time of a neuron averages five milliseconds, then in 100 cycle times of a neuron a decision is reached." If we use the computer analogy that one step of a program is processed for each time cycle, then the brain runs parallel programs that are only 100 steps long. In contrast to large software programs operating in serial on conventional computers, the brain operates with massively parallel programs that have comparatively few steps, possibly explaining why the brain is superior at human information processing problems despite being as many as 6 orders of magnitude slower.

### 2.3.3. Abundance and Complexity

There are a massive number of neurons operating in parallel in the brain at any given moment. The number is estimated to be between $10^{11}$ and $10^{14}$, each with between $10^3$ and $10^4$ abutting connections per neuron. If we consider the brain to be the ultimate ANS model, it appears that interesting applications will require a large number of processing elements (neurons). In addition to the number of neurons, studies have also found that the neuron is not a simple threshold unit, rather it is a complex computing device (Grossberg, 1982a & 1986a). Analysis has shown (Levy, 1982) that all the computing does not take place solely inside the soma; computations also occur outside the neuron body in the dendrites and at the synapses.

### 2.3.4. Knowledge Storage

Another distinction between the computer and the brain is knowledge storage. In the computer, a static copy of the knowledge being stored is placed in an addressed memory location. New information destroys old information. In contrast, because the number of connections between neurons in the brain is relatively fixed and very few new pathways are formed in the adult brain (Crick, 1979), information in the brain is thought to be stored in the interconnections between neurons (Grossberg, 1982a & 1986a). Moreover, it is felt that new information is added to the brain (i.e learned) by adjusting the interconnection strengths — the synaptic efficacy — between neurons. This adaptation premise provides a possible explanation for the brain's ability to generalize. In summary, knowledge in the brain is adaptable, while knowledge in the computer is strictly replaceable.

### 2.3.5. Fault Tolerance

The brain exhibits fault-tolerant characteristics. Damage (faults) to individual neurons can occur in the brain without a severe degradation of its overall performance (Hopfield, 1982; Hopfield, Feinstein, & Palmer, 1983; Hopfield, 1984; Lindsay & Norman, 1977). This graceful degradation is called fault-tolerance. Fault-tolerance supports the theory that the brain carries a distributed representation of the world and each concept or idea is not held in only one neuron, but rather spread across many neurons and their interconnections. If a portion of the brain is removed, the knowledge of the concept or idea is still retained through the redundant, distributed encoding of information. In contrast, most conventional computers are not fault-tolerant, instead they are fault-intolerant. Removing any processing component of a conventional computer leads to an ineffective machine, and the corruption of a conventional computer's memory is irretrievable and leads to failure as well.

### 2.3.6. Processing Control

The brain does not have any specific area with dictatorial control, rather the brain is an anarchic system (Crick, 1979; Feldman & Ballard, 1982; Feldman, 1985; Hecht-Nielsen, 1982 & 1983). There is no homunculus in the brain that monitors each neuron's activity. Each neuron's output is a sum of its synapse's activations thresholded by its signal functions; therefore, each neuron's output is a function of only its locally available information. Local information means each neuron only has access to the information contained in those neurons (or other neural processes) it is directly interconnected to and no others. In sharp contrast, the control in a conventional computer is completely autocratic. The computer's central processing unit monitors all activities and has access to global information, creating both a processing bottleneck and a critical point for failure.

# CHAPTER 3

# Foundations of Artificial Neural Systems

This chapter will introduce a fundamental nomenclature and the rudimentary mathematical concepts used to describe and analyze ANS processing. In a broad sense, ANSs consist of three elements: (1) an organized topology (geometry) of interconnected processing elements (i.e. a network or a neural system), (2) a method of encoding information, and (3) a method of recalling information. The following sections on processing elements and network topologies provide a description of neural system topologies. The sections on threshold elements and, again, processing elements provide an overview of ANS recall; and the sections on memory and learning will provide some insights concerning ANS encoding.

In addition to the three elemental ANS characteristics of topology, encoding, and recall, there are two other key concepts that play important roles and must be addressed — techniques for analyzing ANS dynamics and general taxonomy of all ANS paradigms that minimizes ambiguity. Each of these subjects will be addressed in separate sections.

## 3.1. PROCESSING ELEMENTS

Processing elements (PEs), also referred to as nodes, short-term memory (STM), neurons, populations, or threshold logic units, are the ANS components where most, if not all, of the computing is done. Figure 3-1 displays the anatomy of a generic PE. The input signals come from either the environment or outputs of other PEs and form an input vector $A = (a_1,\ldots,a_i,\ldots,a_n)$, where $a_i$ is the activity level of the $i th$ PE or input. Associated with each connected pair of PEs is an adjustable value (i.e., a system variable) called a weight (also referred to as a connection strength, interconnect, or long-term memory). The collection of weights that abuts the $j th$ PE, $b_j$, forms a vector $W_j = (w_{1j},\ldots,w_{ij},\ldots,w_{nj})$, where the weight $w_{ij}$ represents the connection strength from the PE $a_i$ to the PE $b_j$. Sometimes there is an additional parameter $\Theta_j$ modulated by the weight $w_{0j}$ that is associated with the inputs. This term is considered to be an internal threshold value that must be exceeded for there to be any PE activation. The weights $W_j$, their associated PE values $A$, and the possible extra parameter $\Theta_j$, are used to compute the output value $b_j$. This computation is typically performed by taking the dot product of $A$ and $W_j$, subtracting the threshold, and passing the result through a threshold function $f()$. (See next section for description of threshold functions.) Mathematically this operation (also shown in Figure 3-1) is defined as

$$b_j = f(A \cdot W_j - w_{0j}\Theta_j) \tag{3-1}$$

or, in point-wise notation, as

$$b_j = f\left(\sum_{i=1}^{n} a_i w_{ij} - w_{0j}\Theta_j\right) \tag{3-2}$$

## 3.2. THRESHOLD FUNCTIONS

Threshold functions, also referred to as activation functions, squashing functions, or signal functions, map a PE's (possibly) infinite domain — the input — to a prespecified range — the

7

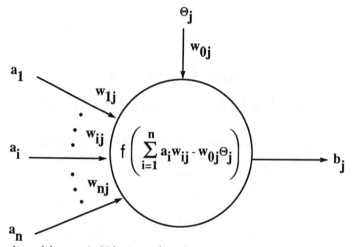

FIGURE 3-1. Topology of the generic PE $b_j$. Inputs form the vector $A = (a_1,\ldots,a_n)$. The threshold is $\Theta_j$. Each input and threshold has a corresponding weight value $w_{ij}$ which represents the connection strength from the $ith$ input $a_i$ to the $jth$ output $b_j$ with the threshold being assigned the weight $w_{0j}$. The collection of the weights forms the n + 1 dimensional vector $W_j = (w_{0j}, w_{1j}, \ldots, w_{nj})$. The output is shown as a function of its inputs, illustrating the local behavior of ANS PEs.

output. Four common threshold functions are the linear, ramp, step, and sigmoid functions. Figure 3-2 shows typical shapes of these functions.

The linear function, shown in Figure 3-2(a), has the equation

$$f(x) = \alpha x \qquad (3\text{-}3)$$

where $\alpha$ is a real-valued constant that regulates the magnification of the PE activity x.

When the linear function is bounded to the range $[-\gamma, +\gamma]$, eq. 3-3 becomes the nonlinear ramp threshold function, shown in Figure 3-2(b) and described by the equation

$$f(x) = \begin{cases} +\gamma & \text{if } x \geq \gamma \\ x & \text{if } |x| < \gamma \\ -\gamma & \text{if } x \leq -\gamma \end{cases} \qquad (3\text{-}4)$$

where $\gamma$ $(-\gamma)$ is the PE's maximum (minimum) output value, a value commonly referred to as the saturation level. Note that although eq. 3-4 is a piece-wise linear function, it is often used to represent a simplified nonlinear operation.

If the threshold function responds only to the sign of the input, emitting $+\gamma$ if the input sum is positive and $-\delta$ if it is not, then the threshold function is called a step threshold function where $\delta$ and $\gamma$ are positive scalars. The step threshold function shown in Figure 3-2(c) is mathematically characterized by the equation

$$f(x) = \begin{cases} +\gamma & \text{if } x > 0 \\ -\delta & \text{otherwise} \end{cases} \qquad (3\text{-}5)$$

Often eq. 3-5 is binary in nature, emitting a 1 if $x > 0$, and 0 otherwise.

The final, and most pervasive, threshold function is the sigmoid threshold function. The sigmoid (S-shaped) function, shown in Figure 3-2(d), is a bounded, monotonic, non-decreasing function that provides a graded, nonlinear response. A common sigmoid function is the logistic function

$$S(x) = (1 + e^{-x})^{-1} \qquad (3\text{-}6)$$

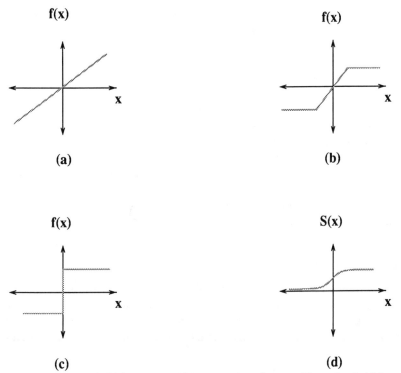

FIGURE 3-2. Four common threshold functions used in processing elements. These threshold functions are: (a) the linear threshold function, (b) the ramp threshold function, (c) the step threshold function, and (d) the sigmoid threshold function. Note that all except (a) are nonlinear functions. See text for a more detailed description.

This function is seen in statistics (as the Gaussian distribution function), chemistry (describing catalytic reactions), and sociology (describing human population growth). The saturation levels of eq. 3-6 are 0 and 1. Two other sigmoid functions are the hyperbolic tangent

$$S(x) = \tanh(x) \qquad (3-7)$$

which has saturation levels at $-1$ and $1$; and the augmented ratio of squares

$$f(x) = \begin{cases} x^2/(1 + x^2) & \text{if } x > 0 \\ 0 & \text{otherwise} \end{cases} \qquad (3-8)$$

which has saturation levels at 0 and 1.

## 3.3. TOPOLOGY CHARACTERISTICS

ANS topologies, or architectures, are formed by organizing PEs into fields (also called slabs or layers) and linking them with weighted interconnections. Characteristics of these topologies include connection types, connection schemes, and field configurations.

### 3.3.1. Connection Types

There are two primary connection types, excitatory and inhibitory. *Excitatory* connections increase a PE's activation and are typically represented by positive signals. *Inhibitory* connections decrease a PE's activation and are typically represented by negative signals. These connections need not be distinguished; rather, a portion of the connections abutting a PE may have negative weights and the remainder have positive weights.

### 3.3.2. Interconnection Schemes

The three primary PE interconnection schemes are intra-field, inter-field, and recurrent connections. *Intra-field* connections, also referred to as intra-layer connections or lateral connections, are connections between PEs in the same layer of PEs. *Inter-field* connections, also referred to as inter-layer connections or field connections, are connections between PEs in different fields. *Recurrent* connections are connections that loop and connect back to the same PE. Interfield connection signals propagate in one of two ways, either feedforward or feedback. *Feedforward* signals only allow information to flow amongst PEs in one direction. *Feedback* signals allow information to flow amongst PEs in either direction and/or recursively. Figure 3-3 offers a pictorial description of these two methods of information recall.

### 3.3.3. Field Configurations

Field (layer) configurations combine fields of PEs, information flow and connection schemes into a coherent architecture. Field configurations include lateral feedback, field feedforward, and field feedback. A field that receives input signals from the environment is called an input field (input layer) and a field that emits signals to the environment is called an output field

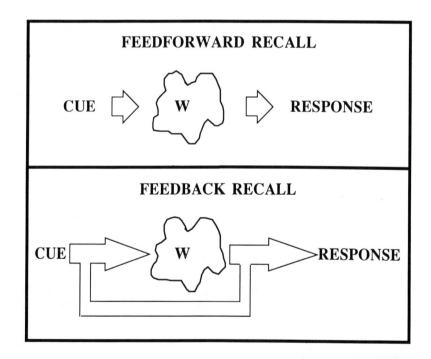

FIGURE 3-3. The difference between feedforward and feedback recall is illustrated. During feedforward recall, the input cue is passed through the memory W and produces an output response in one pass. During feedback recall, the input cue is passed through the memory W and produces an output response that is, in turn, fed back into the memory until the cue and response cease to change.

(output layer). Any fields that lie between the input and output fields are called hidden fields (hidden layers) and have no direct contact with the environment (i.e. input and output PEs).

Figure 3-4 illustrates four common ANS topologies. In each panel of the figure, the arrows denote the direction of information flow. Panel (a) illustrates a one-layer lateral feedback ANS, panel (b) illustrates a two-layer feedforward ANS, panel (c) illustrates a two-layer feedback ANS, and panel (d) illustrates a three-layer feedforward ANS.

An equivalent topology to the one-layer lateral feedback topology shown in panel (a) of Figure 3-4 is the crossbar ANS topology shown in Figure 3-5. A crossbar ANS is a matrix of crossing wires with adaptable connections at each crossing. The crossbar representation is convenient for transitioning ANSs into hardware. This transition is performed by replacing the adaptable connections with resistors and placing amplifiers (shown as triangles in Figure 3-5) at the outputs of each line (PE) prior to feedback (Steinbuch & Piske, 1961; Hopfield, 1984; Hopfield & Tank, 1986).

## 3.4. MEMORY

### 3.4.1. Pattern Types

ANSs store two types of patterns: spatial patterns and spatiotemporal patterns. A *spatial* pattern is a single static image. A *spatiotemporal* (space-time) pattern is a sequence of spatial patterns. A convenient analogy is to consider a spatial pattern as a frame of a movie (i.e. a picture), and a spatiotemporal pattern as the entire movie. Many of the ANS paradigms described here are spatial pattern matchers or spatial pattern classifiers.

### 3.4.2. Memory Types

There are three different types of spatial pattern matching memories: random access memory, content-addressable memory, and associative memory. Random access memory (RAM) is the type of memory found in conventional computers and it maps addresses to data. Content addressable memory (CAM) is found in some computers and signal processing equipment and it maps data to addresses. An associative memory maps data to data. ANSs act as content-addressable and associative memories. When an ANS is acting as a CAM, it stores data at stable states in some memory matrix W. When an ANS is acting as an associative memory, it provides output responses from input stimuli.

### 3.4.3. Mapping Mechanisms

There are two primary ANS mapping mechanisms: autoassociative and heteroassociative mappings. An ANS is *autoassociative* if its memory, W, stores the vectors (patterns) $A_1$, ..., $A_m$. An ANS is *heteroassociative* if W stores the pattern pairs $(A_1,B_1)$, ..., $(A_m,B_m)$.

## 3.5. RECALL

Assume that the pattern pairs $(A_k,B_k)$, k = 1, 2, ..., m, have been stored in W. A hetero-associative recall mechanism is a function g() that takes W (memory) and $A_k$ (stimuli) as input, and returns $B_k$ (response) as output. This relationship is illustrated by the equation

$$B = g(A_k,W) \tag{3-9}$$

Using this notation, we can define the two primary ANS recall mechanisms: nearest-neighbor recall and interpolative recall. *Nearest-neighbor* recall finds the stored input that most closely

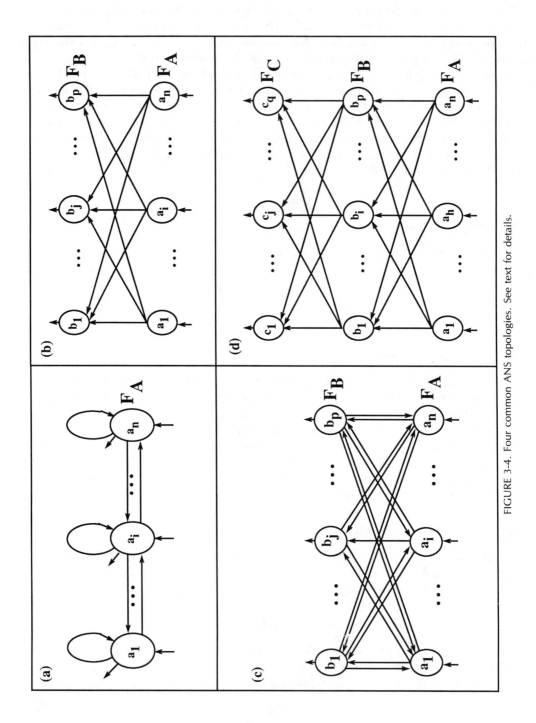

FIGURE 3-4. Four common ANS topologies. See text for details.

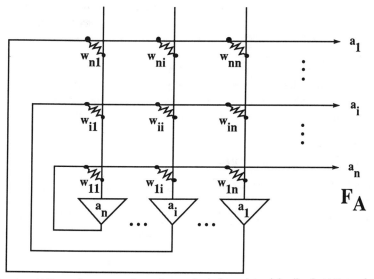

FIGURE 3-5. Crossbar ANS topology—an alternative to single layer lateral feedback ANS topology. See text for details.

matches the stimulus and responds with the corresponding output. This operation can be conveniently illustrated by the equation

$$B_k = g(A',W) \tag{3-10}$$

where

$$\text{dist}(A',A_k) = \underset{q=1}{\overset{m}{\text{MIN}}}\{\text{dist}(A',A_q)\} \tag{3-11}$$

where dist( ) is typically the Hamming or Euclidian distance function. *Interpolative* recall accepts a stimulus and interpolates (in a possibly nonlinear fashion) from the entire set of stored inputs to produce the corresponding output. Assuming that the interpolation is linear, this operation can be illustrated by the equation

$$B' = g(A',W) \tag{3-12}$$

where $A_p \le A' \le A_q$ and $B_p \le B' \le B_q$ for some pattern pairs $(A_p,B_p)$ and $(A_q,B_q)$.

## 3.6. LEARNING

Learning is defined to be in any change in the memory W, defined mathematically as

$$\text{Learning} \equiv dW/dt \ne 0 \tag{3-13}$$

All learning methods can be classified into two categories, supervised learning and unsupervised learning, although aspects of each may co-exist in a given architecture. *Supervised learning* is a process that incorporates an external teacher and/or global information. Supervised learning techniques include: deciding when to turn off the learning, deciding how long and how often to present each association for training, and supplying performance error information. Supervised learning is further classified into two subcategories: structural learning and temporal learning. *Structural learning* encodes the proper autoassociative or heteroassociative mapping into W. *Temporal learning* encodes a sequence of patterns necessary to achieve some final outcome (e.g. the correct sequence of moves necessary to win a chess game) into W. Examples of supervised learning algorithms are error-correction learning, reinforcement learning, stochastic learning, and hardwired systems. *Unsupervised learning,* also referred to as self-organization, is a process that incorporates no external teacher and relies upon only local information and internal control. Unsupervised learning self-organizes presented data and discovers its emergent collective properties. Although they are not learning systems, randomly connected ANSs have also received much attention. Each learning algorithm discussed above is detailed in the following sections.

## 3.6.1. Error-Correction Learning

*Error-correction learning* is a supervised learning procedure that adjusts the connection weights between PEs in proportion to the difference between the desired and computed values of each PE in the output layer. If the desired value of the *jth* output layer PE is $c_j$ and the computed value of the same PE is $b_j$, then a general equation for changing the connection strength $w_{ij}$ is

$$\Delta w_{ij} = \alpha a_i[c_j - b_j] \tag{3-14}$$

where $w_{ij}$ is the memory connection strength from $a_i$ to $b_j$, and $\alpha$ is the learning rate, typically $0 < \alpha \ll 1$. A problem that once plagued error-correction learning ANSs was their inability to extend learning beyond a two-layer ANS. Specifically, the amount of error each hidden layer PE should be credited for the output PEs' errors was not defined. Fortunately this problem, known as the credit assignment problem (Barto, 1984; Minsky, 1961), has been solved (see, for example, backpropagation—section 5.4.3.—and the Boltzmann machine—section 5.4.4.).

## 3.6.2. Reinforcement Learning

*Reinforcement learning* is similar to error-correction learning in that weights are reinforced for properly performed actions and punished for poorly performed actions. The difference is that error-correction learning requires an error value for each output layer PE—a vector of error values—and reinforcement learning requires only one value to describe the output layer's performance—a scalar error value (Widrow, Gupta & Maitra, 1973; Williams, 1986). A general reinforcement learning equation (Williams, 1987) is

$$\Delta w_{ij} = \alpha[r - \Theta_j]e_{ij} \tag{3-15}$$

where r is the scalar success/failure value provided by the environment, $\Theta_j$ is the reinforcement threshold value for the *jth* output PE, $e_{ij}$ is the canonical eligibility of the weight from the *ith* PE to the *jth* PE, and $\alpha$ is a constant ($0 < \alpha < 1$) that regulates the learning rate. Canonical eligibility between the *ith* and the *jth* PEs is dependent on a previously selected probability distribution that is used to determine if the computed output value equals the desired output value and is defined as

$$e_{ij} = \frac{\partial \ln g_i}{\partial w_{ij}} \tag{3-16}$$

where $g_i$ is the probability of the desired output equaling the computed output, defined as

$$g_i = Pr\{b_j = c_j|W_j,A\} \tag{3-17}$$

where $b_j$ is the computed value of the *jth* PE, $c_j$ is the desired value of the *jth* PE, $W_j$ is the weight vector associated with the *jth* PE and A is the vector of inputs to the *jth* output PE.

## 3.6.3. Stochastic Learning

*Stochastic learning* uses random processes, probability, and an energy relationship to adjust the memory connection weights (Ackley, Hinton & Sejnowski, 1985; Szu, 1986a). Stochastic learning makes a random weight change, determines the resultant energy created after the change, and keeps the weight change according to the following criteria: (1) if the ANS energy is lower after the random weight change (i.e. system performed better), accept the change, (2) if the energy is not lower after the random weight change, accept the change according to a pre-chosen probability distribution, otherwise (3) reject the change. The acceptance of some changes, despite poorer performance, allows the ANS to escape local energy minima in favor of a deeper energy minimum, a process called simulated annealing (Geman & Geman, 1984; Kirkpatrick, Gelatt & Vecchi, 1983). This process slowly decreases the number of probabilistically accepted weight changes that result in poorer performance.

## 3.6.4. Hardwired Systems

Hardwired systems are ANS models that have their connections and weights predetermined (hardwired) for the ANS. Resembling finite state automata, such ANS have been constructed to represent the semantics of language (Cottrell & Small, 1983 & 1984; Fanty, 1986b), vision (Feldman, 1980 & 1981b; Fukushima, 1969 & 1970; Grossberg & Mingolla, 1985), concepts in the brain (Feldman, 1981a), and causal relationships (Kosko, 1986a).

## 3.6.5. Hebbian Learning

*Hebbian learning,* named after Donald Hebb (1949)—who articulated the concept of correlation learning but not the mathematical formalization— is the adjustment of a connection weight according to the correlation of the values of two PEs it connects. Hebb describes this idea in the following passage from his book *Organization of Behavior* (1949):

> When an axon of cell A is near enough to excite a cell B and repeatedly or persistently takes part in firing it, some growth process or metabolic change takes place in one or both cells such that A's efficiency as one of the cells firing B is increased.

Panel (a) of Figure 3-6 illustrates the simplest mathematical form of the learning rule— *simple Hebbian* correlation—where the weight value $w_{ij}$ is the correlation (multiplication) of the PE $a_i$ with the PE $a_j$ using the discrete time equation

$$\Delta w_{ij} = a_i a_j \qquad (3\text{-}18)$$

where $\Delta w_{ij}$ represents the discrete time change to $w_{ij}$. Below are several extensions of this simple learning rule.

Sejnowski (1977a & 1977b) has used the covariance correlation of PE activation values in the equation

$$\Delta w_{ij} = \eta[a_i - \bar{a}_i][a_j - \bar{a}_j] \qquad (3\text{-}19)$$

where the bracketed terms represent the covariance and $0 < \eta < 1$. Here, $\eta$ is the adaptation rate constant, the overbar $(-)$ represents the mean, and the quantity in brackets represents

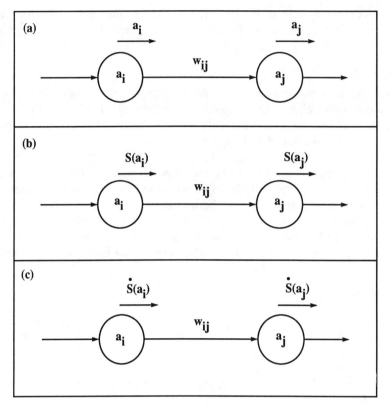

FIGURE 3-6. Three Hebbian learning topologies are illustrated. Panel (a) shows the discrete time correlation of $a_i$ PE activations with $a_j$ PE activations. Panels (b) and (c) display the topology of two continuous time Hebbian correlation equations, Signal Hebbian Learning and Differential Hebbian Learning, respectively.

the variance of the *jth* PE. Sutton & Barto (1981a) have used the correlation of the mean value of $a_i$ with the variance of $a_j$ as expressed by the equation

$$\Delta w_{ij} = \eta \bar{a}_i [a_j - \bar{a}_j] \tag{3-20}$$

Klopf (1986) has proposed a discrete time correlation equation—called drive-reinforcement learning—that correlates the changes in $a_i$ and the changes in $a_j$ which is expressed as (omitting time-lagged variations)

$$\Delta w_{ij} = (\Delta a_i)(\Delta a_j) \tag{3-21}$$

Cheung & Omidvar (1988) have created a discrete time equation, a combination of the Klopf and Sutton-Barto equations, that correlates the activation value of $a_i$ with the changes in $a_j$ regulated by the current connection strength value and a constant as seen by the equation

$$\Delta w_{ij} = \eta a_i w_{ij} (\Delta a_j) \tag{3-22}$$

Casting eq. 3-18 into continuous time and adding a decay term yields the equation

$$\dot{w}_{ij} = -w_{ij} + a_i a_j \tag{3-23}$$

where the overdot ($\cdot$) represents $dw_{ij}/dt$. Grossberg (1968c & 1969b), Hopfield (1984), and many others employ an extension of this continuous time Hebbian learning rule that correlates the activation values after they have been passed through a nonlinear threshold function. This learning rule—called the *passive decay associative law* or the *signal Hebbian learning law*—is illustrated in panel (b) of Figure 3-6 and obeys the equation

$$\dot{w}_{ij} = -w_{ij} + S(a_i)S(a_j) \tag{3-24}$$

where $S()$ is a sigmoid threshold function (see section 3.2.). Kosko (1985, 1986d) has used a continuous time version of Klopf's drive-reinforcement learning equation (eq. 3-21) that correlates the time derivatives of signal functions. This learning rule—called *differential Hebbian learning*—is illustrated in panel (c) of Figure 3-6 and is described by the equation

$$\dot{w}_{ij} = -w_{ij} + \dot{S}(a_i)\dot{S}(a_j) \tag{3-25}$$

where the continuous time derivative of the sigmoid function is

$$\dot{S}(x) = S'(x)\dot{x} \tag{3-26}$$

Later work with the differential Hebbian learning rule has been conducted by Hinton & McClelland (1988) and Gluck, Parker & Reifsnider (1988).

A more thorough examination of these Hebbian learning rules and others can be found in Barto (1984) and Tesauro (1986).

## 3.6.6. Competitive and Cooperative Learning

Competitive and cooperative processes are described as ANSs with self-exciting recurrent connections and neighbor-inhibiting (competitive) and/or neighborhood-exciting (cooperative) connections. More precisely, the system of differential equations $dx_i/dt = F_i(x_1,x_2,\ldots,x_n) = F_i(X)$, $i = 1, 2, \ldots, n$, is *competitive* if

$$\partial F_i/\partial x_j \leq 0 \ \forall \ j \neq i \tag{3-27}$$

and *cooperative* if

$$\partial F_i/\partial x_j \geq 0 \ \forall \ j \neq i \tag{3-28}$$

Competitive learning, introduced by Grossberg (1972b & 1976a) and von der Malsburg (1973) and extensively studied by Amari & Takeuchi (1978), Amari (1983), Bienstock, Cooper & Munro (1982), Grossberg (1982a & 1987), and Rumelhart & Zipser (1985), is a pattern classification procedure for conditioning intra-layer connections in a two-layer ANS. In its simplest form ("winner take all"), competitive learning works in concert with recall in the following manner: (1) an input pattern is presented to the input layer $F_A$ of PEs, (2) the $F_A$ PEs send their activations through the $F_A$ to $F_B$ intra-layer connections to the $F_B$ layer, (3) each $F_B$ PE competes with the others by sending positive signals to itself (recurrent self-excitation) and negative signals to all its neighbors (lateral neighbor-inhibition), and (4) eventually the $F_B$ PE with the greatest activation will be singularly active and all others will be nullified Steps (1) through (4) are often referred to as on-center/off-surround interactions. The $F_B$ PE with the largest activation is called the $F_B$-winner. Once the competition is complete, conditioning of the $F_A$ to $F_B$-winner intra-layer connections takes place using the equation

$$\dot{w}_{ij} = S(a_i)[-w_{ij} + S(b_j)] \tag{3-29}$$

where $w_{ij}$ is the connection strength from the *ith* $F_A$ PE($a_i$) to the *jth* $F_B$-winner PE($b_j$) and $S()$ is a sigmoid function. In summary, eq. 3-29 automatically adjusts only those connections emanating from the winning $F_B$ PE, leaving all other connections unaffected. More generally, activity at $F_B$ is contrast-enhanced, but not to the point where only one PE remains active.

One extension of competitive learning is Grossberg's (1982a) competitive-cooperative learning. A competitive-cooperative learning ANS has separate excitatory (positive) and in-hibitory (negative) connections to each PE. The competitive learning equation (eq. 3-29) is the same, but the activation dynamics are entirely different. In Grossberg (1980) an expla-nation of the benefit of these interactions in the discrimination of signal and noise is concisely summarized in a step-by-step construction of the motivations for such a system.

### 3.6.7. Randomly Connected Systems

Randomly connected ANSs are non-learning networks studied by Farley & Clark (1954), Allanson (1956), Averbukh (1969), Beurles (1962a & 1962b), Minsky & Selfridge (1961), Rozonoer (1969a, 1969b & 1969c), Stubbs & Good (1976), Torioka (1979), Kohonen (1971a & 1973), and Amari (1971 & 1972a). Randomly connected ANSs have been analyzed to support the theory that the brain was truly a randomly connected network when viewed at a macroscopic level. It was hoped that by studying randomly connected ANSs some of the brain's organizational secrets might be unlocked.

## 3.7. STABILITY AND CONVERGENCE

ANS processing is typically governed by two bodies of mathematics: global stability and convergence. *Global stability* is the eventual stabilization of all PE activations from any initial input. *Convergence* is the eventual minimization of error between the desired and computed PE outputs. Stability is a notion usually associated with feedback recall, and convergence is a notion usually associated with supervised learning. There are three general theorems that are used for showing the stability of a wide class of ANS paradigms that employ feedback during recall. Proofs of convergence are specific to each ANS paradigm.

### 3.7.1. A Definition of Global Stability

Equilibria and motions that are only slightly disturbed by negligible deviations are termed stable; those which suffer extensive disturbance are termed unstable (Chetayav, 1961). Glob-ally stable ANSs are defined as nonlinear dynamical systems that rapidly map all inputs to fixed points. These fixed points (limit points, convergence points, equilibria, etc.) are where information can be deliberately stored. Although global stability guarantees all inputs are mapped to a fixed point, it does not guarantee that it will map all inputs into the desired fixed point.

There are three main theorems that are used to prove stability for a wide range of ANS paradigms that employ feedback during recall. Each of these theorems employs the direct method of Lyapunov, a powerful tool that will be reviewed in the following section before the three general stability theorems are summarized.

#### 3.7.1.1. Lyapunov's Direct Method
The direct method of Lyapunov studies stability by finding certain functions of the variables of a dynamical system whose derivatives with respect to time have specific properties. This method is in direct contrast with the alternative method of studying the stability of a system of dynamical equations by integrating its equations of motion. In essence, Lyapunov's direct method is a short cut to global stability analysis of a system of possibly nonlinear differential (difference) equations. The four specific properties of Lyapunov's direct method (Chetayav,

1961) needed to prove global stability for a system of equations $dx/dt = F(t,x_1,x_2,\ldots,x_n) = X_i$ are as follows:

(L1)                    $X_i = 0$ if $x_i = 0$   $\forall\ i = 1, 2, \ldots, n$                    (3-30)

(i.e. 0 only at the origin)

(L2)                            $X_i$ is holomorphic                            (3-31)

(i.e. first derivative exists at all parts of the given domain)

(L3)                    $\sum_{i=1}^{n} x_i \leq H \,\forall\, t \geq t_0$                    (3-32)

where $t_0$ and $H$ are constants and $H$ is always non-vanishing (i.e. $x_i$ is bounded)

(L4)                    $\dot{V} = \sum_{i=1}^{n} \frac{\partial V}{\partial x_i} \leq 0 \,\forall\, \dot{x}_i$                    (3-33)

where $V$ is a Lyapunov energy function of the variables of $X_i$ that maps n dimensions into one, i.e. $V: \mathcal{R}^n \to \mathcal{R}^1$. Lyapunov's direct method states that if the above properties are satisfied for a given energy function $V$, then for all possible system inputs $X = (x_1,x_2,\ldots,x_n)$, the system will converge and become globally stable.

### 3.7.1.2. A Lyapunov Energy Example

To illustrate how this method is used, the following example is provided. Consider the system $X = (x_1,x_2,\ldots,x_n)$, where $x_i$ is a time-dependent variable whose change is described as

$$\dot{x}_i = f_i(x_1,\ldots,x_n) = f_i(X)$$                    (3-34)

where the overdot ($\cdot$) represents continuous time differentiation, i.e. $dx_i/dt$. An example of such a system can be described by the Lyapunov energy function

$$V = x_1^2 + x_2^2 + \cdots + x_n^2$$                    (3-35)

a mapping of all the system variables, $X$, into a scalar. Taking the time derivative of $V$ and replacing each $dx_i/dt$ with its respective function (eq. 3-34) yields

$$\dot{V} = \sum_{i=1}^{n} \frac{\partial V}{\partial x_i} = 2x_1 f_1(X) + 2x_2 f_2(X) + \cdots + 2x_n f_n(X)$$                    (3-36)

Assume each $f_i(X)$ is simply the decay function

$$f_i(X) = -x_i$$                    (3-37)

then

$$\dot{V} = x_1(-x_1) + x_2(-x_2) + \cdots + x_n(-x_n)$$                    (3-38)

$$= -2x_1^2 - 2x_2^2 - \cdots - 2x_n^2$$

$$= -2 \sum_{i=1}^{n} x_i^2 < 0$$

What eq. 3-39 says is when at least one input $x_i$ to the system is changing ($dx_i/dt \neq 0$) then the system will dissipate energy ($dV/dt < 0$) and when the all the inputs to the system cease changing ($dx_i/dt = 0$) then the system will remain stable ($dV/dt = 0$).

## 3.7.2. Three General Stability Theorems

There are three general theorems that describe the stability of a large set of nonlinear dynamical systems. Because many neural networks are nonlinear dynamical systems, these general theorems are very useful for describing the dynamics of autoassociative and heteroassociative continuous time feedback recall neural networks (autoassociators and heteroassociators). The first theorem—the Cohen-Grossberg theorem—is used for showing the stability of non-adaptive autoassociators. The second theorem—the Cohen-Grossberg-Kosko theorem—is used for showing the stability of adaptive autoassociators. In addition, a third theorem—the ABAM theorem—is used for showing the stability of adaptive heteroassociators.

### 3.7.2.1. Non-Adaptive Autoassociator Stability

Non-adaptive autoassociators are ANS paradigms that operate in continuous time, employ feedback recall, and have changes in connection weights that are negligible enough (with respect to the change in PE activation values) that they can be considered constant. The theorem used to prove the stability of such systems was developed by Cohen & Grossberg (1983) and is stated as follows:

**COHEN-GROSSBERG THEOREM:** Any nonlinear dynamical system of the form

$$\dot{x}_i = \alpha_i(x_i)\left[\beta_i(x_i) - \sum_{j=1}^{n} m_{ji}S_j(x_j)\right] \tag{3-39}$$

such that

    a. the matrix $\|m_{ij}\|$ is symmetric and all $m_{ij} \geq 0$;
    b. the function $\alpha_i(\xi)$ is continuous for all $\xi \geq 0$;
    c. the function $\alpha_i(\xi) \geq 0$ for all $\xi \geq 0$; the function $S_i(\xi) \geq 0$ for all $\geq 0$;
    d. the function $S_i(\xi)$ is differentiable and monotone nondecreasing for all $\xi \geq 0$;
    e. eq. 3-39 describes the time-dependent activation of possibly multilayer networks with symmetric coefficients $m_{ij}$;

then the function

$$V = 1/2 \sum_{i=1}^{n} \sum_{j=1}^{n} m_{ji}S_i(x_i)S_j(x_j) - \sum_{i=1}^{n} \int_0^{x_i} S_i'(\Theta_i)\beta_i(\Theta_i)d\Theta_i \tag{3-40}$$

is a Lyapunov energy function for the system and the system is stable.

    The proof for this theorem is very tricky, requiring a very complicated argument that shows the system is bounded, and then showing that the time derivative of the system (eq. 3-40) is constantly decreasing or zero. See Cohen & Grossberg (1983) for the detailed proof. There are several ANSs that utilize this theorem in proving their stability simply by making the proper algebraic identifications and being mindful of the corresponding restrictions.

### 3.7.2.2. Adaptive Autoassociator Stability

Kosko (1988c) has extended the Cohen-Grossberg theorem by removing the restriction that the system must not learn when it is recalling information. The new theorem—the Cohen-Grossberg-Kosko theorem—is stated as follows:

**COHEN-GROSSBERG-KOSKO THEOREM:** Any nonlinear dynamical system of the form

$$\dot{x}_i = \alpha_i(x_i)\left[\beta_i(x_i) - \sum_{j=1}^{n} m_{ji}S_j(x_j)\right] \tag{3-41}$$

and

$$\dot{m}_{ji} = -m_{ji} + S_i(x_i)S_j(x_j) \tag{3-42}$$

such that

a. the matrix $\|m_{ij}\|$ is symmetric and all $m_{ij} \geq 0$;
b. the function $\alpha_i(\xi)$ is continuous for all $\xi > 0$;
c. the function $\alpha_i(\xi) \geq 0$ for all $\xi \geq 0$; the function $S_i(\xi) \geq 0$ for all $\xi \geq 0$;
d. the function $S_i(\xi)$ is differentiable and monotone nondecreasing for all $\xi \geq 0$;
e. eq. 3-41 describes the time-dependent activation of the possibly multilayer networks with symmetric coefficients $m_{ij}$;
f. eq. 3-42 describes the changes in the interconnection strengths $m_{ij}$;

then the function

$$V = 1/2 \sum_{i=1}^{n} \sum_{j=1}^{n} m_{ji}S_i(x_i)S_j(x_j) - \sum_{i=1}^{n} \int_0^{x_i} S_i'(\Theta_i)\beta_i(\Theta_i)d\Theta_i - 1/4 \sum_{i=1}^{n} \sum_{j=1}^{p} m_{ji}^2 \tag{3-43}$$

is a Lyapunov energy function for the system and the system is stable.

Like the Cohen-Grossberg theorem, the Cohen-Grossberg-Kosko theorem is proven by first showing that the system (eqs. 3-41 & 3-42) is bounded for all inputs and that the time derivative of the Lyapunov energy function (eq. 3-43) is constantly decreasing or zero. Refer to Kosko (1988c) for details.

### 3.7.2.3. Adaptive Heteroassociator Stability
The ABAM theorem (Kosko, 1988c) describes, in three general equations, the activations of globally stable two layer ANSs that can learn and adapt at the same time. This theorem represents a specific two-layer implementation of the more general Cohen-Grossberg-Kosko theorem. The theorem is as follows:

**ABAM THEOREM:** Every signal Hebbian dynamical system of the form

$$\dot{x}_i = -\alpha_i(x_i)\left[\beta_i(x_i) - \sum_{j=1}^{p} m_{ji}S_j(y_j)\right] \tag{3-44}$$

$$\dot{y}_j = -\alpha_j(y_j)\left[\beta_j(y_j) - \sum_{i=1}^{n} m_{ij}S_i(x_i)\right] \tag{3-45}$$

$$\dot{m}_{ij} = -m_{ij} + S_i(x_i)S_j(y_j) \tag{3-46}$$

such that

a. the matrix $\|m_{ij}\|$ is symmetric and all $m_{ij} \geq 0$;
b. the functions $\alpha_i(\xi)$ & $\alpha_j(\xi)$ are continuous for all $\xi \geq 0$;
c. the functions $\alpha_i(\xi)$ & $\alpha_j(\xi) \geq 0$ for all $\xi \geq 0$;

d. the functions $S_i(\xi)$ & $S_j(\xi) \geq 0$ for all $\xi \geq 0$;

e. the functions $S_i(\xi)$ & $S_j(\xi)$ are differentiable and monotone nondecreasing for all $\xi \geq 0$;

f. eqs. 3-45 & 3-46 describe the time-dependent activation of the layer $F_X \in \mathcal{R}^n$ & $F_Y \in \mathcal{R}^p$, respectively;

g. eq. 3-46 describes the changes in the interconnection strengths between $F_X$ & $F_Y$ PEs contained in the matrix $M \in \mathcal{R}^{n \times p}$;

then the function

$$V = -\sum_{i=1}^{n}\sum_{j=1}^{p} m_{ij}S_i(x_i)S_j(y_j) + \sum_{i=1}^{n}\int_0^{x_i} S_i'(\Theta_i)\beta_i(\Theta_i)d\Theta_i \qquad \textbf{(3-47)}$$

$$+ \sum_{j=1}^{p}\int_0^{y_j} S_j'(\zeta_j)b_j(\zeta_j)d\zeta_j + 1/2\sum_{i=1}^{n}\sum_{j=1}^{p} m_{ij}^2$$

is a Lyapunov energy function for the system and the system is stable.

One important characteristic of this system, as well as the first two, is that the system is at equilibrium ($dV/dt = 0$) if and only if $dx_i/dt = dy_j/dt = dm_{ij}/dt = 0$ for all i and j, and stability is achieved in exponential time. As a point of interest, the ABAM theorem can be placed in an algebraic framework that makes it immediately identifiable with the Cohen-Grossberg-Kosko theorem, and vice versa.

## 3.7.3. A Definition of Convergence

*Convergence* is defined as a sequence of numbers $x_n$ that tends to a limit x if, given some $\epsilon > 0$, we can find an integer $n_0$ such that $|x_n - x| < \epsilon$ for every $n > n_0$. Restated,

$$\lim_{n \to \infty} x_n = x \qquad \textbf{(3-48)}$$

There are two convergence methods based upon this general principle of convergence that are common to many ANS paradigms: (1) convergence with probability 1 — convergence almost everywhere — and (2) convergence in the mean-square sense. *Convergence with probability 1* is defined as

$$\lim_{n \to \infty} P\{x_n = x\} = 1 \qquad \textbf{(3-49)}$$

where $P\{x\}$ represents the probability of x, and *convergence in the mean-square sense* is defined as

$$\lim_{n \to \infty} E\{|x_n - x|^2\} = 0 \qquad \textbf{(3-50)}$$

where $E\{x\}$ represents the estimated value of x (Papoulis, 1965). Convergence is strictly related to the learning in a system. In a more rigorous sense, convergence is a means of analyzing the ability of a given learning procedure to properly capture the mapping between presented data. If the mapping converges to a fixed value, or to some fixed set, then the learning procedure is properly capturing the mapping. The degree of error that is measured during learning describes how well this mapping is being acquired.

# CHAPTER 4

# Artificial Neural System Implementations

A wide variety of ANS implementations have been developed that attempt to streamline the computation and take advantage of the inherent parallelism. In this chapter we will present an overview of the various hardware technologies being used to implement ANSs and place them into a coherent taxonomy that will provide an easy reference during the later paradigm descriptions.

ANS implementations have three key implementation characteristics:

1. *Computationally intensive:* The output of each processing element in an ANS is the sum of several products; hence, the primary ANS operation is the multiply-accumulate. For every connection in the network, there is a multiply-accumulate operation required.

2. *Massively parallel:* ANSs typically have completely local processing; hence, each processing element (PE) can be treated as an individual processor operating in parallel. This means, assuming that each PE has its own dedicated processor, that an ANS' speed is only dependent on the number of multiply-accumulates per PE and not the number of PEs. As an example, if each PE had the same number of connections, a network with 10 PEs could operate just as fast as a network with 10,000.

3. *Tremendous memory requirement:* ANSs typically have many connections. Each connection has an associated weight that must be stored. This creates a serious problem as the size of the network scales up. As an example, a fully connected two-layer network with 10 PEs in each layer has 100 connections. Doubling the number of PEs (20 in each layer) results in 400 connections. A factor of two increase in the number of PEs resulted in a factor of four increase in the number of connections. In general, networks must be very large to carry out useful tasks; hence, they must have an adequate amount of storage.

## 4.1. HISTORICAL PERSPECTIVE

ANS implementations date back to as early as 1913, when the first ANS implementation, using hydraulics, was proposed (in great detail) but never implemented (Russell, 1913). In 1951, Minsky and Edmonds created the first physical ANS implementation. This 40-element learning machine, based upon the Hebbian learning rule, consisted of self-made clutches, tubes, and motors and it worked with some success. Minsky and Edmonds' effort was closely followed by several innovative ANS implementations: the machina speculatrix (Walter, 1950), the homeostat (Ashby, 1952), the maze-solving mouse (Shannon, 1951), the machina docilis (Walter, 1952), "rerons" (Gilstrap, 1960), and digital computer simulations (Farley & Clark, 1954).

In 1960, three significant advances were made in ANS implementations. The first was the MARK I, a pattern recognition device built by Hay, Martin, and Wightman (1960) that learned using Rosenblatt's (1958) Perceptron learning rule. This early ANS implementation consisted of 400 photoresistive cells (20 × 20 array) that fed data into as many as 512 PEs. The size of this machine was approximately 3 ft. × 15 ft. × 6 ft.

During the same year, Widrow (1960) introduced an ANS implementation of his Adaline

(Widrow & Hoff, 1960). This implementation was constructed of memistors, small electro-chemical devices that adpated by changing the amount of plating on a conducting surface. This device led to a company of the same name — Memistor, Inc. — that marketed the adaptive learning and signal processing capabilities of this new system (Rosenfeld, 1987).

The third ANS implementation introduced in 1960 was the neurally inspired transistor called the neuristor (Crane, 1960 & 1962). The neuristor was motivated by a desire to construct new wiring schemes for highly miniaturized electronic systems and enjoyed some success in signal processing (Czarnul, Kiruthi & Newcomb, 1979), robotics (Chande, DeCleris & Newcomb, 1983) and vision (Ajmera, Newcomb, Chitale & Nilsson, 1983).

This early flurry of new ANS implementations did not last. During the period from 1960 to the mid 1980's the majority of ANS implementations were performed using software simulations on digital computers. Because of the computer's versatility, cost, and ever-increasing capability, these efforts have continued and represent the most popular ANS implementation medium today. In addition, the advent of supercomputers, massively parallel computers, and specialized coprocessors/attached processors has provided even greater capabilities in these areas.

In 1984 two pioneering ANS implementations were introduced that rekindled the enthusiasm and, in turn, the creation of innovative ANS implementations. The first of these 1984 efforts introduced the concept of a virtual ANS implementation, a neurocomputer, that could be used to implement and rapidly process a wide variety of ANS paradigms. This neurocomputer, called the TRW MARK III, was developed by Hecht-Nielsen & Gutschow (1986a) out of their growing frustration with the slow processing speeds garnered from their MARK I and MARK II software simulations running on a DEC VAX mainframe.

The second of these 1984 efforts introduced the natural marriage of ANSs and optics. Farhat and Psaltis (1984), two noted optical engineers, saw that the high connectivity and extraordinary computational requirements of ANSs could be naturally handled using various intensities of light modulated by a holographic film (see Figure 4-1). This work is still in its infancy and shows great promise for future ANS implementations. Most of the current implementations of this type combine electronic and optical components into a hybrid electro-optical system.

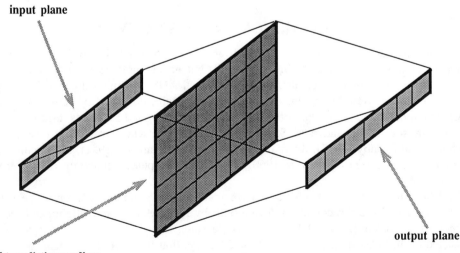

FIGURE 4-1. General configuration for an optical/electro-optical implementation of a two-layer ANS.

More ANS implementations were announced in 1986 when several major research laboratories (AT&T, JPL, CalTech, MIT/Lincoln Lab) all developed electronic implementations of ANSs. (See Denker, 1986a.) Because electronic (i.e. transistor level) implementations are currently restricted to a two-dimensional topology, these implementations are well suited for ANSs that require near-neighbor connectivity or networks that can be arranged into a crossbar structure (see Figure 3-5). Like most optical implementations, most electronic implementations assume that the weights for the ANS have already been determined and are being hard-wired into the electronics. Research on adaptive methods can be found in Mead (1989).

## 4.2. ANS IMPLEMENTATIONS

The broad range of ANS implementations that exist today can be placed into a three class taxonomy that includes:

1. *computer implementations*—defined as any software implementation that is created on a machine that was not made explicitly for ANS processing;

2. *electronic implementations*—defined as any electronic implementation that is made with the sole purpose of performing ANS processing; and

3. *optical/electro-optical implementations*—defined as any ANS implementation that involves the use of optical components.

Each of these classes and their subclasses are shown in Figure 4-2. The following sections describe each subclass in greater detail.

### 4.2.1. Computer ANS Implementations

*4.2.1.1. Supercomputers*
A supercomputer is defined as a very high-speed computer used primarily for computationally intensive programs that are amenable to batch processing (i.e. no user interaction). These computers do not rely on a large number of processing units to attain their tremendous speed; rather they typically make use of vector processing, very efficient and specialized system

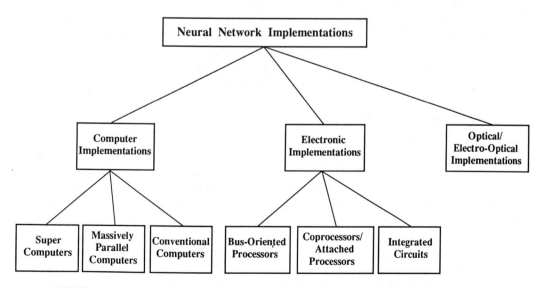

FIGURE 4-2. Taxonomy of ANS implementations. See text for detailed description of each node.

designs, and advanced semiconductor materials that provide exceptionally quick processing speeds. The ANS implementations on supercomputers consist of software simulations that require very little, or no, man-machine interaction.

Examples of supercomputers include the SCS-40 from Scientific Computer Systems, the Cray 123 and XYZ lines from Cray Research, Fujitsu's VP/2600/20, NEC's SX-2, and many others from Alliant Computer Systems, Ardent Computer, Control Data, and Convex Computer Corporation. Supercomputers are limited by their inability to provide efficient processing with extensive human interaction and the expensive purchase/operation costs.

### 4.2.1.2. Massivelly Parallel Computers

A massively parallel computer is characterized by an architecture that produces high-speed computations through a large number of individual processors. These computers typically have restricted communication throughput and simple one-bit arithmetic logic unit (ALU) processors—but this is not always the case. Each of these computers have architectures that range from Single-Instruction/Multiple-Data Stream (SIMD)—that is architectures where one instruction after another is broadcast to all the processors for simultaneous application to individual pieces of data—to Multiple-Instruction/Multiple-Data Stream (MIMD)—where each processor can execute its own set of instructions on its own data.

ANS implementations are programmed in languages that are often unique to each machine and offer very little portability. There have been some attempts to produce very general ANS simulation environments that have met with some success. The processing speed of these implementations is slightly-slower to much-slower than supercomputer implementations, but they have the valuable ability to interact with the ANS as it is processing. Table 4-1 lists some of the most prominent massively parallel computers being employed for ANS implementations.

### 4.2.1.3. Conventional Computers

The majority of ANS implementations are software simulations. Conventional computers using any programming language can implement virtually any ANS; it just takes longer to process. There are several versatile ANS simulation packages available today that are developed for common computers such as the Apple Macintosh, the IBM PC and its compatibles, SUN, Texas Instruments Explorer, Apollo, Symbolics Workstations, and all forms of VAX, Hewlett-Packard, UNISYS, NCR, and MASSCOMP (etc.) micro-computers. The conventional computer is the first step to any engineering project concerning ANSs and, depending on the size of the application, it could be sufficient for the entire project.

## 4.2.2. Electronic ANS Implementations

### 4.4.2.1. Bus-Oriented Processors

A bus-oriented processor is a specific computer architecture that is designed using existing processors arranged on a data bus for the express purpose of providing tremendous data throughput. The bus-oriented processors are specialized hardware implementations that bridge the gap between the massively parallel computers that utilize crossbar switches and hypercube configurations for data communication, and the coprocessor/attached processor implementations that rely on a high-speed bus that provides tremendous data throughput to a single processor. Bus-oriented processors can implement a wide variety of ANSs, making them very verstatile. Examples of bus-oriented processor ANS implementations include the TRW Mark III, the TRW Mark V, and the MIT Lincoln Lab MX-1.

| MASSIVELY PARALLEL COMPUTERS | | | |
|---|---|---|---|
| **MODEL** | **MANUFACTURER** | **ARCHITECTURE TYPE** | **MAX NO. OF PROCESSORS** |
| Butterfly | Bolt, Beranek, & Newman | MIMD | 256 |
| CAPP — Content Addressable Parallel Processor | University of Massachusetts | SIMD | 262,144 |
| Connection Machine II | Thinking Machines Corp. | SIMD | 65,536 |
| GAPP — Geometric Array Parallel Processor | Martin Marietta Corp./ NCR Corp. | SIMD | 72 (6x12) |
| iPSC | Intel Scientific Computers | MIMD | 128 |
| MPP — Massively Parallel Processor | Goodyear Aerospace Corp./ NASA Goddard Flight Center | SIMD | 16,384 |
| RP3 — Research Parallel Processor Project | IBM | MIMD | 512 |
| WARP | Carnegie Mellon University | MIMD | 20 |
| Parallon 1 | Human Devices, Inc. | MIMD | 2048 |

TABLE 4-1. A listing of several massively parallel computers that can be used for ANS implementations is shown. The model, the architecture type, the manufacturing company, the maximum number of processors, and the processor type of each computer are included.

## 4.2.2.2. Coprocessors/Attached Processors

The coprocessor/attached processor ANS implementations are specialized hardware systems that are attached to a conventional computer and provide magnitudes of improvement in the processing speed of ANS applications. These implementations use processors that provide extremely fast multiply-accumulate operations. They are able to implement virtually any ANS paradigm, and they have the added ability to develop applications in a familiar software environment. A listing of some of the primary coprocessor/attached processor ANS implementations can be found in Table 4-2.

## 4.2.2.3. Integrated Circuits

The integrated circuit ANS implementations are strictly a research-oriented issue at this time, although there have been several small start-up companies, like Synaptics, Universal Learning Systems, and Syntonics, that are hoping to produce commercial VLSI ANS implementations in the near future. The advantages of a VLSI implementation include significant increases in processing speed and reduced size and power requirements. The limitations include the difficulty in producing highly connected implementations on a chip's planar surface and the relative immaturity and inexperience in applying the materials necessary for these implementations to be viable. Integrated circuit implementations carry great promise for the future, especially in areas now being explored such as advanced bonding methods that will allow ANS hierarchies to be formed at the chip level, the advent of three-dimensional integrated circuits, and the latest hybrid electronic-optical combinations.

## COPROCESSORS / ATTACHED PROCESSORS

| MODEL | MANUFACTURER | HOST MACHINE | COPROCESSOR |
|---|---|---|---|
| ANZA | Hecht-Nielsen Neurocomputer Corporation | Zenith 248 PC | Motorola MC68020/ MC68881 |
| ANZA Plus | Hecht-Nielsen Neurocomputer Corporation | Zenith 348 PC | Wietek XL RISC Processor |
| Δ-1 Floating Point Processor | SAIC | Wyse 386 PC | BIT Technology Emmitter coupled with a logic based multiply-accumulator |
| Transputer Development System | INMOS | IBM PC AT/ Macintosh | INMOS IMS T414 or IMS T800 |
| Odyssey | Texas Instruments | TI Explorer | TI TMS 32020 DSP Processor |
| Network Emulation Processor | IBM Palo Alto Scientific Center | IBM PC AT | TI TMS 32020 DSP Processor |
| Neuro-Engine | NEC Corp. | NEC PC-9801 | NEC ImPP (Micro PD7281) data-flow-type microprocessors |

TABLE 4-2. A listing of several coprocessor/attached processor ANS implementations is shown. The model, the host machine, the processor employed, and the manufacturing company of each are included.

## 4.2.3. Optical/Electro-Optical ANS Implementations

The optical/electro-optical implementations of ANSs are the furthest from becoming widely available. The work in this area is currently restricted to precise, sensitive equipment in optical laboratories. Conversely, optics is where the most promising ANS implementations exist. The light-speed performance of multiply-accumulate operations, coupled with the ability to provide dense connectivity in a three-dimensional computing environment (light can interfere without being destructive), makes optical and electro-optical implementations worth the effort.

# CHAPTER 5

# Artificial Neural System Paradigms and their Applications and Implementations

In this chapter a description of 27 ANS paradigms is provided. Each paradigm discussed has been successfully used in applications or has application potential. This is not an exhaustive list of ANS paradigms. Hence, the ANS paradigms (ANS models) reviewed represent only a fraction of those that have been, and continue to be, developed. In this report we have reserved judgment and opinion concerning each model's overall comparative worth, choosing instead to focus upon the principles of each model, a brief and general discussion of its strengths and limitations, its application(s), and its implementation(s). The references provide further details.

Each paradigm description includes a complete mathematical and topological overview of its original form. The extensions, analysis and comparative performance of each paradigm are cited as well as comprehensive listings of known applications and implementations.

To properly describe the ANS paradigms that are available requires a taxonomy that is minimally ambiguous and extremely general. It is for this reason that the two characteristics ubiquitous to both encoding and recall have been chosen as taxonomical discriminators. Each ANS paradigm has two inherent encoding qualities—supervised and unsupervised learning—and each paradigm has two inherent recall qualities—feedforward and feedback recall. The paradigms presented in this chapter have been classified using these characteristics— encoding supervision and recall information flow. Table 5-1 lists each of the paradigms discussed in this chapter in its appropriate category. Each of the following four sections discuss each taxonomical combination.

## 5.1. UNSUPERVISED LEARNING AND FEEDBACK RECALL ARTIFICIAL NEURAL SYSTEMS

### 5.1.1. Additive Grossberg (AG)

The additive Grossberg (AG) ANS—introduced by Grossberg (1968c)—is a single-layer, autoassociative, nearest-neighbor classifier that stores arbitrary analog spatial patterns $A_k = (a_1^k,\ldots,a_n^k)$, $k = 1, 2, \ldots, m$, using either signal Hebbian or competitive learning. The AG learns online, operates in continuous time, and displays the one-layer feedback topology shown in Figure 5-1, where the n $F_A$ processing elements (PEs) correspond to $A_k$'s components.

#### 5.1.1.1. Encoding
AG learning typically uses the signal Hebbian learning correlation equation

$$\dot{w}_{ij} = -\alpha w_{ij} + \beta S(a_i^k)S(a_j^k) \tag{5-1}$$

where $w_{ij}$ is the symmetric ($w_{ij} = w_{ji}$) connection strength from the $i$th to the $j$th $F_A$ PE, S() is a sigmoid function (see section 3.2. for a description of threshold functions), $\alpha$ is a positive constant controlling the passive decay, and $\beta$ is a positive constant controlling the signal

| | FEEDBACK RECALL | FEEDFORWARD RECALL |
|---|---|---|
| **UNSUPERVISED LEARNING** | • Additive Grossberg (AG)<br>• Shunting Grossberg (SG)<br>• Binary Adaptive Resonance Theory (ART1)<br>• Analog Adaptive Resonance Theory (ART2)<br>• Discrete Hopfield (DH)<br>• Continuous Hopfield (CH)<br>• Discrete Bidirectional Associative Memory (BAM)<br>• Temporal Associative Memory (TAM)<br>• Adaptive Bidirectional Associative Memory (ABAM) | • Learning Matrix (LM)<br>• Driver-Reinforcement Learning (DR)<br>• Linear Associative Memory (LAM)<br>• Optimal Linear Associative Memory (OLAM)<br>• Sparse Distributed Associative Memory (SDM)<br>• Fuzzy Associative Memory (FAM)<br>• Learning Vector Quantization (LVQ)<br>• Counterpropagation (CPN) |
| **SUPERVISED LEARNING** | • Brain-State-in-a-Box (BSB)<br>• Fuzzy Cognitive Map (FCM) | • Perceptron<br>• Adaline & Madaline<br>• Backpropagation (BP)<br>• Boltzmann Machine (BM)<br>• Cauchy Machine (CM)<br>• Adaptive Heuristic Critic (AHC)<br>• Associative Reward Penalty (ARP)<br>• Avalanche Matched Filter (AMF) |

*Learning* →
↓ *Recall*

TABLE 5-1. Taxonomy of ANS paradigms showing the models that belong to each class. See text for a description of the taxonomy.

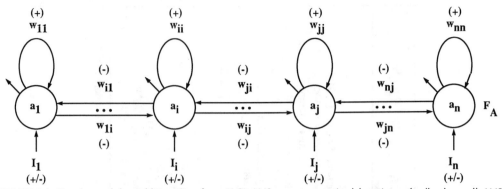

FIGURE 5-1. Topology of the Additive Grossberg (AG) ANS, an unsupervised learning—feedback recall ANS. This one-layer ANS utilizes positive valued recurrent connections and negative valued lateral connections. The input to each PE can be either positive or negative. This is a continuous time ANS that classifies analog patterns. To keep the presentation uncluttered, all connections are not shown—there is actually a lateral connection from each $F_A$ PE to every other $F_A$ PE, and a recurrent connection from every $F_A$ PE to itself.

Hebbian learning term. Grossberg refers to the $w_{ij}$ connections as long term memory (LTM) and refers to eq. 5-1 as the passive decay LTM equation.

An alternative encoding procedure is the gated decay (competitive learning) LTM equation

$$\dot{w}_{ij} = S(a_i^k)[-\alpha w_{ij} + \beta S(a_j^k)] \tag{5-2}$$

which only allows changes to the LTM connections that have non-zero signals being emitted from $a_i^k$.

### 5.1.1.2. Recall
$F_A$ activations are competitive, facilitated through the self-exciting (+) and neighbor-inhibiting (−) lateral feedback connections as shown in Figure 5-1. These $F_A$ activations are described by the equation

$$\dot{a}_i = -\mu a_i + \delta \sum_{j=1}^{n} S(a_j)w_{ji} + I_i \tag{5-3}$$

where $a_i$ and $a_j$ are the activation values of the $i$th and $j$th $F_A$ PEs, respectively, $I_i$ is the $i$th input value, $\mu$ is a positive constant controlling activation decay, and $\delta$ is a positive constant controlling lateral (intra-layer) feedback. Grossberg refers to the $F_A$ PE activation values as short term memory (STM) and refers to eq. 5-3 as the additive STM equation. Nearest-neighbor classification of each input is provided by eq. 5-3's dynamics in that the $F_A$ PEs most closely resembling the presented input pattern will become maximally activated and those least resembling the presented input will be nullified. During recall, the winning $F_A$ PEs typically saturate to 1 and the nullified $F_A$ PEs saturate to 0. If the activations are processed long enough, only one PE, $a_h$, will remain active. In this situation the winning PE is determined by the equation

$$a_h = \underset{i=1}{\overset{n}{\text{MAX}}}\{a_i\} \tag{5-4}$$

### 5.1.1.3. Stability
The AG ANS is proven globally stable using the Cohen-Grossberg theorem (1983). Using the notation described in section 3.7.2.1., we need only make algebraic identifications that do not violate the five listed restrictions, and the AG ANS is automatically proven stable by

virtue of the Cohen-Grossberg equations being stable. Referring to eq. 3-40, we substitute the Cohen-Grossberg terms (left hand side) with the AG ANS terms (right hand side) as follows:

$$\alpha_i(x_i) = 1$$

$$\beta_i(x_i) = -\alpha a_i + I_i$$

$$m_{ij} = w_{ij}$$

$$S_i(x_i) = S(a_i)$$

and

$$x_i = a_i$$

### 5.1.1.4. Discussion, Analysis, Applications, and Implementations

The AG ANS represents the first step in an evolutionary development of successively more powerful ANS paradigms and, accordingly, it exhibits more limitations than its successors. One AG ANS limitation is that signal and noise are equally regarded and therefore both noise and signal are encoded—a problem aptly titled by Grossberg as the noise-saturation dilemma. The dilemma is resolved by the addition of an automatic gain control over the input signal that nullifies noise while abstracting and encoding the signal (see Shunting Grossberg ANS, section 5.1.2.). An additional AG ANS limitation is that later input patterns can be similar enough to encoded patterns that the input pattern will create similar activations, resulting in re-encoding over the previously encoded pattern and irretrievable loss of that information—a problem that Grossberg calls the stability-plasticity dilemma. This problem has been solved by the introduction of adaptive resonance theory (Grossberg, 1976b). AG ANS strengths include its ability to classify data in an unsupervised fashion and its provisions for online adaptation, important qualities for applications unable to obtain *a priori* data patterns.

Several analysis efforts and extensions have been described for the AG ANS. Recent analysis by Guez, Protopopsecu & Barhen (1988) has shown that the AG ANS has the capacity to store $m = n^3$ patterns, where n is number of $F_A$ PEs. Lemmon and Kumar (1988) have introduced an algorithm that will predict which PEs will become active without having to perform an extensive amount of computation. Standley & Wyatt (1988) and Wyatt & Standley (1988) have shown that the AG ANS is stable when placed in VLSI despite the presence of unwanted spurious oscillations that readily occur in assemblies with a large number of amplifiers. Sutton, Marsog & Reggia (1988) have extended the current recall scheme to allow the competitive mechanism to minimize the number of connections. Karayiannis & Venetsanopoulos (1988) have studied the changes in dynamics created by replacing the sigmoid threshold function in eq. 5-3 with the step threshold function (see section 3.2. for a description of threshold functions).

Several applications of the AG ANS have been suggested (see Table 5-2). The applications that have the most promise are those that require pattern classification or signal enhancement.

AG ANS implementations have just recently begun to surface (see Table 5-3). The inherent stability and fault-tolerance of the AG ANS make the optical/electro-optical and integrated circuit implementations very promising.

## 5.1.2. Shunting Grossberg (SG)

The shunting, or multiplicative, Grossberg (SG) ANS—introduced by Grossberg (1973) and inspired by the results of Hodgkin (1964) and Hodgkin & Huxley (1952)—is a single-layer, competitive-cooperative, autoassociative, nearest-neighbor classifier that stores arbitrary an-

| Additive Grossberg Applications | |
|---|---|
| **Application** | **Reference** |
| Signal Processing | Petsche & Dickson, 1988 |
| Control | Guez, Eilbert & Kam, 1988 |
| Ecological Systems | Matsuo, 1987 |
| Pattern Recognition | Grossberg, 1970a & 1970b |
| Image Processing | Grossberg, 1987b |
| Speech & Language | Grossberg, 1969b, 1969c & 1986c<br>Grossberg & Pepe, 1971 |

TABLE 5-2.

| Additive Grossberg Implementations | |
|---|---|
| **Implementation** | **Reference** |
| Optical/Electro-Optical | D. Anderson, 1987<br>TeKolste & Guest, 1987<br>Jenkins & Wang, 1988<br>Wang & Jenkins, 1988 & 1988b<br>Stirk, 1987<br>Wagner & Psaltis, 1987b |
| Integrated Circuits | Standley & Wyatt, 1988<br>Alspector, et al., 1988 |
| Analog Electronics | Nabet & Darling, 1988 |
| Coprocessor/Attached Processor | SAIC, 1988<br>HNC, 1987b |

TABLE 5-3.

alog spatial patterns $A_k = (a_1^k, \ldots, a_n^k)$, $k = 1, 2, \ldots, m$, using either signal Hebbian or competitive learning. The SG learns online, operates in continuous time, and has the topology shown in Figure 5-2, where the n $F_A$ PEs correspond to $A_k$'s components. The differences between the AG and SG are their activation dynamics and their delineation of positive and negative inputs. The SG activation dynamics also contain automatic gain control recall dynamics that contrast enhance inputs and nullifies noise, hence, transmitting only signal.

### 5.1.2.1. Encoding

SG encoding is performed with either the passive decay LTM equation (eq. 5-1) or the gated decay (competitive learning) LTM equation (eq. 5-2) that are described in section 5.1.1.

### 5.1.2.2. Recall

The SG ANS employs the recall equation

$$\dot{a}_i = -\alpha a_i + (\beta - a_i)[S(a_i) + I_i] - (a_i + \mu)\left[\sum_{j=1}^{n} S(a_j)w_{ji} + J_i\right] \qquad (5\text{-}5)$$

where $a_i$ is the $i$th $F_A$ PE's activation value, $I_i$ is the excitatory (positive) input, $J_i$ is the inhibitory (negative) input, $w_{ij}$ is the symmetric LTM connection from the $i$th to the $j$th $F_A$ PE, $\alpha$ is a positive constant controlling passive decay term, $\beta$ is a positive constant controlling excitatory input and recurrent feedback, and $\mu$ is a positive constant controlling inhibitory input and lateral feedback. Automatic gain control—the amplification of signal and nullification of noise—is implemented through the shunting terms $(\beta - a_i)$ and $(a_i + \mu)$. These terms balance the input and feedback signals, allowing the $i$th PE's activation to remain sensitive to the input signal and shunt noise, hence, Grossberg calls eq. 5-5 the shunting STM equation.

### 5.1.2.3. Stability

The SG ANS is proven globally stable using the Cohen-Grossberg theorem (Cohen & Grossberg, 1983). As was done in the previous section, by using the notation described in section 3.7.2.1. we need only make algebraic identifications that do not violate the five listed restrictions, and the SG ANS is automatically proven stable. Referring to eq. 3-40, we sub-

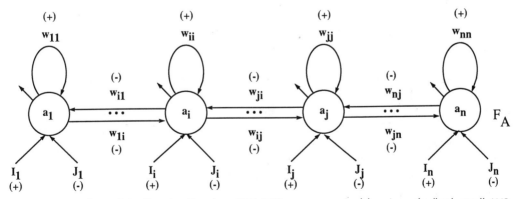

FIGURE 5-2. Topology of the Shunting Grossberg (SG) ANS, an unsupervised learning—feedback recall ANS. This one-layer ANS utilizes positive valued recurrent connections and negative valued lateral connections. There are separate positive and negative inputs to each $F_A$ PE. This is a continuous time ANS that classifies analog patterns. To keep the presentation uncluttered, all connections are not shown—there is actually a lateral connection from each $F_A$ PE to every other $F_A$ PE, and a recurrent connection from every $F_A$ PE to itself.

stitute the Cohen-Grossberg terms (left hand side) with the SG ANS terms (right hand side) as follows:

$$x_i = a_i + \mu$$

$$\alpha_i(x_i) = a_i$$

$$\beta_i(x_i) = 1/2[\alpha\mu - (\alpha + J_i)a_i + (\beta + \mu - a_i)(I_i + S(a_i - \mu))]$$

$$m_{ij} = w_{ij}$$

and

$$S_j(x_j) = S(a_j - \mu)$$

### 5.1.2.4. Discussion, Analysis, Applications, and Implementations

SG limitations include the stability-plasticity dilemma and limited storage. SG strengths include online adaptation and unsupervised learning. The AG applications (see table 5-2) are equally analogous to this paradigm. In addition, the SG has a great amount of mathematical (Hirsch, 1982 & 1985) and neurological support (Hodgkin, 1964; Kandel, 1979; Kandel & Schwartz, 1985; Plonsey & Fleming, 1969; Grossberg, 1986c) which adds validity to its use as an application paradigm for human information processing problems. Another important aspect of this paradigm is its ease of combination with other ANS architectures to create hybrid ANS architectures, exemplified by the SG's use in ART1's and ART2's recall dynamics. A variant of the SG ANS has been discussed by Lopez (1988) that casts the recall dynamics into a feedforward framework and analyzes its relationship to higher-order correlation ANSs. In addition, Johnson (1988) has proposed an electro-optical implementation of the SG ANS.

## 5.1.3. Binary Adaptive Resonance Theory (ART1)

The binary adaptive resonance theory (ART1) ANS — introduced by Carpenter and Grossberg (1986a, 1986b, & 1987b) and based upon the initial concept of adaptive resonance theory introduced by Grossberg (1976b) — is a two-layer, nearest-neighbor classifier that stores an arbitrary number of binary spatial patterns $A_k = (a_1^k, \ldots, a_n^k)$, $k = 1, 2, \ldots, m$, using competitive (gated decay LTM) learning. ART1 learns online, operates in discrete or continuous time, and has the topology shown in Figure 5-3, where the n $F_A$ PEs correspond to $A_k$'s components and the p $F_B$ PEs each represent a pattern class.

Although ART1 is principally a two-layer architecture, it is also transparently framed within two subsystems — the attentional subsystem and the orienting subsystem. As shown in Figure 5-4, the attentional subsystem allows the $F_A$ PEs to be engaged only when an input pattern is present, and the orienting subsystem removes $F_B$ PEs from the set of allowable winners, an operation termed STM reset. These operations are inherent to the sequence of steps used by ART1 during its pattern processing.

ART1 is a field feedback paradigm: $F_A$ PEs receive signals from both the external inputs ($a_i^k$) and the top-down ($v_{ji}$) connections, and $F_B$ PEs receive signals from bottom-up ($w_{ij}$) connections. The encoding procedure is outlined as follows:

1. Present an input pattern $A_k = (a_1^k, \ldots, a_n^k)$ to the $F_A$ PEs, where $F_A = (a_1, \ldots, a_n)$.
2. Each $F_A$ PE activation $a_i$ sends a signal through its LTM connections $w_{ij}$ to every $F_B$ PE $b_j$.

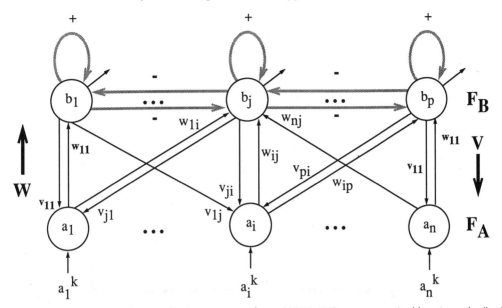

FIGURE 5-3. Topology of the binary adaptive resonance theory (ART1) ANS, an unsupervised learning—feedback recall ANS. There are inter-layer feedback connections between the $F_A$ and $F_B$ PEs that facilitate a resonation upon proper match between encoded and input patterns. The $F_A$ PEs accept inputs from the environment and the $F_B$ PEs each represent a pattern class (sometimes referred to as a grandmother cell in this context). During operation the $F_B$ PEs employ an invisible on-center/off-surround competition that is used to choose the proper class for the presented input. These lateral interactions are shown in the figure as shaded self-exciting/neighbor-inhibiting connections to emphasize this point. This is a continuous time ANS that classifies binary patterns. To keep the presentation uncluttered, all connections are not shown—there is actually a connection from each $F_A$ PE to each $F_B$ PE and vice versa, a shaded negative lateral connection from each $F_B$ PE to every other $F_B$ PE, and a shaded positive recurrent connection from every $F_B$ PE to itself.

3. Each $F_B$ PE competes with the others using Shunting Grossberg (SG) interactions until only one $F_B$ PE remains active.

4. The winning $F_B$ PE, e.g. $b_h$, sends a top-down signal through its LTM connections, $v_{hi}$, back to $F_A$ and (possibly) creates a new set of $F_A$ PE activations.

5. The input, $A_k = (a_1^k, \ldots, a_n^k)$, is compared with the top-down—$F_B$ to $F_A$—feedback activations, X, created by the winning $F_B$ PE.

6. If the relative difference between these two activations—input and top-down—exceeds a value—determined by the vigilance parameter—then the winning $F_B$ PE does not represent the proper class for $A_k$ and it is removed from the set of allowable $F_B$ winners. Control branches at this point in one of two directions:
   a. If there are still $F_B$ PEs remaining in the set of allowable winners, go to step 2.
   b. If there are no remaining $F_B$ PEs in the set of allowable winners, recruit an uncommitted $F_B$ PE and encode $A_k$ onto this PE's connections.

7. If the difference between the two activations does not exceed the amount determined by the vigilance parameter, then the $F_B$ PE is determined to be the proper class for the input pattern $A_k$, and the input pattern is then merged with the stored pattern.

In summary, the above sequence of events conducts a search through the encoded patterns associated with each class trying to find a sufficiently close match with the input pattern. If no class exists, a new class is made. The test for a sufficient match between the top-down feedback pattern and the bottom-up input pattern is called hypothesis testing.

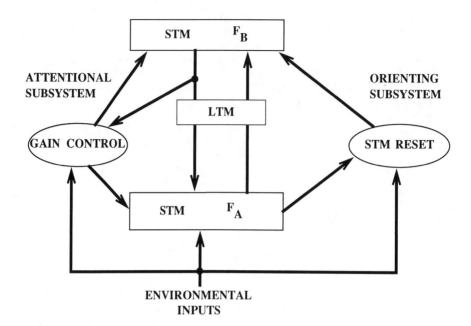

FIGURE 5-4. A pictorial representation of the placement of the orienting and attentional subsystems. These subsystems do not require specific physical connections within the ART1 topology, rather they are dynamical constraints that affect how information is processed.

### 5.1.3.1. Recall

The recall equation for the $F_A$ PEs is the STM competitive-cooperative Shunting Grossberg equation

$$\dot{a}_i = -a_i + (1 - \mu_1 a_i)\left[\gamma_1 \sum_{j=1}^{m} f(b_j)v_{ji} + a_i^k\right] - (\delta_1 + \epsilon_1 a_i)\sum_{j=1}^{m} f(b_j) \qquad (5\text{-}6)$$

where $a_i$ and $b_j$ are the activations of the $i$th $F_A$ and $j$th $F_B$ PEs, f() is the threshold function described by eq. 5-10, $\mu_1$ is a positive constant controlling bottom-up input and top-down feedback, $\delta_1$ and $\epsilon_1$ are positive constants regulating attentional gain control, and $\gamma_1$ is a positive constant regulating bottom-up input and top-down feedback. The analogous $F_B$ recall equation is

$$\dot{b}_j = -b_j + (1 - \mu_2 b_j)\left[\gamma_2 \sum_{i=1}^{n} S(a_i)w_{ij} + f(b_j)\right] - (\delta_2 + \epsilon_2 a_i)\sum_{k \neq j}^{m} S(b_k) \qquad (5\text{-}7)$$

where $\mu_2$ is a positive constant regulating bottom-up input and top-down feedback terms, $\delta_2$ and $\epsilon_2$ are positive constants regulating attentional gain control, and $\gamma_2$ is a positive constant regulating bottom-up input.

### 5.1.3.2. Encoding

Once the proper $F_B$ PE is selected, there are two ways that ART1 can learn—slow learning or fast learning. Slow learning allows only a small portion of the input pattern to seep into the weights. After repeated presentations of the entire training set, the most prominent characteristics of each pattern will emerge and become committed to long-term memory. This form of learning is well suited to large dimension problems that are subject to noisy training sets. Fast learning immediately encodes the input pattern directly onto the weights and does not require more than one or a few passes through the training set. During fast learning a heuristic can also be employed that allows the immediate jump to an uncommitted $F_B$ PE when there is top-down/input pattern mismatch. Note that the pattern classes formed using fast learning are not as statistically representative as those found using slow learning. Fast learning is well suited to applications that have crisp data sets and require immediate learning. The specifics of each form of learning are detailed in the following two sections.

Slow Learning Equations. Once the proper $F_B$ PE has been selected, ART1 employs gated decay LTM encoding on both the top-down and bottom-up connections. The top-down LTM connections are adjusted with the equation

$$\dot{v}_{ji} = \alpha_1 f(b_j)[-\beta_1 v_{ji} + S(a_i^k)] \tag{5-8}$$

and the bottom-up LTM connections are adjusted using

$$\dot{w}_{ij} = \alpha_2 f(b_j)[-\beta_2 w_{ij} + S(a_i^k)] \tag{5-9}$$

where $\alpha_1$ and $\alpha_2$ are positive constants controlling the learning rate, $\beta_1$ and $\beta_2$ are positive constants controlling passive decay, $v_{ji}$ is the connection strength from the $j$th $F_B$ to the $i$th $F_A$ PE, $w_{ij}$ is the connection strength from the $i$th $F_A$ to the $j$th $F_B$ PE. The threshold function employed for the $F_A$ PEs, $S()$, is a sigmoid function (see section 3.2. for a description of threshold functions) and the $F_B$ threshold function, $f()$, is defined as

$$f(b_j) = \begin{cases} 1 & \text{if } b_j = \underset{k \in B}{\text{MAX}} \{b_k\} \\ 0 & \text{otherwise} \end{cases} \tag{5-10}$$

where B is the set of $F_B$ PEs allowed to win. Note that the initial values of the weights can be random if slow learning is used.

Fast Learning Equations. For fast learning to work correctly the top-down and bottom-up weights must first be initialized to insure that encoded patterns are always accessed in the proper manner. The initial conditions for the bottom-up—$F_A$ to $F_B$—weights must satisfy a condition Carpenter & Grossberg call the *Direct Access Inequality* which is defined as

$$0 < w_{ij} < L/(L - 1 + n) \tag{5-11}$$

where L is the recoding constant ($L > 1$) and n is the number of $F_A$ PEs. The initial conditions for the top-down—$F_B$ to $F_A$—weights must satisfy a condition called the *Template Learning Inequality* defined as

$$1/2 < v_{ji} \leq 1 \tag{5-12}$$

Once the proper $F_B$ PE has been selected, ART1 calculates the top-down feedback/input correlations and stores them in the temporary vector X. Each element of X is determined using the equation

$$x_i = \sum_{j=1}^{n} a_i^k \cap v_{ji} \tag{5-13}$$

where $X = (x_1, x_2, \ldots, x_n)$ is the top-down/input match vector and $\cap$ is the binary intersection operator (remember all the patterns are binary and using fast learning the weights will also be binary). We now use X to encode the input pattern onto the top-down and bottom-up weights. The bottom-up weights are encoded using the equation

$$w_{ij} = \begin{cases} L/(L - 1 + |X|) & \text{if } x_i \text{ and } b_j = 1 \\ 0 & \text{otherwise} \end{cases} \qquad (5\text{-}14)$$

where $|X|$ is the sum of components of the vector $X$. The top-down weights are adjusted using the equation

$$v_{ji} = \begin{cases} 1 & \text{if } x_i = 1 \\ 0 & \text{otherwise} \end{cases} \qquad (5\text{-}15)$$

The equation that determines if the winning $F_B$ PE has a pattern associated with it that sufficiently matches the input pattern is called the STM reset equation. This equation is very important in that the vigilance parameter $\rho$ is used to determine the granularity of classifications. This STM reset equation is a ratio of the sizes of the top-down feedback pattern and the bottom-up input pattern defined as

$$\frac{|A_k \cap X|}{|A_k|} < \rho \qquad (5\text{-}16)$$

where $\rho$ is the vigilance parameter with a value between 0 and 1, $X = (x_1,\ldots,x_n)$ is the vector of top-down/input values determined by eq. 5-13, and $|*|$ is an operator that adds all the elements of the vector enclosed within the braces. As the vigilance parameter $\rho$ becomes closer to 1, the granularity of classifications becomes finer.

### 5.1.3.3. Stability
A series of theorems proven by Carpenter and Grossberg (1986c) predict both the order of search and the categorization properties of ART1. It has been shown, through the introduction of a 2/3 rule that allows $F_A$ PEs to become active only if they receive two of their three possible inputs—environment inputs, gain control inputs, top-down inputs—that ART1 encoding is stable using fast learning.

### 5.1.3.4. Discussion, Extensions, Applications, and Implementations
ART1 strengths include its ability to place an arbitrary number of patterns into categories of varying degrees of complexity, its stable encoding, and its online learning abilities. An ART1 limitation is its restriction to binary pattern classification—a problem clearly understood by its creators and corrected in a recent extension of ART1 called ART2 (see section 5.1.4.).

SAIC's Tucson AI Technology Center has developed a system based upon ART1, entitled the property inheritance network (Ryan & Winter, 1987), that is an associative memory capable of hierarchical search (Ryan, Winter & Turner, 1987). Ryan (1988) has also extended ART1 to allow any length of input pattern to be encoded without performing an extensive serial search through all the stored patterns. Kam, Naim & Alteson (1988) have studied a version of ART1 that reacts symmetrically during weight changes, and have developed a new set of learning rules based upon standard estimation procedures. Moore (1988) has repeated the stability and convergence proofs of Carpenter & Grossberg (1987b) within the framework of pattern analysis mathematics, and has examined some of its properties. McDuff & Simpson (1989) have extended ART1 to allow pattern matching. And, Menon & Kolodzy (1988), Kolodzy & Menon (1988) and McDuff & Simpson (1989) have compared the classification power of ART1 with several other ANS paradigms.

ART1 is an ANS paradigm that is extremely well suited to applications that need immediate encoding of binary representations. Areas where this is applicable include digital image processing and diagnostics. Table 5-4 lists ART1's applications and Table 5-5 lists ART1's implementations.

| ART1 Applications | |
|:---:|:---:|
| **Application** | **Reference** |
| Image Processing | Carpenter & Grossberg, 1986c<br>Grossberg, 1986b & 1987b<br>Grossberg & Mingolla, 1985<br>Rak & Kolodzy, 1988<br>Kadar, et al., 1988<br>Zmuda, 1988 |
| Speech Processing | Cohen, Grossberg & Stork, 1987<br>Grossberg, 1986 b & 1986c<br>Grossberg & Stone, 1986a & 1986b |
| Temporal Pattern Recognition | Sung, Priebe & Marchette, 1988 |
| Decision Making Under Risk | Grossberg & Gutowski, 1987 |
| Neurobiological Connections | Banquet, 1988 |
| Classical Conditioning | Grossberg, 1982b<br>Grossberg & Levine, 1987<br>Grossberg & Schmajuk, 1987 |
| Control | Ryan & Winter, 1988<br>Winter, 1988<br>Ryan, Winter & Turner, 1987 |
| Diagnostics | Winter, Ryan & Turner, 1987<br>McDuff & Simpson, 1989 |
| Knowledge Processing | Leven, 1988<br>Leven & Yoon, 1988 |

TABLE 5-4.

## 5.1.4. Analog Adaptive Resonance Theory (ART2)

The analog adaptive resonance theory (ART2) ANS—introduced by Carpenter and Grossberg (1987c & 1987d)—is an extension of the ART1 ANS (see previous section). ART2 is a two-layer, nearest-neighbor classifier that stores an arbitrary number of analog spatial patterns $A_k = (a_1^k, \ldots, a_n^k)$, k = 1, 2, ..., m, using competitive (gated decay LTM) learning. ART2 learns online, operates in discrete or continuous time, and has the topology shown in Figure 5-5, where the n $F_G$ PEs correspond to $A_k$'s components and the p $F_H$ PEs each represent a pattern class.

Although ART2 is principally a two-layer architecture, each input layer PE actually consists of six inter-PEs working in synchrony as shown in Figure 5-6. These inter-PEs normalize the input and stored patterns to allow for equitable comparison. The function of each inter-PE in the *ith* $F_G$ PE is as follows: $a_i$ holds the analog input value for the *ith* component of

| ART1 Implementations | |
|---|---|
| **Implementation** | **Reference** |
| Integrated Circuits | Syntonics, 1988a & 1988b |
| Coprocessor/Attached Processor | SAIC, 1988<br>HNC, 1987b |

TABLE 5-5.

the k*th* input pattern ($a_i^k$), $b_i$ holds a normalized representation of $a_i$'s value, $c_i$ holds a normalized LTM/input pattern comparison, $d_i$ holds the analog LTM pattern readout/input pattern comparison, $e_i$ holds the normalized LTM pattern readout, and $g_i$ holds the analog LTM pattern readout. The links between $g_i$ and $e_i$, $d_i$ and $c_i$, and $a_i$ and $b_i$, are transparent (note the shaded lines) and unit valued. The link from $e_i$ to $d_i$ carries a linearly regulated sigmoid-thresholded signal ($\beta\phi(e_i)$), the link from $b_i$ to $d_i$ carries a sigmoid-thresholded signal, the link from $c_i$ to $g_i$ carries the value of $c_i$, and the link from $c_i$ to $a_i$ carries a linearly regulated $c_i$ signal (see section 3.2. for a description of threshold functions).

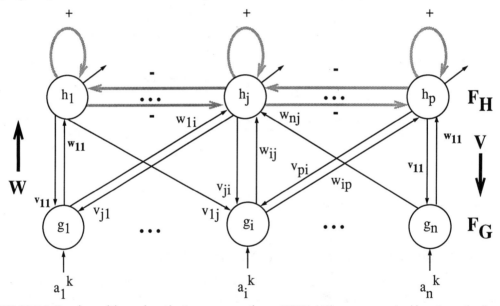

FIGURE 5-5. Topology of the analog adaptive resonance theory (ART2) ANS, an unsupervised learning — feedback recall ANS. There are inter-layer connections between the $F_G$ and $F_H$ PEs that store analog spatial patterns. When the input pattern and the stored pattern sufficiently match, the network is said to be in a state of resonance — this is when learning occurs. The $F_G$ PEs accept input patterns from the environment and the $F_H$ PEs each represent a pattern class (sometimes referred to as a grandmother cell in this context). During operation, the $F_B$ PEs employ an invisible on-center/off-surround competition that is used to choose the proper class for the presented input. These lateral interactions are shown in the figure as shaded self-exciting/neighbor-inhibiting connections to emphasize this point. This is a continuous time ANS that classifies analog patterns. To keep the presentation uncluttered, all connections are not shown — there is actually a connection from each $F_G$ PE to each $F_H$ PE and vice versa, a shaded negative lateral connection from each $F_G$ PE to every other $F_H$ PE, and a shaded positive recurrent connection from every $F_H$ PE to itself.

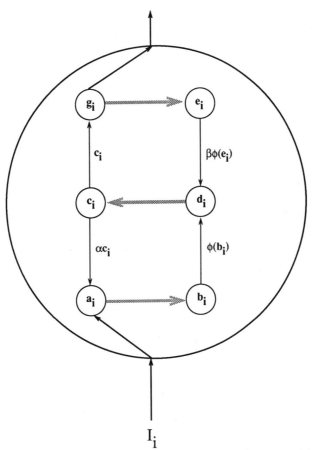

FIGURE 5-6. An expanded view of the *ith* $F_G$ PE showing the six inter-PEs that are used for normalization of the analog patterns stored in LTM (the connections between $F_G$ and $F_H$) and the input patterns. The shaded connections inherently carry information concerning the other PEs of the same type (information necessary for the normalization process to occur). Pattern normalization allows an equitable comparison to be made between the stored and input pattern.

Like ART1, ART2 is a field feedback paradigm: $F_G$ PEs receive signals from both the external inputs ($A_k$) and the top-down ($v_{ji}$) connections, and $F_H$ PEs receive signals from bottom-up ($w_{ij}$) connections. The encoding procedure is outlined as follows:

1. Present an input pattern $A_k = (a_1^k, \ldots, a_n^k)$ to the $F_G$ PEs.
2. Inside each $F_G$ PE the analog input pattern is normalized and fed through the $a_i \rightarrow b_i \rightarrow d_i \rightarrow c_i \rightarrow g_i$ inter-PE path, and sends the resultant signal through the $F_G$ to $F_H$ LTM connections.
3. Each $F_H$ PE competes with the others using Shunting Grossberg (see section 5.1.2) interactions until only one $F_H$ PE remains active.
4. The winning $F_H$ PE, e.g. $h_j$, sends a top-down signal through its LTM connections, $v_{ji}$, back to $F_G$.
5. The top-down signal is sent through the $g_i \rightarrow e_i \rightarrow d_i \rightarrow c_i$ inter-PE path resulting in a possibly new $c_i$ signal.
6. The combined normalized top-down LTM/bottom-up input signal at $c_i$ is compared with the top-down stored signal $g_i$.

7. If the difference between these two activations — $c_i$ and $g_i$ — exceeds a value — determined by the vigilance parameter — then the winning $F_H$ PE does not represent the proper class for $A_k$ and it is removed from the set of allowable $F_H$ winners. Control branches at this point in one of two directions:

   a. If there are still $F_H$ PEs remaining in the set of allowable winners, go to step 2.

   b. If there are no remaining $F_H$ PEs in the set of allowable winners, recruit an uncommitted $F_H$ PE and encode the normalized input (held at $c_i$ and fed to $g_i$) onto this PE's connections.

8. If the difference between the two activations meets the criterion established by the vigilance parameter, then the $F_H$ PE is determined to be the proper class for the input pattern $A_k$ and the input pattern is merged onto the weights with the stored pattern. We will call this match between the input and stored patterns resonation, and we shall call the length of time that the match occurs the resonation period.

In summary, the above sequence of events conducts a search through the encoded patterns associated with each class trying to find a sufficiently close match with the input pattern. If no class exists, a new class is made.

### 5.1.4.1. Recall

The inter-PE recall equations are as follows:

$$a_i = a_i^k + \alpha c_i \tag{5-17}$$

where $0 < \alpha < 1$;

$$b_i = a_i/(\gamma + \|A\|) \tag{5-18}$$

where $A = (a_1, a_2, \ldots, a_n)$, $\gamma > 0$ is a constant, and $\|*\|$ represents the Euclidian norm of the vector;

$$c_i = d_i/(\gamma + \|D\|) \tag{5-19}$$

where $D = (d_1, d_2, \ldots, d_n)$;

$$d_i = \phi(b_i) + \beta\phi(e_i) \tag{5-20}$$

where $\beta > 0$ is a constant and $\phi()$ is the sigmoid threshold function

$$f(x) = \begin{cases} 2\theta x^2/(x^2 + \theta^2) & \text{if } 0 \le x \le \theta \\ x & \text{otherwise} \end{cases} \tag{5-21}$$

and

$$e_i = g_i/(\gamma + \|G\|) \tag{5-22}$$

where $G = (g_1, g_2, \ldots, g_n)$. The output of the $i$th $F_G$ PE, $g_i$, depends upon the use of fast learning or slow learning dynamics. If slow learning is used, the $i$th $F_G$ PE's value is calculated using the equation

$$g_i = c_i + \sum_{j=1}^{p} \varphi(h_j)v_{ji} \tag{5-23}$$

where $v_{ji}$ is the connection strength from the $j$th $F_H$ PE to the $i$th $F_G$ PE and the function $\varphi()$ is defined as

$$\varphi(h_j) = \begin{cases} \delta & \text{if } h_j = \underset{k \in H}{\text{MAX}} \{h_k\} \\ 0 & \text{otherwise} \end{cases} \tag{5-24}$$

where $0 < \delta < 1$ and H is the set of $F_H$ PEs allowed to win. If fast learning is employed, the $ith$ $F_G$ PE's value is calculated using the equation

$$g_i = \begin{cases} c_i & \text{if } F_H \text{ is receiving bottom-up input} \\ c_i + \delta w_{Ji} & \text{if } h_J \text{ is active} \end{cases} \tag{5-25}$$

The $F_H$ PE values are calculated in a straight-forward dot-product fashion using the equation

$$h_j = \sum_{i=1}^{n} g_i w_{ij} \tag{5-26}$$

### 5.1.4.2. Encoding

Like ART1, once the proper $F_H$ PE is selected, there are two ways that ART2 can learn — slow learning or fast learning. Slow learning allows only a small portion of the input pattern to seep into the weights during any given resonation period. After repeated presentations of the entire training set, the most prominent characteristics of each pattern will emerge and become committed to long-term memory. This form of learning is well suited to large dimension problems that are subject to noisy training sets. Fast learning immediately encodes the input pattern directly onto the weights and does not require more than a few passes through the training set. During fast learning an immediate jump to an uncommitted $F_H$ PE can occur after the first top-down/input pattern mismatch. Note that the pattern classes formed using fast learning are not as statistically representative as those found using slow learning. The initial conditions on the weights during both fast learning and slow learning are only that they are close to zero.

Slow Learning Equations. The $F_H$ to $F_G$ connections are adjusted using the equation

$$\dot{v}_{ji} = \varphi(h_j)[g_i - v_{ji}] \tag{5-27}$$

The $F_G$ to $F_H$ connections are adjusted using the equation

$$\dot{w}_{ij} = \varphi(h_j)[g_i - w_{ij}] \tag{5-28}$$

Fast Learning Equations. The $F_H$ to $F_G$ connections are adjusted using the equation

$$\dot{v}_{ji} = \begin{cases} \delta[g_i - v_{ji}] = \delta(1 - \delta)[[c_i/(1 - \delta)] - v_{ji}] & \text{if } h_j = \underset{k \in H}{\text{MAX}} \{h_k\} \\ 0 & \text{otherwise} \end{cases} \tag{5-29}$$

and the $F_G$ to $F_H$ connections are adjusted using the equation

$$\dot{w}_{ij} = \begin{cases} \delta[g_i - w_{ij}] = \delta(1 - \delta)[[c_i/(1 - \delta)] - w_{ij}] & \text{if } h_j = \underset{k \in H}{\text{MAX}} \{h_k\} \\ 0 & \text{otherwise} \end{cases} \tag{5-30}$$

where $0 < \delta < 1$.

The final piece that ties the entire system together is the reset equation that determines if the input pattern sufficiently matches the stored pattern. The reset condition — the condition that determines that the input pattern does not sufficiently match the pattern associated with the maximally activated $F_H$ PE — is dependent upon the vigilance parameter $\rho$, a value between 0 and 1. The closer $\rho$ is to 1, the finer the classification granularity. The reset condition is

$$\rho/(\gamma + \|F\|) > 1 \tag{5-31}$$

where F is a vector of the match $c_i$ — the normalized input signal — and $g_i$ — the stored pattern. Each element of F is found using the equation

$$f_i = (c_i + \zeta g_i)/(\gamma + \|C\| + \zeta\|G\|) \tag{5-32}$$

where $0 < \zeta \ll 1$ is a constant, $C = (c_1, c_2, \ldots, c_n)$ and $G = (g_1, g_2, \ldots, g_n)$.

### 5.1.4.3. Discussion, Extensions, Applications, and Implementations

Empirical and analytical analysis by Carpenter and Grossberg (1987c & 1987d) have shown that poor parameter selection can degrade the stable encoding of patterns by ART1 and ART2, but for a wide range of parameters the systems do stably encode patterns. ART2 strengths include its ability to place an arbitrary number of analog patterns into categories of varying degrees of granularity, its stable encoding, and its online learning abilities. Two ART2 alternatives have been proposed by Carpenter & Grossberg (1987d) that combine some of the functionality of the model presented here. ART2 can be applied as a pattern-classifying subsystem in a more complex ANS application. Examples of this are shown in Carpenter & Grossberg (1987a & 1988) for radar image classification and speech perception and production. In addition, SAIC (1988) and HNC (1987b) have developed coprocessor/attached processor simulations of the ART2 ANS.

## 5.1.5. Discrete Autocorrelator (DA)

A Discrete Autocorrelator (DA) is a single-layer, symmetric, non-linear, autoassociative, nearest-neighbor pattern encoder that stores binary/bipolar spatial patterns $A_k = (a_1^k, \ldots, a_n^k)$, $k = 1, 2, \ldots, m$, using Hebbian learning. The DA learns offline, asynchronously updates its PEs, operates in discrete time (hence its name), and has the topology shown in Figure 5-7, where the n $F_A$ PEs correspond to $A_k$'s components. Because this ANS paradigm is simple to implement and its operation easy to understand, it has been one of the most studied and applied of all the existing ANS paradigms.

### 5.1.5.1. Brief History

DAs were introduced as a theoretical notion by McCulloch & Pitts (1943) and first rigorously analyzed by Amari (1972, 1977). Other researchers that studied the dynamics of discrete autocorrelators include Little (1974), Little & Shaw (1978), and later Hopfield (1982). Hopfield's work is of particular importance in that he introduced an alternative stability procedure

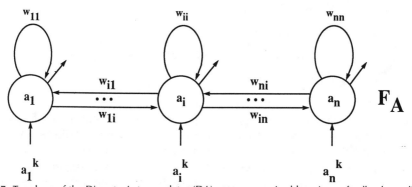

FIGURE 5-7. Topology of the Discrete Autocorrelator (DA), an unsupervised learning—feedback recall ANS. This single-layered ANS paradigm has lateral and recurrent connections. The input vector's components $A_k = (a_1^k, a_2^k, \ldots, a_n^k)$ feed directly into the $F_A$ layer, and outputs can be read from the $F_A$ layer at any time. This is a discrete time ANS that stores binary/bipolar patterns. To keep the presentation uncluttered, all connections are not shown—there is actually a lateral connection from each $F_A$ PE to every other $F_A$ PE, and a recurrent connections from every $F_A$ PE to itself.

(using an Ising spin-glass analogy that is now commonly referred to as Lyapunov energy functions) for this class of ANSs, and was able to excite a large number of scientists and engineers with these simple yet extremely powerful associative memories. The seminal DA work has been performed by Amari. He presented the simple autocorrelator and several variants in 1972, and strictly analyzed the stability of these models using a method he pioneered, entitled statistical neurodynamics. A description of functions very similar to the Lyapunov functions described by Hopfield (1982) can also be found in Amari's (1977) treatment of autocorrelators using stochastic approximation. Nevertheless, Hopfield's promulgation to a large audience of the autocorrelator's capability initiated much of the recent interest in ANSs. Because of this, the autocorrelator is often called the Hopfield Associative Memory or Hopfield Net.

### 5.1.5.2. Encoding

First-Order DA Encoding. The DA encoding equation is

$$W = \sum_{k=1}^{m} A_k^T A_k \tag{5-33}$$

where W is the n-by-n matrix of $F_A$ PE interconnections. In point-wise notation the encoding equation is

$$w_{ij} = \sum_{k=1}^{m} a_i^k a_j^k \tag{5-34}$$

for all ($\forall$) i and j = 1, 2, ..., n, where $w_{ij}$ is the strength of the symmetric connection strength ($w_{ij} = w_{ji}$) from the ith to the jth $F_A$ PE. In some of the presentations of this ANS paradigm (e.g. Hopfield, 1982) there is the further restriction that the diagonal terms of W must be zero (i.e. $w_{ii} = 0\ \forall\ i = 1,2,...,n$), but recently it has been shown by McEliece, et al., (1987) and Gindi, Gmitro, & Parthasarathay (1988) that this restriction can be relaxed.

Higher-Order DA Encoding. An immediate and straightforward DA encoding extension is to develop second-order (and higher if desired) extensions. First-order connections correlate one PE's activation with another's activation. Second-order connections correlate a pair of PE activations with another PE's activation. A pictorial representation of the difference between first- and second-order connections is shown in Figure 5-8. First-order correlations, those encoded by eq. 5-33 and eq. 5-34, are limited in that they can develop only linearly separable mappings. Second-order correlations can capture nonlinear mappings. As an example, some scale and rotation invariances for image processing can be captured by second-order correlations but not by first-order correlations (Giles & Maxwell, 1987). The second-order correlations are stored in an n-by-n-by-n matrix V using the equation

$$v_{hij} = \sum_{k=1}^{m} a_h^k a_i^k a_j^k \tag{5-35}$$

for all ($\forall$) h, i & j = 1, 2, ..., n, where $v_{hij}$ is the strength of the symmetric connection strength ($v_{hij} = v_{ijh} = v_{jhi}$) from the hth and ith $F_A$ PEs to the jth $F_A$ PE. These correlations can continue for third-order ($u_{ghij}$), fourth-order ($t_{fghij}$), and so on.

### 5.1.5.3. Recall

The DA ANS uses a discrete-time relative of the additive STM equation (see section 5.1.1.), without a decay term. The recall equation for the first-order DA is

$$a_i(t + 1) = f\left(\sum_{j=1}^{n} w_{ij}a_j(t)\right) \qquad \text{(5-36)}$$

where $a_j(t)$ is the activation of the $jth$ PEs at time t, and f() is the binary/bipolar step threshold function

$$f(x) = \begin{cases} 1 & \text{if } x > 0 \\ 0 & \text{otherwise} \end{cases} \qquad \text{(5-37)}$$

DA recall is a feedback operation that requires repeated application of eq. 5-36 until all $F_A$ PEs cease to change. When all the $F_A$ PEs have ceased to change, the DA ANS is said to be stable. An example of the DA encoding and recall procedures is provided in Box 5-1.

The recall equation for the second-order DA is

$$a_j(t + 1) = f\left(\sum_{h=1}^{n} \sum_{i=1}^{n} a_h(t)a_i(t)v_{hij}\right) \qquad \text{(5-38)}$$

which is also repeatedly applied until all the $F_A$ PE values cease to change.

### 5.1.5.4. Stability and Capacity

The key question that must be answered for all feedback recall associative memories is, "Is the system stable for all inputs?" Several different proofs have affirmatively answered this question.

Hopfield (1982) used the discrete time Lyapunov function

$$L(A) = -1/2 \sum_{\substack{i=1 \\ i \neq j}}^{n} \sum_{j=1}^{n} a_i a_j w_{ij} \qquad \text{(5-39)}$$

where $A = (a_1, \ldots, a_n)$ is an arbitrary vector of $F_A$ PE activations and the weight matrix has zero-diagonal terms. Taking the discrete-time derivative of $L(A)$ with respect to $a_i$ and applying some algebraic manipulations yields

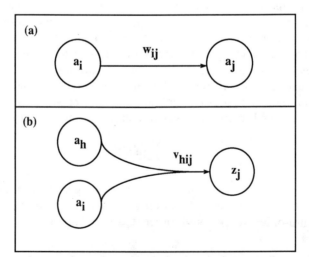

FIGURE 5-8. The difference between first-order and second-order correlations is illustrated. Panel (a) shows first-order correlations — correlations of one PE with another. Panel (b) shows second-order correlations — correlations of a pair of PE's with another. Third-order correlations (not shown) correlate a triplet of PEs with another, and so on.

$$\Delta L(A) = -\left[\sum_{j=1}^{n} a_j w_{ij}\right]\Delta a_i \tag{5-40}$$

which, for any $\Delta a_i$, results in $\Delta L(A) < 0$, hence the system is globally stable (see section 3.7.1). Recent work by McEliece, et al., (1987) has extended this proof to allow for diagonal terms no larger than n.

---

## Discrete Autcorrelator (DA) Example

**ENCODING:**

DA encoding forms the memory matrix W from the sum of m vector outer products using the equation:

$$W = \sum_{k=1}^{m}\left[A_k^T A_k - I\right]$$

where the row vector $A_k = (a_1^k, a_2^k, ..., a_n^k)$, $A_k \in \{-1,+1\}^n$, and I is the n-by-n identity matrix. Using this equation we form the matrix W from the two 4-dimensional row vectors $A_1$ and $A_2$ as follows:

$$A_1 = (1\ \text{-}1\ 1\ \text{-}1) \qquad\qquad A_2 = (1\ 1\ 1\ 1)$$

$$A_1^T A_1 - I = \begin{bmatrix} 1 \\ -1 \\ 1 \\ -1 \end{bmatrix}\begin{bmatrix} 1 \ \text{-}1 \ 1 \ \text{-}1 \end{bmatrix} - \begin{bmatrix} 1 & 0 & 0 & 0 \\ 0 & 1 & 0 & 0 \\ 0 & 0 & 1 & 0 \\ 0 & 0 & 0 & 1 \end{bmatrix}$$

$$A_2^T A_2 - I = \begin{bmatrix} 1 \\ 1 \\ 1 \\ 1 \end{bmatrix}\begin{bmatrix} 1\ 1\ 1\ 1 \end{bmatrix} - \begin{bmatrix} 1 & 0 & 0 & 0 \\ 0 & 1 & 0 & 0 \\ 0 & 0 & 1 & 0 \\ 0 & 0 & 0 & 1 \end{bmatrix}$$

$$W = \sum_{k=1}^{2}\left[A_k^T A_k - I\right] = \begin{bmatrix} 0 & 0 & 2 & 0 \\ 0 & 0 & 0 & 2 \\ 2 & 0 & 0 & 0 \\ 0 & 2 & 0 & 0 \end{bmatrix}$$

---

BOX 5-1. An example of how the encoding and recall operations of the Discrete Autoassociator (DA) operate. This example stores two patterns and then demonstrates how a pattern close to $A_2$ will recall the pattern $A_2$ when presented to the DA.

# Discrete Autocorrelator (DA) Example (cont'd)

**RECALL:**

   Recall in the DA ANS uses simple asynchronous updating, meaning only one PE is updated at a time. Mathematically this means that only one row-column vector matrix multiplication can be performed during any given clock cycle. The recall equation used for the DA ANS is

$$a_j = f\left( \sum_{i=1}^{n} a_i w_{ij} \right)$$

where the threshold function f() is defined as

$$f(x) = \begin{cases} 1 & \text{if } x \geq 0 \\ \\ 0 & \text{otherwise} \end{cases}$$

Using the above equations we will test the recall of the vector $A = (1\ -1\ 1\ 1) \approx A_2$

$$\text{Update } a_1: \quad a_1 = f\left( \sum_{i=1}^{4} a_i w_{i1} \right) \ = \ f(2) = 1 \quad \text{and } A = (1\ -1\ 1\ 1)$$

$$\text{Update } a_2: \quad a_2 = f\left( \sum_{i=1}^{4} a_i w_{i2} \right) \ = \ f(2) = 1 \quad \text{and } A = (1\ 1\ 1\ 1)$$

$$\text{Update } a_3: \quad a_3 = f\left( \sum_{i=1}^{4} a_i w_{i3} \right) \ = \ f(2) = 1 \quad \text{and } A = (1\ 1\ 1\ 1)$$

$$\text{Update } a_4: \quad a_4 = f\left( \sum_{i=1}^{4} a_i w_{i4} \right) \ = \ f(2) = 1 \quad \text{and } A = (1\ 1\ 1\ 1)$$

and so on forever, recalling the vector $A = (1\ 1\ 1\ 1) = A_2$, hence the memory W corrected the error in A, producing $A_2$.

BOX 5-1. *Continued*

   Grossberg (1988a) has shown, through the application of a signal-sum algebraic translation and a discrete-to-continuous time transformation, that the DA ANS is amenable to the Cohen-Grossberg theorem (1983) and is therefore a globally stable system.

   Also, Amari and Maginu (1988) have used Amari's method of statistical neurodynamics (Amari, 1974) to show the DA ANS is stable. Amari's method uses the strong law of large numbers to show that the probability of perfect recall of all stored patterns is 1, provided the memory capacity does not exceed a logarithmic function that decreases for increasing n.

Mathematically restated,

$$\lim_{n \to \infty} P_n(m) = 1 \qquad \qquad \textbf{(5-41)}$$

provided the capacity (i.e. number of patterns stored in W) does not exceed

$$m = \frac{n}{2 \log n + \log \log n} \qquad \qquad \textbf{(5-42)}$$

where log is the natural logarithm. Similar stability/capacity work has also been done by McEliece, et al. (1987), and Baldi and Venkatesh (1987).

### 5.1.5.5. Discussion, Analysis, Applications, and Implementations

The most prominent DA limitation is its limited storage capacity (see eq. 5-42), the larger the number $F_A$ PEs there are, the worse the storage capacity. It is possible to implement an online learning version of this system, but there must be special care taken not to exceed the capacity in such situations. The other primary limitation is the restriction to only binary patterns. DA strengths include its ability to reconstruct entire patterns from partial or incomplete input — making it useful in noisy environments, its stability under asynchronous updating — making it extremely appealing for integrated circuit implementations, and its fault-tolerance.

Studies of the DA's network dynamics have been performed by Amari (1972b, 1974 & 1977b), Amari, Yoshida & Kanatani (1977), Peretto (1984 & 1988), Amit, Gutfruend & Sompolinksy (1985 & 1987), Peretto & Niez (1986a & 1986b), Babcock & Westervelt (1986a & 1986b), Goles & Vichniac (1986), Keeler (1986), Sitte (1988), Marcus & Westervelt (1988a & 1988b), M. Cottrell (1988), Kemlos & Paturi (1988), and Godbeer, Lipscomb & Luby (1988).

There have also been several studies of the DA's memory capacity by Hopfield (1982), Abu-Mostafa & St. Jacques (1985), Bruce, et al. (1986), Hirtz, Grinstein & Solla (1986), Venkatesh (1986), McEliece, et al. (1987), Venkatesh & Psaltis (1987), Xu, Tsai & Huang (1988a), Amari & Maginu (1988), and Newman (1988).

Studies of higher-ordered DAs include Chen, et al. (1986), Lee, et al. (1986), Peretto & Niez (1986a), Baldi & Venkatesh (1987 & 1988), Maxwell, Giles & Lee (1987), Bak & Little (1988), Busch & Trainer (1988), Xu, Tsai & Huang (1988b), Guyon, et al., (1988), Giles, Griffin & Maxwell (1988), Newman (1988), and Little & Bak (1988).

Other variants and analysis of the DA are voluminous. Hopfield, Feinstein & Palmer (1983) and Sasiela (1986) have introduced the idea of partial memory erasure as a means of improving the DA's storage capacity. C. Anderson & Abrahams have incorporated Bayesian probabilities into the network dynamics. Platt & Hopfield (1986) have studied the error-correction properties of the DA. Keeler (1987) has compared the DA's performance with that of the Sparse Distributed Memory (see section 5.2.5). Jacyna & Malaret (1987) have studied the DA's classification performance under a wide variety of conditions. Conwell (1987) has studied the effects of placing time-delays on the DA's interconnections. Buhman and Schulten (1986) have studied the effects of noise on the DA's performance. Pearson (1988) and Baldi & Baum (1986) have studied the relationship between ultrametrics and DAs. Montgomery & Vijaya Kumar (1986) and Lippman (1988) have compared the DA's performance to that of other nearest-neighbor classifiers. Fleisher (1988) has developed a multi-threshold variant of the DA recall equation and studied its effects on pattern storage. Tai & Jang (1988) have analyzed the trade-offs between binary and bipolar encoding with respect to error-correction properties and storage capacity. Parker (1987) has developed a variant of the learning rule entitled second-order Hebbian learning. Gindi, Gmitro & Parthasarathy (1988) have extended the Hopfield version of the DA to include non-zero diagonal terms. Willshaw, Buneman & Longuet-Higgins (1969) have developed an associative memory that uses only binary valued weights, and Palm (1980) has analyzed the capacity of this scheme. Finally, Wong — while in high school! — has developed a technique for improving the storage capacity of a DA by performing transformations on the memory matrix.

The DA is well suited for applications that require the capability to remove noise from large binary patterns. Other application areas include pattern matching and pattern classification. Table 5-6 lists several DA applications. Because the DA is stable under asynchronous updating and because of its extreme simplicity, there have been several proposed and realized DA implementations (see Table 5-7).

| Discrete Autocorrelator Applications | |
|---|---|
| **Application** | **Reference** |
| Image Processing | Psaltis & Hong, 1986<br>Maxwell, Lee & Giles, 1986<br>Giles & Maxwell, 1987<br>Horn, 1988 |
| Speech Processing | Gold, 1986<br>Alspector, 1987<br>Solomon, 1987<br>An, et al., 1988 |
| Control | Hoteuse, 1988<br>Guez, Eilbert & Kam, 1988<br>Pourboghrat & Sayeh, 1988a & 1988b |
| Signal Processing | Goles & Vichniac, 1986<br>Gardner, 1986<br>Farhat, 1987a<br>Gallagher & Coyle, 1987 |
| Database Retrieval | Hecht-Nielsen, 1986a & 1988b |
| Fault-Tolerant Computing | Hopfield, 1982 |
| Pattern Classification | Lippmann, Gold & Malpass, 1986<br>Alspector, 1987 |
| Pattern Recognition | Farhat, 1985 & 1987a<br>Grant & Sage, 1986<br>Soffer, 1987<br>Solomon, 1987<br>Pawlicki, 1988<br>Chieuh & Goodman, 1988 |
| Olfactory Processing | Getz, 1988 |
| Knowledge Processing | Parey & Bonemay, 1988<br>Lendaris, 1988 |

TABLE 5-6.

## Discrete Autocorrelator Implementations

| Implementation | Reference |
|---|---|
| Integrated Circuits | Hubbard, et al., 1986<br>Thakoor, 1986 & 1987<br>Alspector, 1987<br>Sage, 1987<br>Kung & Huang, 1988a<br>Verlyson, Serletti & Jespers, 1988<br><br>Thakoor, et al., 1986<br>Sage, Thompson & Whithers, 1986<br>Agranat, 1987<br>Solomon, 1987<br>Marcus & Westervelt, 1988a |
| Coprocessor/Attached Processor | HNC, 1987b<br>Field & Navlakha, 1988<br><br>SAIC, 1988 |
| Bus-Oriented Processor | TRW, 1987<br><br>Myers, 1987 |
| Massively Parallel Computer | Brown, 1988 |
| Optical/Electro-Optical | Psaltis & Farhat, 1984 & 1985<br>Dunning, et al., 1986 & 1987<br>Soffer, et al., 1986a & 1986b<br>Farhat, 1987a & 1987b<br>Soffer, 1987<br>Macukow & Arsenault, 1987<br>Song, Hong & Bhattascharya, 1988<br>Psaltis, Park & Hong, 1988<br><br>Farhat, et al., 1985<br>Farhat, Miyahara & Lee, 1986<br>Psaltis & Hong, 1986<br>Farhat & Shae, 1987 & 1988<br>White, Aldridge & Lindsay, 1988<br>Vecchi & Salchji, 1988<br>Hsu, Brady & Psaltis, 1988 |

TABLE 5-7.

## 5.1.6. Continuous Hopfield (CH)

The continuous Hopfield (CH) ANS—introduced by Cohen & Grossberg (1983) and Hopfield (1984)—is a single layer, autoassociative, nearest-neighbor encoder that operates in continuous time, stores arbitrary analog spatial patterns $A_k = (a_1^k, \ldots, a_n^k)$, $k = 1, 2, \ldots, m$, and is represented by the one-layer feedback topology shown in Figure 5-9, where the n $F_A$ PEs correspond to each of $A_k$'s components. The CH ANS is a move from the discrete time DA ANS, that could only handle binary/bipolar data to a continuous-time system that can handle analog data. This transition has opened up several new applications, particularly with respect to unconstrained optimization problems.

### 5.1.6.1. Encoding
The conductance value (connection strength) from the *ith* to the *jth* $F_A$ PE is the inverse of some resistance $R_{ij}$

$$w_{ij} = \frac{\alpha}{R_{ij}} \qquad (5\text{-}43)$$

where $\alpha$ is the sign (+ or −) of the connection value being emitted from the *jth* PE. Since the values of $R_{ij}$ are not determined through some specific encoding process, alternative methods of determining the $w_{ij}$ values could include signal Hebbian learning (eq. 5-1) or competitive learning (eq. 5-2).

### 5.1.6.2. Recall
CH recall uses the equation

$$c_i \dot{a}_i = \sum_{j=1}^{n} S(a_j) w_{ji} - \frac{a_i}{R_i} + I_i \qquad (5\text{-}44)$$

where $c_i$ is a positive constant representing the *ith* PE's input capacitance, $R_i$ is a positive constant controlling the *ith* PE's decay resistance, $I_i$ is the external input to the *ith* $F_A$ PE, S() is a sigmoid function (see section 3.2. for a description of threshold functions), and $w_{ji}$ is the symmetric connection from the *jth* to the *ith* $F_A$ PE. The dynamics of eq. 5-44 are very similar to those of Kirchoff's law used to describe the dynamics of electrical circuits.

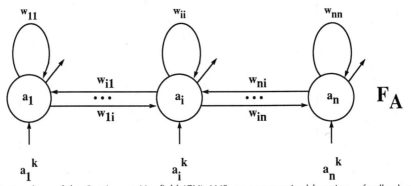

FIGURE 5-9. Topology of the Continuous Hopfield (CH) ANS, an unsupervised learning—feedback recall ANS. This single-layered ANS paradigm has lateral and recurrent connections. The input vector's components $A_k = (a_1^k, a_2^k, \ldots, a_n^k)$ feed directly into the $F_A$ layer and outputs can be read from the $F_A$ layer at any time. This is a continuous time ANS that stores analog patterns. To keep the presentation uncluttered, all connections are not shown—there is actually a lateral connection from each $F_A$ PE to every other $F_A$ PE, and a recurrent connection from every $F_A$ PE to itself.

### 5.1.6.3. Stability

CH stability can be proven using any one of the three global stability theorems presented in section 3.7.2. We will prevail upon the Cohen-Grossberg theorem as it yields the result with the least amount of mathematical difficulty. Using the notation described in section 3.7.2.1., we need only make algebraic identifications that do not violate the five listed restrictions and the CH ANS is automatically proven stable. Referring to eq. 3-40, we substitute the Cohen-Grossberg terms (left hand side) with the CH ANS terms (right hand side) as follows:

$$x_i = a_i$$

$$\alpha_i(x_i) = \frac{1}{c_i}$$

$$\beta_i(x_i) = -\frac{1}{R_i} a_i + I_i$$

$$m_{ij} = -w_{ij}$$

and

$$S_j(x_j) = S(a_j)$$

### 5.1.6.4. Discussion, Analysis, Applications, and Implementations

The strength of the CH ANS is its ability to handle analog data in continuous time. These qualities allow the CH ANS to be almost immediately transitioned into analog hardware implementations (Hopfield, 1985; Hopfield & Tank, 1986). Unfortunately, like its discrete autocorrelator ANS predecessor, the CH ANS has a low storage capacity. Also, this ANS lacks a straight-forward encoding scheme and it is restricted to offline learning.

There have been several extensions and careful analyses of the CH ANS. Anderson & Abrahams (1986) have extended the CH ANS to include the use of Bayesian probabilities. Studies of the CH's dynamics have been performed by Babcock & Westervelt (1986a & 1986b), Davis & Ansari (1987), and Denker (1987). Platt & Hopfield (1986) have evaluated the error correction properties of the CH ANS. Marcus & Westervelt (1988a, 1988b & 1988c) have analyzed CH dynamics when time-delays are introduced to the weight connections. And, Michael, Farrell & Porod (1988) have applied the theory of large-scale interconnected dynamical systems to the CH ANS and studied the CH's dynamical properties.

The CH ANS has been successfully applied to many combinatorial optimization problems—situations that require the minimization of a multiple-constraint cost function to determine the set of optimal system parameters. Hopfield and Tank (1985)—inspired by the work of Kirkpatrick, Gelatt & Vecchi (1983)—were the first to introduce this idea in an ANS framework. The way that the CH ANS is applied is by finding an unconstrained cost function that, when minimized, finds the solution for a combinatorial optimization problem. Then, by manipulating the cost function, algebraic identifications are made between the terms in the CH Lyapunov energy function and the terms in the cost function. Finally, the CH-identified terms are "back-engineered" into the appropriate ANS. When this newly created ANS is presented an initial set of parameters, it produces a near-optimal response in real-time through the minimization of energy. Table 5-8 lists several of the application areas where this approach has been used.

Other than combinatorial optimization applications, the CH ANS's ability to reconstruct entire patterns from partial cues stands out as one of its primary application strengths. In addition, the CH ANS' nearest-neighbor response and fault tolerance qualities are also ap-

# Combinatorial Optimization Applications

| Application | Reference |
|---|---|
| Image Processing | Bilbro, White & Snyder, 1988 — Koch, 1988<br>Koch, Marroquin & Yuille, 1986 — Koch, et al., 1988<br>Winters, 1988 — Zhou & Chellappa, 1988a & 1988b<br>Zhou, Chellappa & Jenkins, 1987 — Troudel & Tabatabai, 1988<br>Furman, Liang & Szu, 1988 — Castelez, 1988<br>Zhou, et al., 1988 — Basenberg & Rossi, 1988<br>Gellard & Lawton, 1988 — Mjolsness, Gindi & Anandan, 1988<br>Barnard & Casasent, 1988 |
| Signal Processing | Tank & Hopfield, 1986 — Platt & Barr, 1988<br>Provence, 1987 — Anastassiou, 1988<br>Zhao & Mendel, 1988 — Bayley, et al., 1988<br>Culhane, Peckerar & Marrian, 1988a&1988b — Pati, et al., 1988 |
| Graph Coloring, Graph Flow & Graph Manipulation | Dahl, 1987b — Marcus, 1987<br>Tagliarina & Page, 1987 — Goldstein, Toomarian & Barhen, 1988<br>Ramanujam & Sadayappan, 1988 — Chen, et al., 1988<br>Peterson & Anderson, 1987 — Stork & Saylor, 1986 |
| Load Balancing & Programming Parallel Computers | Barhen, Toomarian & Protopopsecu, 1987a — Simmes, 1987<br>Barhen, et al., 1987 — Barbosa & Huang, 1988 |
| ANS Programming | Lapedes & Farber, 1986a & 1986b — Mjolsness, 1987<br>Lee & Shey, 1988 |
| Data Deconvolution | Marrian & Peckerar, 1987 |
| Abductive Reasoning | Goel, Ramanujam & Sadayappan, 1986 |

TABLE 5-8.

## Combinatorial Optimization Applications (cont)

| Application | Reference | |
|---|---|---|
| Control | Tsutsumi & Matsumoto, 1987 | Pourboghrat & Sayeh, 1988a & 1988b |
| Stress Measurement | Tsutsumi, Katayama & Matsumoto, 1988 | |
| Pattern Matching | Wong, Banick & Bower, 1988<br>Derthick & Tebelskis, 1988<br>Leung, 1988<br>Zador, et al., 1988 | Ramanujam & Sadayappan, 1988<br>Moopen, Thakoor & Duong, 1988<br>Kamgar-Parsi & Kamgar-Parsi, 1988<br>Peterson, 1988 |
| Solving Equations & Optimizing Functions | Jeffrey & Rosner, 1986<br>Jang, Lee & Shin, 1988<br>Altes, 1988 | Takeda & Goodman, 1986<br>Barnard & Casasent, 1988 |
| Traveling Salesman, Scheduling & Resource Allocation | Bagherzadeh, et al., 1987<br>Alspector, 1987<br>Takeda & Goodman, 1986<br>Tagliarina & Page, 1987 & 1988<br>Szu, 1988<br>Wilson & Pawley, 1988<br>Hegde, Sweet & Levy, 1988<br>Wacholder, Han & Mann, 1988a & 1988b<br>Noetzel & Grazinni, 1988<br>Tanaka, et al., 1988<br>Vichniac, Lepp & Steenstrap, 1988<br>Earle & Szu, 1988<br>Yanai, Hayakawa & Sawaka, 1988 | Simmes, 1987<br>Davis & Ansari, 1987<br>Platt & Barr, 1988<br>Gutzman, 1987<br>Gulati & Iyengar, 1987<br>Foo & Takefuji, 1988<br>Bout & Miller, 1988<br>Toomarian, 1988<br>Brandt, et al., 1988<br>Hopfield & Tank, 1985 & 1986<br>Chen, et al., 1988<br>W. Lee, 1988 |

TABLE 5-8. *Continued*

pealing. Because of these qualities, pattern classification and noise removal from patterns are key CH ANS applications. Table 5-9 lists those areas where the CH ANS has been applied.

Although the CH ANS has not enjoyed the same number of implementation efforts as its DA ANS predecessor, it has enjoyed the diversity of implementations. Table 5-10 lists several CH ANS implementations.

## 5.1.7. Discrete Bidirectional Associative Memory (BAM)

The discrete bidirectional associative memory (BAM) ANS represents the logical extension of autocorrelators to heterocorrelators—the encoding of pattern pairs and not just single patterns. The key point that is made with heterocorrelators is that feedback between the layers stabilizes and, at the point of stability, is a stored pattern pair. This operation was introduced by Soffer, et al. (1986a & 1986b) for use in an optical resonating associative memory. Later, Kosko (1988b) refined first-order heterocorrelators and gave them the title of bidirectional associative memories (BAMs). The BAM is a two-layer, heteroassociative, nearest-neighbor pattern matcher that encodes aribtrary binary/bipolar spatial pattern pairs $(A_k, B_k)$, $k = 1, 2,$ ..., m, using Hebbian learning, where the $k$th pattern pair is represented by the vectors $A_k$ = $(a_1^k, ..., a_n^k)$ and $B_k = (b_1^k, ..., b_p^k)$. The BAM has the ability to learn online, it operates in discrete time, and it is represented by the two-layer feedback topology shown in Figure 5-10, where the n $F_A$ PEs correspond to $A_k$'s components and the p $F_B$ PEs correspond to $B_k$'s components. In addition, the BAM is similar to the ART1 system (section 5.1.3.).

*5.1.7.1. Encoding*
BAM encoding is performed by summing together the outer products of the m pattern pairs (vectors) using the equation

$$W = \sum_{k=1}^{m} A_k^T B_k \tag{5-45}$$

| Continuous Hopfield Applications | |
|---|---|
| **Application** | **Reference** |
| Image Processing | Alspector, et al, 1988 Koch, 1987 Myers, 1987 Sage, 1987 |
| Control | Barhen, et al., 1987 |
| Signal Processing | Herault & Jutten, 1986 |
| Olfactory Processing | Baird, 1986 |
| Pattern Recognition | Alspector, et al., 1988 Solomon, 1987 |

TABLE 5-9.

# Continuous Hopfield Implementations

| Implementation | Reference |
| --- | --- |
| Integrated Circuit | Graf, et al., 1986<br>Solomon, 1987<br>Moopen, et al., 1988<br>Marcus & Westervelt, 1988b & 1988c<br>Moopen, Thakoor & Duong, 1988<br><br>Alspector, 1987<br>Sage, 1987<br>Symon, et al, 1988<br>Troudel & Tabatabai, 1988 |
| Optical/Electro-Optical | TeKolste & Guest, 1987<br>Stoll & Lee, 1988<br><br>Farhat, 1987a<br>Soffer, et al., 1986a & 1986b |
| Bus-Oriented Processors | TRW, 1987 |
| Coprocessor/Attached Processor | HNC, 1987b<br><br>SAIC, 1988 |
| Massively Parallel Computers | Brown, 1988<br>Barhen, Toomarian & Protopopsecu, 1987<br><br>Toomarian, 1988<br>Barhen, et al., 1987 |

TABLE 5-10.

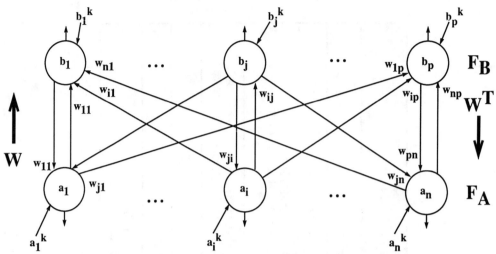

FIGURE 5-10. Topology of the discrete Bidirectional Associative Memory (BAM), an unsupervised learning—feedback recall ANS. This two-layer ANS stores pattern pairs in the weight matrix W formed from the connections between the $F_A$ and $F_B$ layers. This is a discrete time ANS that stores binary/bipolar pattern pairs. To keep the presentation uncluttered, all connections are not shown—there is actually a connection from each $F_A$ PE to each $F_B$ PE and vice versa.

where W is the n-by-p memory matrix that stores the pattern pair associations. In point-wise form, the encoding equation is

$$w_{ij} = \sum_{k=1}^{m} a_i^k b_j^k \qquad \text{(5-46)}$$

where $w_{ij}$ is the connection strength from the *ith* $F_A$ to the *jth* $F_B$ PE.

### 5.1.7.2. Recall

Like ART1, BAM recall employs inter-layer feedback between $F_A$ and $F_B$ PEs. Given an initial pattern or two incomplete pattern pairs, the BAM immediately reaches a resonant state where the final pattern pairs are found. The recall operation is described as follows:

1. Present a pattern to $F_A$ or $F_B$ or present partial patterns to both $F_A$ and $F_B$.
2. Feed the $F_A$ PE activation values asynchronously (or synchronously) through W to $F_B$.
3. Calculate the $F_B$ PE activation values.
4. Feed back the $F_B$ PE activation values asynchronously (or synchronously) through $W^T$ to $F_A$.
5. Calculate the $F_A$ PE activation values.
6. Repeat steps (3)–(6) until all $F_A$ and $F_B$ activations cease to change. This state of equilibrium is called resonation.

When the BAM updates are synchronous, it means that all the PEs from one layer are activated simultaneously. When the BAM updates are asynchronous, it means that less than all the PEs from one layer are activated at any given time.

The $F_B$ PE activation values are calculated using the equation

$$b_j(t + 1) = \begin{cases} 1 & \text{if } y_j > 0 \\ b_j(t) & \text{if } y_j = 0 \\ -1 & \text{if } y_j < 0 \end{cases} \qquad \text{(5-47)}$$

# Bidirectional Associative Memory (BAM) Example

**ENCODING:**

Pattern pair associations are encoded in a discrete Bidirectional Associative Memory (BAM) matrix W by summing the outer products of the m pattern pairs using the equation

$$W = \sum_{k=1}^{m} A_k^T B_k$$

where each $A_k \in \{-1,+1\}^n$ and $B_k \in \{-1,+1\}^p$. Using this equation we will encode the two pattern pairs $(A_1, B_1)$ and $(A_2, B_2)$ in W as follows:

$$A_1 = (1\ \text{-}1\ 1) \qquad\qquad B_1 = (1\ \text{-}1\ 1\ \text{-}1)$$
$$A_2 = (\text{-}1\ 1\ 1) \qquad\qquad B_2 = (\text{-}1\ 1\ \text{-}1\ 1)$$

$$A_1^T B_1 = \begin{bmatrix} 1 \\ \text{-}1 \\ 1 \end{bmatrix} \begin{bmatrix} 1\ \text{-}1\ 1\ \text{-}1 \end{bmatrix} \qquad\qquad A_2^T B_2 = \begin{bmatrix} \text{-}1 \\ 1 \\ 1 \end{bmatrix} \begin{bmatrix} \text{-}1\ 1\ \text{-}1\ 1 \end{bmatrix}$$

$$W = \sum_{k=1}^{2} A_k^T A_k \quad = \begin{bmatrix} 2 & \text{-}2 & 2 & \text{-}2 \\ \text{-}2 & 2 & \text{-}2 & 2 \\ 0 & 0 & 0 & 0 \end{bmatrix}$$

**RECALL:**

$F_A$ recall uses the equations

$$b_j(t+1) = \begin{cases} 1 & \text{if } y_j > 0 \\ b_j(t) & \text{if } y_j = 0 \\ \text{-}1 & \text{if } y_j < 0 \end{cases} \text{, where } \quad y_j = \sum_{i=1}^{n} a_i(t) w_{ij} \quad \forall i \& j = F(AW)$$

and $F_B$ recall uses the equations

$$a_i(t+1) = \begin{cases} 1 & \text{if } x_i > 0 \\ a_i(t) & \text{if } x_i = 0 \\ \text{-}1 & \text{if } x_i < 0 \end{cases} \text{, where } \quad x_i = \sum_{j=1}^{p} b_j(t) w_{ji} \quad \forall i \& j = F(BW^T)$$

BOX 5-2. An example of how the encoding and recall operations of the Bidirectional Associative Memory (BAM) operate. This example stores two pattern pairs and then demonstrates how a stored input pattern will recall the proper output pattern, and how an input that is slightly corrupted will also recall the proper output pattern.

# Bidirectional Associative Memory (BAM) Example (cont'd)

Using the above equations we will test the recall of the vector $A_1 = (1 -1\ 1)$ we get:

$$A_1W = (4\ -4\ 4\ -4) \Rightarrow threshold \Rightarrow (1\ -1\ 1\ -1) = B_1$$

$$B_1W^T = (8\ -8\ 0) \Rightarrow threshold \Rightarrow (1\ -1\ 1) = A_1$$

Repeating this process for the vector $A_2 = (-1\ 1\ 1)$ we get:

$$A_2W = (-4\ 4\ -4\ 4) \Rightarrow threshold \Rightarrow (-1\ 1\ -1\ 1) = B_2$$

$$B_2W^T = (-8\ 8\ 0) \Rightarrow threshold \Rightarrow (-1\ 1\ 1) = A_2$$

Therefore, both patterns are stored in the BAM W. Taking the example a step further, we present the vector $B = (1\ 1\ 1\ -1)$, a vector that has equal Hamming distance from both $B_1$ and $B_2$:

$$BW^T = (4\ -4\ 0) \Rightarrow threshold \Rightarrow (1\ -1\ -1) = A$$

$$AW = (4\ -4\ 4\ -4) \Rightarrow threshold \Rightarrow (1\ -1\ 1\ -1) = B'$$

$$B'W^T = (8\ -8\ 0) \Rightarrow threshold \Rightarrow (1\ -1\ -1) = A$$

and so on forever, recalling the vector $A = (1\ -1\ 1)$ and $B' = (1\ -1\ 1\ -1) = B_1$. Hence, the memory W corrected the error in B, producing $B_1$, and recalled the vector $A = (1\ -1\ -1)$, a vector closer in Hamming distance to $A_1$ than $A_2$.

BOX 5-2. *Continued*

where $b_j(t + 1)$ is the activation of the $j$th $F_B$ PE at time $t + 1$, and $y_j$ is the $j$th $F_B$ PE's pre-activation value found by the equation

$$y_j = \sum_{i=1}^{n} a_i(t)w_{ij} \qquad (5\text{-}48)$$

where $a_i(t)$ is the activation value of the $i$th $F_A$ PE at time t. The $F_A$ PE activation values are calculated using the equation

$$a_i(t + 1) = \begin{cases} 1 & \text{if } x_i > 0 \\ a_i(t) & \text{if } x_i = 0 \\ -1 & \text{if } x_i < 0 \end{cases} \qquad (5\text{-}49)$$

where $x_i$ is the $i$th $F_A$ PE's pre-activation value found by the equation

$$x_i = \sum_{j=1}^{p} b_j(t)w_{ji} \qquad (5\text{-}50)$$

and $w_{ji}$ is the connection strength from the $jth$ $F_B$ to the $ith$ $F_A$ PE. An example of the BAM encoding and recall operations is provided in Box 5-2.

### 5.1.7.3. Stability

BAM stability has been proven by Kosko (1988b) using a discrete-time Lyapunov energy function similar to the Discrete Autocorrelator's. The BAM energy function incorporates all the BAM's system parameters; the energy function only decreases when an $F_A$ and/or $F_B$ PE's activation value changes, and it is stable only when all the $F_A$ and $F_B$ PE activation values cease to change. The BAM's Lyapunov energy function, in vector notation, is

$$L(A,B) = -1/2AWB^T - 1/2AW^TB^T = -AWB^T \qquad (5\text{-}51)$$

where A is the vector of $F_A$ PE activation values, B is the vector of $F_B$ PE activation values, W is the matrix of $F_A$ to $F_B$ connections, and $W^T$ is the matrix transpose of W. Converting eq. 5-51 to pointwise notation yields

$$L(A,B) = -\sum_{i=1}^{n} \sum_{j=1}^{p} a_i b_j w_{ij} \qquad (5\text{-}52)$$

Calculating the change in energy (eq. 5-52) with respect to the change in A, $\Delta L_A(A,B)$, produces

$$\Delta L_A(A,B) = -(\Delta A)WB^T = -\sum_{i=1}^{n} \Delta a_i \sum_{j=1}^{p} b_j w_{ij} \qquad (5\text{-}53)$$

where $\Delta A = (\Delta a_1, \Delta a_2, \ldots, \Delta a_n)$. Through a careful case-by-case analysis of the effects on eq. 5-52 for changes in $F_A$ PE activation values shows: if $\Delta A \neq 0$ then $\Delta L(A,B) < 0$, and if $\Delta A = 0$, then $\Delta L(A,B) = 0$. Therefore, the system is stable. See Kosko (1988b) for details. Performing similar analysis for the $F_B$ layer, the change in energy (eq. 5-53) with respect to the change in B, $\Delta L_B(A,B)$, is

$$\Delta L_B(A,B) = -AW(\Delta B)^T = -\sum_{j=1}^{p} \Delta b_j \sum_{i=1}^{n} a_i w_{ij} \qquad (5\text{-}54)$$

which also decreases for all $\Delta B \neq 0$ and is stable when $\Delta B = 0$. Therefore, since all possible non-zero PE activation changes lead to a decrease in energy and all zero PE activation changes result in equilibrium, the BAM is globally stable. Moreover, since the weight matrix W had no effect on the stability analysis, *all* W are bidirectionally stable.

### 5.1.7.4. Discussion, Analysis, Applications, and Implementations

The BAM's strengths include its unconditional stability, its instructive simplicity—easily demonstrating how a heteroassociative, nearest-neighbor, pattern matching ANS can be constructed and operate—and its ability to add new pattern pairs quickly. The BAM's limitations include its inability to encode a large number of pattern pairs and its restriction to binary/bipolar valued pattern pairs.

BAM analysis and extensions have recently been emerging. Loos (1988) has described a version of the BAM that increases the pattern storage through the use of matrix transformations. Haines & Hecht-Nielsen (1988) have extended the capacity work of McEliece, et al. (1987) and found the BAM's capacity to be

$$m = \frac{q}{4 \log q} \tag{5-55}$$

where $q = \min(n,p)$. Haines & Hecht-Nielsen have also extended the BAM to include thresholds and they have improved the storage capacity through the use of Willshaw-type (Willshaw, Buneman & Longuet-Higgins, 1969) correlations. Lui (1988) has shown how the BAM is a special case of the Discrete Autocorrelator, and has discussed the use of the perceptron encoding algorithm (Rosenblatt, 1957) to improve storage capacity. Simpson (1988c) has compared the performance of the BAM against the Discrete Autocorrelator for pattern matching problems, and has extended the BAM to include higher-order correlations and intra-layer connections. Simpson (1988a & 1988b) has also developed an algorithm that stores patterns in a system of BAMs and demonstrated how to maximize the potential of each individual BAM in the system through the use of orthogonal encoding techniques.

The BAM is best applied in situations that require nearest-neighbor pattern matching of only a few patterns. A list of BAM applications can be found on Table 5-11. Like the Discrete Autocorrelator, the BAM is extremely amendable to optical implementations because of its simple dynamics. A list of the optical/electro-optical, and other, implementations can be found on Table 5-12.

### 5.1.8. Adaptive Bidirectional Associative Memory (ABAM)

The adaptive bidirectional associative memory (ABAM) ANS — introduced by Kosko (1987c) — is a two-layer, heteroassociative nearest-neighbor pattern matcher that stores arbitrary analog spatial pattern pairs $(A_k, B_k)$, $k = 1, 2, \ldots, m$, using signal Hebbian encoding, where the $k$th pattern pair is represented by the vectors $A_k = (a_1^k, \ldots, a_n^k)$ and $B_k = (b_1^k, \ldots, b_p^k)$. The ABAM learns online, operates in continuous time, and is represented by the two-layer feedback topology shown in Figure 5-11, where the n $F_A$ PEs correspond to $A_k$'s components and the p $F_B$ PEs correspond to $B_k$'s components. The ABAM is a step in the evolution of the Discrete BAM (see previous section) in that it operates with analog values in continuous time.

*5.1.8.1. Encoding*

Vanilla ABAM Encoding. Pattern pairs are encoded using the signal Hebbian (passive decay LTM) correlation equation

| BAM Applications ||
|---|---|
| **Application** | **Reference** |
| Image Processing | Kosko, 1988b<br>Dunning, et al., 1986 & 1987<br>Soffer, et al., 1986a & 1986b |
| Control | Bavarian, 1988 |
| Resource Allocation | AMC, 1988 |

TABLE 5-11.

| BAM Implementations | |
| --- | --- |
| **Implementation** | **Reference** |
| Optical/Electro-Optical | Kinser, Caulfield & Shamir, 1988a & 1988b<br>Dunning, et al., 1986 & 1987<br>Soffer, et al., 1986a & 1986b<br>Kosko & Guest, 1987<br>TeKolste & Guest, 1987<br>Owechko, 1987<br>D. Anderson, 1986 |
| Coprocessor/Attached    Processor | HNC, 1987b<br>SAIC, 1988 |

TABLE 5-12.

$$\dot{w}_{ij} = \alpha[-w_{ij} + S(a_i^k)S(b_j^k)] \qquad (5\text{-}56)$$

where $\alpha$ is a positive constant controlling the learning rate, $w_{ij}$ is the connection strength from the $i$th $F_A$ to the $j$th $F_B$ PE, and $S()$ is a sigmoid function (see section 3.2. for a description of threshold functions). The ABAM's memory is extremely plastic. Any pattern pair presented for an extended period of time is imprinted in the memory to the point that no other patterns can be stored in the memory. Sampling learning is employed to overcome this obstacle (Diaconis & Efrom, 1983; Kosko, 1987e). During sampling learning, brief glimpses of pattern pairs are selected randomly from a large set of noisy $(A_k, B_k)$ images and are encoded in W over an extended period of time. Combining sampling learning with a low learning rate (i.e. $\alpha \ll 1$), the ABAM's Lyapunov energy surface is gently sculpted, yielding more abundant pattern storage.

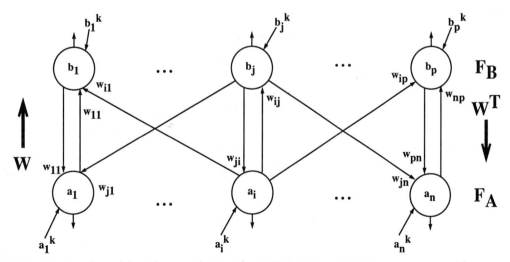

FIGURE 5-11. Topology of the Adaptive Bidirectional Associative Memory (ABAM), an unsupervised learning—feedback recall ANS. This two-layer ANS stores pattern pairs in the weight matrix W formed from the connections between the $F_A$ and $F_B$ layers. This is a continuous time ANS that stores analog pattern pairs. To keep the presentation uncluttered, all connections are not shown—there is actually a connection from each $F_A$ PE to each $F_B$ PE and vice versa

Higher-Order ABAM Encoding. The ABAM can be made a better pattern matcher (at the cost of higher connectivity) through the use of higher-order correlations—a procedure that offers some invariances to shift, rotation and scale in the mapping (Kosko, 1987e). Figure 5-8 shows the difference between first-order and second-order connections in a one-layer ANS topology; the extension to two-layer topologies is direct. Higher-order correlations couple several PE activations with another PE. The second-order $F_A$ to $F_B$ correlations are stored in the n-by-n-by-p matrix U using the equation

$$\dot{u}_{hij} = -u_{hij} + S(a_h^k)S(a_i^k)S(b_j^k) \tag{5-57}$$

which connects the h*th* and i*th* $F_A$ PEs with the j*th* $F_B$ PE. The second-order $F_B$ to $F_A$ correlations are stored in the p-by-p-by-n matrix V using the equation

$$\dot{v}_{jih} = -v_{jih} + S(b_j^k)S(b_i^k)S(a_h^k) \tag{5-58}$$

which connects the j*th* and i*th* $F_B$ PEs with the h*th* $F_A$ PE.

Differential Hebbian ABAM Encoding. Another ABAM encoding extension adds a continuous time differential Hebbian (Kosko, 1986e & 1988c) correlation term to eq. 5-56, allowing the correlation of both PE activations and their velocities as shown by the learning equation

$$\dot{w}_{ij} = -w_{ij} + S(a_i^k)S(b_j^k) + \dot{S}(a_i^k)\dot{S}(b_j^k) \tag{5-59}$$

The one drawback to adding the differential Hebbian correlation terms is that stability of the system is jeopardized.

Competitive ABAM Encoding. One final encoding extension of the ABAM requires the addition of intra-layer ($F_A$ to $F_A$ and $F_B$ to $F_B$) connections as shown in Figure 5-12 (Kosko, 1987d). These intra-layer connections provide contrast enhancement of signals during encoding and recall (Cohen & Grossberg, 1983; Grossberg, 1973) and the combined architecture is entitled a Competitive ABAM or CABAM. Three matrices are now used to store connection values:

1. Inter-layer ($F_A$ to $F_B$) connection values are stored in W,

2. $F_A$ intra-layer ($F_A$ to $F_A$) connection values are stored in U,

and

3. $F_B$ intra-layer ($F_B$ to $F_B$) connection values are stored in V.

The intra-layer connections are preset with non-adaptive self-exciting and neighbor-inhibiting connection values. The $F_A$ intra-layer connections are assigned values using the equation

$$u_{gh} = \begin{cases} +\alpha & \text{if } g = h \\ -\alpha & \text{if } g \neq h \end{cases} \tag{5-60}$$

and the $F_B$ intra-layer connections are assigned values using the equation

$$v_{ij} = \begin{cases} +\beta & \text{if } i = j \\ -\beta & \text{if } i \neq j \end{cases} \tag{5-61}$$

where $u_{gh}$ is the connection strength between the g*th* and h*th* $F_A$ PEs, $v_{ij}$ is the connection strength between the i*th* and j*th* $F_B$ PEs, and $\alpha$ and $\beta$ are positive constants. The $F_A$ to $F_B$ inter-field connections are adjusted using eq. 5-56.

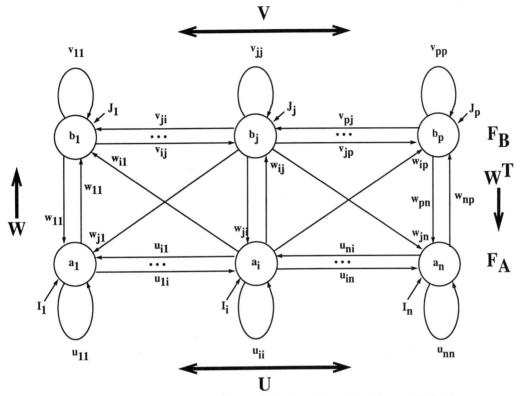

FIGURE 5-12. Toplology of the Competitive Adaptive Bidirectional Associative Memory (CABAM), an unsupervised learning — feedback recall ANS. This two-layer ANS stores pattern pairs in the weight matrix W formed from the connections between the $F_A$ and $F_B$ layers. The CABAM also uses the weight matrices U and V to contrast enhance the $F_A$ and $F_B$ pattern activations, respectively. This is a continuous time ANS that stores analog pattern pairs. To keep the presentation uncluttered, all connections are not shown — there is actually a connection from each $F_A$ PE to each $F_B$ PE (and vice versa), a negative lateral connection from each $F_A$ ($F_B$) PE to every other $F_A$ ($F_B$) PE, a positive recurrent connection from every $F_A$ ($F_B$) PE to itself.

### 5.1.8.2. Recall

General ABAM Recall. ABAM recall uses the same processing sequence as the BAM — a pattern is presented to $F_A$ or $F_B$ (or partial patterns to both), feedback between the layers ensues, and eventually the ABAM stabilizes on a resonant pattern pair. The $F_A$ PE recall equation in the general form is (cf. Cohen-Grossberg theorem eq. 3-40)

$$\dot{a}_i = -\alpha_i(a_i)\left[\beta_i(a_i) - \sum_{j=1}^{p} w_{ji}S_j(b_j)\right] \tag{5-62}$$

where $a_i$ is the *ith* $F_A$ PE's activation value, $b_j$ is the *jth* $F_B$ PE's activation value, $\alpha_i()$ is a non-decreasing function, $\beta_i()$ is an arbitrary bounded function, and $w_{ij}$ is the symmetric connection strength from the *jth* $F_B$ to the *ith* $F_A$ PE. The corresponding $F_B$ PE recall equation is

$$\dot{b}_j = -\alpha_j(b_j)\left[\beta_j(b_j) - \sum_{i=1}^{n} w_{ij}S_i(a_i)\right] \tag{5-63}$$

where $\alpha_j()$ is a non-decreasing function, and $\beta_j()$ is an arbitrary bounded function.

Vanilla ABAM Recall. The less general, yet more common, recall equations are (cf. Additive Grossberg recall eq. 5-3)

$$\dot{a}_i = -a_i + \sum_{j=1}^{P} S(b_j)w_{ji} + I_i \tag{5-64}$$

where $I_i$ is the external input to the $ith$ $F_A$ PE and

$$\dot{b}_j = -b_j + \sum_{i=1}^{n} S(a_i)w_{ij} + J_j \tag{5-65}$$

where $J_i$ is the external input to the $jth$ $F_B$ PE. The vanilla and general forms of the higher-ordered, differential Hebbian, and competitive versions of the ABAM are direct extensions of eqs. 5-62 through 5-65. A detailed explanation of each can be found in Kosko (1988c).

### 5.1.8.3. Stability

General ABAM Stability. The ABAM theorem (section 3.7.2.3.) proves the general ABAM system created by eq. 5-56, eq. 5-62 and eq. 5-63 is globally stable. Using the notation described in section 3.7.2.3., we need only make algebraic identifications that do not violate the five listed restrictions, and the ABAM is automatically proven stable by virtue of the ABAM theorem equations being stable. Referring to eq. 3-40, we substitute the ABAM theorem terms — left hand side — with the terms of eq. 5-56, eq. 5-62 and eq. 5-63 — right hand side — as follows:

$$x_i = a_i$$

$$y_j = b_j$$

and

$$m_{ij} = w_{ij}$$

Vanilla ABAM Stability. The less general ABAM system, eq. 5-56, eq. 5-64 and eq. 5-65, is also proven stable using the ABAM theorem by substituting the terms of the ABAM theorem — left hand side — with the terms of eq. 5-56, eq. 5-64 and eq. 5-65 — right hand side — as follows:

$$\alpha_i(x_i) = \beta_j(y_j) = 1$$

$$\beta_i(x_i) = -a_i + I_i$$

$$\beta_j(y_j) = -b_j + J_j$$

$$x_i = a_i$$

$$y_j = b_j$$

and

$$m_{ij} = w_{ij}$$

Vanilla Competitive ABAM Stability. CABAM stability is most easily shown by collapsing the two-layer CABAM into a one-layer ANS by treating the $F_A$ and $F_B$ layers as a single layer, and creating a new weight matrix of suitable dimensions and filling it with the values from W, $W^T$, U and V. Once this transformation has been made, the resulting system can be shown to be stable using the Cohen-Grossberg-Kosko theorem of section 3.7.2.2. Also note that the CABAM connection topology can be collapsed into a one matrix system with dynamics almost identical to that of the Additive Grossberg ANS (section 5.1.1.) and the Continuous Hopfield ANS (section 5.1.6.). The primary difference between these paradigms is that the CABAM has a rigid field-feedback information flow while the others have a more flexible asynchronous or synchronous information flow.

### 5.1.8.4. Discussion, Applications, and Implementations

A primary limitation of the ABAMs is their poor storage—storing far fewer patterns than the smaller of the two dimensionalities of the $F_A$ and $F_B$ layers. A key strength of the ABAMs is their extreme memory plasticity. Having an extremely plastic memory allows emergent statistical similarities to emerge from excessively noisy data sets. Areas where this type of data is common include image processing (Kosko, 1987c), speech processing, and statistical analysis. Applications are only now being discovered for this relatively new ANS paradigm. Implementations have been sold commercially by HNC (1987b) and SAIC (1988).

## 5.1.9. Temporal Associative Memory (TAM)

The temporal associative memory (TAM) ANS—introduced by Amari (1972b)—is a two-layer, nearest-neighbor sequence encoder that stores arbitrary binary/bipolar spatiotemporal pattern loops $(A_1,\ldots,A_m,A_1)$, $A_k = (a_1^k,\ldots,a_n^k)$, using Hebbian learning. The TAM learns offline, operates in discrete time, and is represented by the two-layer feedback topology shown in Figure 5-13, where the n PEs in both $F_A$ and $F_B$ represent the $kth$ and $k+1st$ patterns of the sequence, $A_k$ and $A_{k+1}$, respectively.

### 5.1.9.1. Encoding

The TAM encodes a spatial pattern by associating $A_1$ with $A_2$, $A_2$ with $A_3$, and so on, eventually forming a pattern loop by associating $A_m$ with $A_1$. The encoding equation uses the

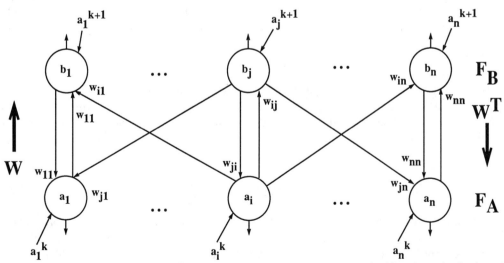

FIGURE 5-13. Topology of the Temporal Associative Memory (TAM), an unsupervised learning—feedback recall ANS. This two-layer ANS stores sequences of patterns in the weight matrix W formed from the connections between the $F_A$ and $F_B$ layers. This is a discrete time ANS that stores binary/bipolar pattern pairs. To keep the presentation uncluttered, all connections are not shown—there is actually a connection from each $F_A$ PE to each $F_B$ PE and vice versa.

same operation as that of the Discrete Autocorrelator (section 5.1.5.) or the Bidirectional Associative Memory (section 5.1.7.), the sum of outer products

$$W = A_m^T A_1 + \sum_{k=1}^{m-1} A_k^T A_{k+1} \qquad (5\text{-}66)$$

where $A_k^T$ is the vector transpose of $A_k$, and $W$ is the $F_A$ to $F_B$ connection matrix storing the m-pattern sequence. In point-wise notation, eq. 5-66 is

$$\Delta w_{ij} = a_i^k a_j^{k+1} \qquad (5\text{-}67)$$

where $a_i^k$ is the $ith$ component of $A_k$, $a_j^{k+1}$ is the $jth$ component of $A_{k+1}$, $\Delta w_{ij}$ is the change in connection strength from the $ith$ $F_A$ to the $jth$ $F_B$ PE, and

$$a_j^{m+1} \equiv a_j^1 \qquad (5\text{-}68)$$

### 5.1.9.2. Recall

During TAM recall, once a pattern is activated, the sequence loop is entered and it begins to infinitely repeat — a limit cycle. The recall equation for the $F_B$ PEs — corresponding to the activation values of the k + 1st pattern — is

$$a_j^{k+1}(t + 1) = \begin{cases} 1 & \text{if } x_j > 0 \\ a_j^{k+1}(t) & \text{if } x_j = 0 \\ -1 & \text{if } x_j < 0 \end{cases} \qquad (5\text{-}69)$$

where $a_i^{k+1}(t + 1)$ is the $jth$ $F_B$ PE's value at time $t + 1$, and $x_j$, the $jth$ $F_B$ PE's pre-activation value computed using the equation

$$x_j = \sum_{i=1}^{n} a_i^k(t) w_{ij} \qquad (5\text{-}70)$$

Note that the TAM will automatically recall patterns in the opposite order if the input pattern primes the $F_B$ layer and continuously uses the transpose of the weight matrix during the cyclic recall phase. An example of the TAM encoding and recall operations is provided in Box 5-3.

### 5.1.9.3. Stability

TAM stability requires proving a limit cycle of length m reverberates stably — a task much different than proving stability at a fixed point. To do this, TAM stability, shown by Kosko (1988b) to be an extension of discrete BAM stability, is proven using a Lyapunov energy function constructed from the entire sequence of m patterns. The resulting energy function, in vector notation, is

$$L(A_1, \ldots, A_m, A_1) = -A_m W A_1^T - \sum_{k=1}^{m-1} A_k W A_{k+1}^T \qquad (5\text{-}71)$$

Without a loss in generality and for the sake of easier analysis, the first term of eq. 5-71 is dropped. Because only one pattern will be active at a time, e.g. the $hth$ pattern, and all other patterns are not being primed, eq. 5-71 can be expanded around the $hth$ pattern's activation as follows

$$L(A_1, \ldots, A_m) = -A_{h-1} W A_h^T - A_h W A_{h+1}^T - \sum_{\substack{k=1 \\ k \neq h \\ k \neq h-1}}^{m-1} A_k W A_{k+1}^T \qquad (5\text{-}72)$$

# Temporal Associative Memory (TAM) Example

**ENCODING:**

A pattern sequence is encoded in a Temporal Associative Memory (TAM) matrix W by summing together the outer products of the m patterns correlations

$$W = \sum_{k=1}^{m-1} A_k^T A_{k+1} + A_m^T A_1$$

where each $A_k \in \{-1,+1\}^n$. Using this equation we encode the sequence $A_1$, $A_2$, $A_3$ in W as follows:

$$A_1 = (1\ -1\ 1\ -1\ 1) \qquad A_2 = (1\ 1\ 1\ -1\ -1) \qquad A_3 = (-1\ -1\ -1\ 1\ 1)$$

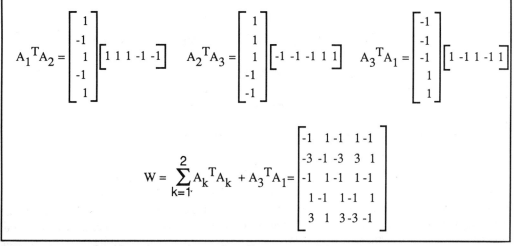

$$A_1^T A_2 = \begin{bmatrix} 1 \\ -1 \\ 1 \\ -1 \\ 1 \end{bmatrix} \begin{bmatrix} 1\ 1\ 1\ -1\ -1 \end{bmatrix} \quad A_2^T A_3 = \begin{bmatrix} 1 \\ 1 \\ 1 \\ -1 \\ -1 \end{bmatrix} \begin{bmatrix} -1\ -1\ -1\ 1\ 1 \end{bmatrix} \quad A_3^T A_1 = \begin{bmatrix} -1 \\ -1 \\ -1 \\ 1 \\ 1 \end{bmatrix} \begin{bmatrix} 1\ -1\ 1\ -1\ 1 \end{bmatrix}$$

$$W = \sum_{k=1}^{2} A_k^T A_k + A_3^T A_1 = \begin{bmatrix} -1 & 1 & -1 & 1 & -1 \\ -3 & -1 & -3 & 3 & 1 \\ -1 & 1 & -1 & 1 & -1 \\ 1 & -1 & 1 & -1 & 1 \\ 3 & 1 & 3 & -3 & -1 \end{bmatrix}$$

BOX 5-3. An example of how the encoding and recall operations of the Temporal Associative Memory (TAM) operate. This example stores a sequence of three patterns and then demonstrates how one pattern in the sequence will cause the TAM to enter a limit cycle that repeatedly recalls the entire sequence.

Calculating the change in energy with respect to the change in $A_h$ produces the equation

$$\Delta L_{A_h}(A_1,\ldots,A_m) = -A_{h-1} W \Delta A_h^T - \Delta A_h W A_{h+1}^T \qquad (5\text{-}73)$$

$$= -\sum_{i=1}^{n} \Delta a_i^h \sum_{j=1}^{n} a_j^{h-1} w_{ij} - \sum_{i=1}^{n} \Delta a_i^h \sum_{j=1}^{n} a_j^{h+1} w_{ij}$$

where $A_{h-1}$ is the $h-1st$ pattern and $A_{h+1}$ is the $h+1st$ pattern. Because each $\Delta A_h \neq 0$ results in a $\Delta L(A_1,\ldots,A_m) < 0$ and all $\Delta A_h = 0$ results in $\Delta L(A_1,\ldots,A_m) = 0$, the TAM is globally stable.

## 5.1.9.4. Discussion, Extensions, Applications, and Implementations

The TAM's primary strength is its ability to store spatiotemporal patterns that can be quickly recalled in either the forward or backward direction. One of the TAM's limitations is its need for specific preprocessing or encoding considerations to allow the same pattern to occur more

## Temporal Associative Memory (TAM) Example (cont'd)

**RECALL:**

$F_A$ and $F_B$ recall uses the equation

$$a_j^{k+1}(t+1) = \begin{cases} 1 & \text{if } x_j > 0 \\ a_j^{k+1}(t) & \text{if } x_j = 0, \text{ where } \quad x_j = \sum_{i=1}^{n} a_i^k(t)\, w_{ij} \quad \forall i\&j = F(AW) \\ -1 & \text{if } x_j < 0 \end{cases}$$

Using the above equation we will test the recall of the sequence loop $\{A_1, A_2, A_3, A_1\}$ by presenting the pattern $A_1 = (1\ -1\ 1\ -1\ 1)$ as follows:

$$A_1 W = (3\ 5\ 3\ -3\ -5) \quad \Rightarrow \text{threshold} \Rightarrow (1\ 1\ 1\ -1\ -1) = A_2$$

$$A_2 W^T = (-1\ -11\ -1\ 1\ 11) \quad \Rightarrow \text{threshold} \Rightarrow (-1\ -1\ -1\ 1\ 1) = A_3$$

$$A_3 W = (9\ -1\ 9\ -9\ 1) \quad \Rightarrow \text{threshold} \Rightarrow (1\ -1\ 1\ -1\ 1) = A_1$$

Therefore, the entire sequence of patterns is stored in the TAM W.

BOX 5-3. *Continued*

than once in the same, or another, sequence. Other restrictions include the inability to store a large number of sequences and the restriction to binary/bipolar patterns.

Some analysis of the TAM has been recently conducted addressing the TAM's limitations. Buhman & Schulten (1988) have studied the similarities between the TAM and other temporal pattern processors. Gardner, Stroud & Wallace (1988) have used noise to increase the storage capacity of the TAM. And, Guyon, Personnaz & Dreyfus (1988) have developed techniques that allow the same pattern to occur in separate sequences.

The TAM is very useful in situations where a succession of sequences must be carried out when a specific cue has been received. This type of temporal processing is most easily identified as a parallel finite state machine (Kohonen, 1984). Another TAM application is text storage and retrieval (Gardner, Stroud & Wallace, 1988; Guyon, Personnaz & Dreyfus, 1988). In addition, Owechko (1987) has discussed an electro-optical implementation of the TAM.

## 5.2. UNSUPERVISED LEARNING AND FEEDFORWARD RECALL ARTIFICIAL NEURAL SYSTEMS

### 5.2.1. Learning Matrix (LM)

The learning matrix (LM) ANS—introduced by Steinbuch (1961)—is a crossbar, heteroassociative, nearest-neighbor pattern classifier that stores arbitrary binary spatial patterns $A_k$, $k = 1, 2, \ldots, m$, into one of p classes using Hebbian learning, where the *kth* pattern is represented by the vector $A_k = (a_1^k, \ldots, a_n^k)$ and the classes are represented by individual components of the vector $B_k = (b_1^k, \ldots, b_p^k)$. The LM learns offline, operates in discrete time, and is represented by the crossbar topology shown in Figure 5-14 where the n $F_A$ lines along the top of the crossbar correspond to $A_k$'s components and the p $F_B$ lines along the left side of the crossbar represent $B_k$'s components.

### 5.2.1.1. Encoding

The LM stores information by conditioning the connections between the $F_A$ and $F_B$ lines. During encoding, one component of $B_k$ is held high (0 = low, 1 = high) to delineate $A_k$'s class, and all others are left low. The LM encoding equation is

$$\Delta w_{ij} = \begin{cases} +\alpha & \text{if } a_i^k = 1 \text{ and } b_j^k = 1 \\ -\alpha & \text{if } a_i^k = 0 \text{ and } b_j^k = 1 \\ 0 & \text{otherwise} \end{cases} \qquad \text{(5-74)}$$

where $w_{ij}$ is the connection strength between the $i$th $F_A$ and $j$th $F_B$ lines and $\alpha$ is a positive constant.

### 5.2.1.2. Recall

LM recall can occur in both directions. The $F_A$ to $F_B$ information flow determines the pattern class by employing the equation

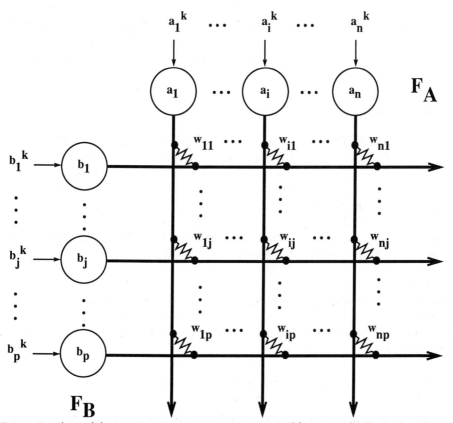

FIGURE 5-14. Topology of the Learning Matrix (LM), an unsupervised learning—feedforward recall ANS. This crossbar ANS stores sequences of patterns in the weight matrix W formed from the connections between the $F_A$ and $F_B$ lines. This is a discrete time ANS that classifies binary patterns. To keep the presentation uncluttered, all connections are not shown—there is actually a connection from each $F_A$ line to each $F_B$ line.

$$b_j = \begin{cases} 1 & \text{if } \sum_{i=1}^{n} a_i w_{ij} = \underset{h=1}{\overset{p}{\text{MAX}}} \left[ \sum_{i=1}^{n} a_i w_{ih} \right] \\ 0 & \text{otherwise} \end{cases} \tag{5-75}$$

where $b_j$ is the $j$th $F_B$ line's activation, and $a_i$ is the $i$th $F_A$ line's activation. The $F_B$ to $F_A$ information flow recalls an $F_A$ pattern given the $j$th $F_B$ class using the equation

$$a_i = \sum_{j=1}^{p} b_j w_{ji} \tag{5-76}$$

### 5.2.1.3. Discussion, Applications, and Implementations

LM convergence was never addressed by Steinbuch. This paradigm was the first crossbar ANS and served as an important foundational construct for the later work of Hopfield (1982) and Kohonen (1984). This paradigm created some excitement in the early 1960's that resulted in some analysis and extensions. Ullman (1962) developed a technique that improved LM encoding. Steinbuch & Piske (1963) extended the LM to perform classification of analog valued patterns and discussed how combination of LMs could be used to create dipoles and layered classifiers. In addition, Steinbuch & Widrow (1965) performed a rigorous comparison of the storage capacities and performance of the LM and the Adaline (see section 5.4.2).

LM applications include self-correcting translator circuits (Steinbuch & Zendeh, 1963), adaptive pattern recognition (Kazmierczak & Steinbuch, 1963), and monitoring production processes (Steinbuch & Piske, 1963). Also, several LM implementations were designed by Steinbuch & Piske (1963), including mechanical, magnetic, electrochemical, capacitive component, and wound ribbon core.

## 5.2.2. Drive-Reinforcement (DR)

The drive-reinforcement (DR) ANS—a development introduced by Klopf (1986) that evolved from his hedonistic neuronal conditioning theory (Klopf, 1972, 1979 & 1982)—is a two-layer, heteroassociative, performance optimizer that stores analog stimulus-response pairs $(A_k, B_k)$, k = 1, 2, ..., m, using discrete-time, time-lagged, differential Hebbian learning, where the $k$th pattern pair is represented by the vectors $A_k = (a_1^k, \ldots, a_n^k)$ and $B_k = (b_1^k, \ldots, b_p^k)$. DR learns offline, operates in discrete time, and is represented by the two-layer feedforward topology shown in Figure 5-15, where the n $F_A$ PEs correspond to $A_k$'s components and the p $F_B$ PEs correspond to $B_k$'s components.

### 5.2.2.1. Encoding

DR encodes stimulus-response pairs by correlating earlier pre-synaptic changes—drives—with later post-synaptic changes—reinforcements. These temporal adjustments condition the $F_A$ to $F_B$ connections by capturing lagged variations, not just instantaneous changes. The DR encoding equation is

$$\Delta w_{ij}(t) = \Delta b_j^k(t) \sum_{h=1}^{\tau} \alpha(t) |w_{ij}(t-h)| \Delta a_i^k(t-h) \tag{5-77}$$

where t is the interstimulus interval, $a_i^k(t)$ is the $i$th $F_A$ PE's value at time t during the encoding of the $k$th pattern pair, $a_i^k(1) = a_i^k$, $b_j^k(t)$ is the $j$th $F_B$ PE's value at time t during the encoding of $k$th pattern pair, $b_j^k(1) = b_j^k$, $w_{ij}$ is the connection strength from the $i$th $F_A$ to the $j$th $F_B$ PE, and $\alpha(t)$ is a positive valued decreasing function proportional to the efficacy of $w_{ij}$ that

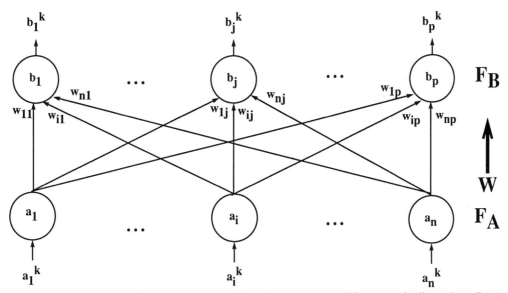

FIGURE 5-15. Topology of the Drive-Reinforcement (DR) ANS, an unsupervised learning—feedforward recall ANS. This two-layer ANS optimizes control sequences by properly conditioning the weight matrix W formed from the connections between the $F_A$ and $F_B$ PEs. To keep the presentation uncluttered, all connections are not shown— there is actually a connection from each $F_A$ PE to each $F_B$ PE.

controls the rate of learning and ranges from $\alpha(1) = 1$ to $\alpha(t) = 0$. The post-synaptic change of the $jth$ $F_B$ PE at time t during presentation of the $kth$ pattern pair is defined as

$$\Delta b_j^k(t) = b_j^k(t) - b_j^k(t - 1) \tag{5-78}$$

and the pre-synaptic change of the $ith$ $F_A$ PE at time t during the presentation of the $kth$ pattern pair is

$$\Delta a_i^k(t) = f(a_i^k(t - h)) - f(a_i^k(t - h - 1)) \tag{5-79}$$

where $f()$ is the step threshold function defined as

$$f(x) = \begin{cases} 1 & \text{if } x \geq 0 \\ 0 & \text{otherwise} \end{cases} \tag{5-80}$$

### 5.2.2.2. Recall
The DR $F_B$ recall equation is

$$b_j(t) = \sum_{i=1}^{n} w_{ij}(t) a_i(t) - \Theta_j \tag{5-81}$$

where $b_j(t)$ is the $jth$ $F_B$ PE's value at time t, $a_i(t)$ is the $ith$ $F_A$ PE's value at time t, and $\Theta_j$ is the $jth$ $F_B$ PE's threshold value.

### 5.2.2.3. Stability, Discussion, Applications, and Implementations
Although there is no DR convergence proof, Kosko's (1986d) analysis of continuous-time differential Hebbian learning and the recent work of Gluck, Parker & Reifsnider (1988) has shown that there are reasonable assumptions that can be made that will lead to a stable system.

A DR strength is its ability to optimize temporal actions. This property has been demonstrated for robotics simulations (Klopf, 1987a) and classical conditioning experiments (Klopf, 1987b & 1987c), making it an ideal candidate for control applications. Another strength is seen in the DR's recent extension to an online learning system (Morgan, Patterson & Klopf, 1988). A primary DR limitation is its inability to learn more than one sequence at a time.

Candidate DR application areas are primarily in the area of control. Existing applications have used the DR ANS for target tracking (McAulay, 1988) and real-time control (Klopf, 1987a; Morgan, Patterson & Klopf, 1988).

### 5.2.3. Sparse Distributed Memory (SDM)

The Sparse Distributed Memory (SDM) ANS — introduced by Kanerva (1984) — is a three-layer, heteroassociative, nearest-neighbor pattern matcher that stores bipolar pattern pairs $(A_k, C_k)$, $k = 1, 2, \ldots, m$, using a random vector preprocessing scheme in combination with Hebbian learning, where the $k$th pattern pair is represented by the vectors $A_k = (a_1^k, \ldots, a_n^k)$ and $C_k = (c_1^k, \ldots, c_q^k)$. The SDM learns offline, operates in discrete time, and is represented by the three-layer feedforward topology shown in Figure 5-16, where the n $F_A$ PEs correspond

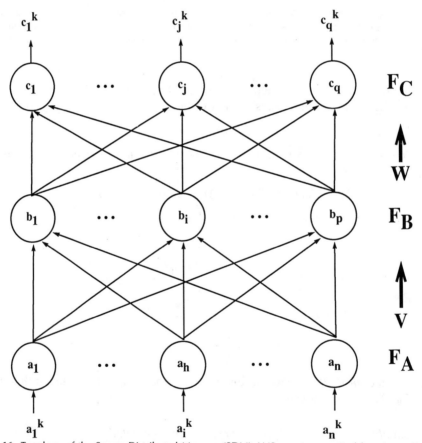

FIGURE 5-16. Topology of the Sparse Distributed Memory (SDM) ANS, an unsupervised learning—feedforward recall ANS. This three-layer ANS utilizes a randomly connected $F_A$ to $F_B$ weight matrix V to create a sparse internal representation, and the pattern pairs are encoded in the weight matrix W formed from the connections between the $F_B$ and $F_C$ PEs. To keep the presentation uncluttered, all connections are not shown—there is actually a connection from each $F_A$ PE to each $F_B$ PE and from each $F_B$ PE to each $F_C$ PE.

to $A_k$'s components, the p $F_B$ PEs correspond to an internal sparse coding representation layer, and the q $F_C$ PEs correspond to $C_k$'s components.

### 5.2.3.1. Encoding

The SDM encodes pattern pairs by creating a random matrix of connections, V, from the $F_A$ to $F_B$ PEs, where the number of $F_B$ PEs is much larger than either the $F_A$ or $F_C$ layers, and by using it as a preprocessor. This technique, similar to the extensive work of Rosenblatt (see the Perceptron in section 5.4.1), allows a transformation from the n-dimensional bipolar cube to a much larger p-dimensional bipolar cube which then allows for improved storage capacity over the Discrete Autocorrelator (see section 5.1.5). In summary, the SDM is a Discrete Autoassociator with a clever preprocessing scheme and no feedback during recall.

The $F_A$ to $F_B$ connections are stored in the n-by-p matrix V — called the address matrix — and are each randomly assigned a bipolar value (+1 or −1). The $F_B$ to $F_C$ connections are stored in the p-by-q matrix W — called the counter matrix — and are found using the equation

$$W = \sum_{k=1}^{m} B_k^T C_k \tag{5-82}$$

where $B_k = (b_{1k},\ldots,b_{ik},\ldots,b_{pk})$ is the internal representation during the encoding of the kth pattern pair. The internal representation for each pattern pair is calculated using the equation

$$b_{hk} = \begin{cases} 1 & \text{if } H(A_k,V_i) \leq n - 2\rho \\ 0 & \text{otherwise} \end{cases} \tag{5-83}$$

where $V_i = (v_{1i},\ldots,v_{hi},\ldots,v_{ni})$ is the vector of connections abutting the ith $F_B$ PE, H() is the Hamming distance function — a function that calculates the number of similar components between two vectors, and $\rho$ is the Hamming radius used to control the number of bits in the internal representation.

### 5.2.3.2. Recall

The recall process accepts an arbitrary bipolar valued input at the $F_A$ PEs, passes the $F_A$ PE values through the randomly connected weight matrix V and creates an internal representation on the $F_B$ PEs, passes these values through the Hebbian correlated connections to $F_C$ and creates the output.

The $F_B$ PE values are calculated using the equation

$$b_i = \Phi\left(\sum_{h=1}^{n} a_h v_{hi}, \rho\right) \tag{5-84}$$

where the two-parameter threshold function is defined as

$$\Phi(\alpha,\beta) = \begin{cases} 1 & \text{if } 1/2(n - \alpha) \leq \beta \\ 0 & \text{otherwise} \end{cases} \tag{5-85}$$

The $F_C$ PE values are then found using the equation

$$c_j = f\left(\sum_{i=1}^{p} b_i w_{ij}\right) \tag{5-86}$$

where f() is the step threshold function defined as

$$f(x) = \begin{cases} 1 & \text{if } x \geq 0 \\ 0 & \text{otherwise} \end{cases} \tag{5-87}$$

*5.2.3.3. Discussion, Applications, and Implementations*

The SDM ANS represents an encoding methodology designed to eliminate the storage capacity limitation. The potentially unlimited storage capacity of the SDM ANS is a primary strength. The SDM's pattern storage is offset by an excessive amount of storage required for large $F_B$ layers. Other limitations of the SDM include its restriction to bipolar-valued patterns, its offline learning requirement, and the lack of means for determining an optimal $F_B$ layer size.

The SDM's memory capacity has been analyzed by Keller (1987 & 1988a) and Chou (1988), and is estimated to be $0.13n$ for n between 100 and 1000. Keeler (1988a & 1988b) has compared the SDM ANS with other Discrete Autocorrelators. Rogers (1988) has developed a tagging scheme to improve the SDM's performance. And Kanerva (1988b) has performed a wide range of analyses and experiments on the SDM and bound them into a book aptly titled *Sparse Distributed Memory*.

The primary SDM application areas are pattern matching and temporal sequence encoding. Kanerva (1988a) has used the SDM to encode and recognize sequences presented at various tempos. Joglekar (1988) has used the SDM to perform a text to phoneme mapping for speech processing. Rogers (1989b) has applied the SDM to statistical prediction. Kanerva (1986) has argued that the SDM ANS is biologically plausible. And, Rogers (1989a) has discussed why the SDM ANS is an ideal ANS for massively parallel computer implementation.

## 5.2.4. Linear Associative Memory (LAM)

The linear associative memory (LAM) ANS — introduced by J. Anderson (1968) and refined by J. Anderson (1970, 1972 & 1973) and Kohonen (1972a, 1972b & 1977) — is a two-layer, heteroassociative, interpolative pattern matcher that stores arbitrary analog spatial pattern pairs $(A_k, B_k)$, k = 1, 2, ..., m, using Hebbian learning, where the *k*th pattern pair is represented by the vectors $A_k = (a_1^k, ..., a_n^k)$ and $B_k = (b_1^k, ..., b_p^k)$. The LAM learns offline, operates in discrete time, and is represented by the two-layer feedforward topology shown in Figure 5-17, where n $F_A$ PE's correspond to $A_k$'s components and the p $F_B$ PEs correspond to $B_k$'s components.

*5.2.4.1. Encoding*

Pattern pairs are encoded in the LAM using the Hebbian correlation equation (i.e. the sum of outer products)

$$W = \sum_{k=1}^{m} A_k^T B_k \tag{5-88}$$

where W is the n-by-p matrix of $F_A$ to $F_B$ connections. In pointwise notation the encoding equation is

$$w_{ij} = \sum_{k=1}^{m} a_i^k b_j^k \tag{5-89}$$

where $a_i$ is the *i*th $F_A$ PE's value, $b_j$ is the *j*th $F_B$ PE's value and $w_{ij}$ is the connection strength from the *i*th $F_A$ PE to the *j*th $F_B$ PE.

*5.2.4.2. Recall*

The $F_B$ PE recall equation is the simple vector-matrix multiplication

$$B = AW \tag{5-90}$$

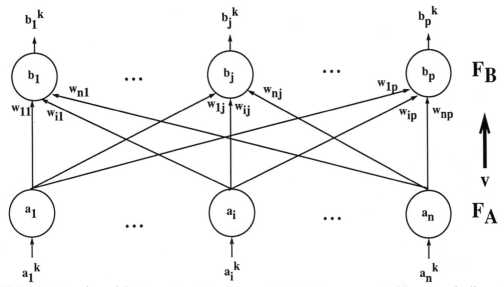

FIGURE 5-17. Topology of the Linear Associative Memory (LAM) ANS, an unsupervised learning—feedforward recall ANS. This two-layer ANS encodes pattern pairs in the weight matrix W formed from the connections between the $F_A$ and $F_B$ PEs. To keep the presentation uncluttered, all connections are not shown—there is actually a connection from each $F_A$ PE to each $F_B$ PE.

where A is the vector of $F_A$ PE values and B is the resultant vector of $F_B$ PE values. In pointwise notation the $F_B$ PEs are calculated using the equation

$$b_j = \sum_{i=1}^{n} a_i w_{ij} \qquad (5\text{-}91)$$

### 5.2.4.3. Recall Analysis

Perfect recall is guaranteed for each vector pair $(A_k, B_k)$ when the following conditions are met:

1. All $A_k$ are normalized to unit length

$$\sum_{i=1}^{n} (a_i^k)^2 = 1 \ \forall \ k = 1, 2, \ldots, m \qquad (5\text{-}92)$$

and

2. All $A_k$ are mutually orthogonal

$$A_i A_j^T = 0 \ \forall \ i \neq j \qquad (5\text{-}93)$$

The relevance of these requirements is realized by breaking eq. 5-88 into signal and noise terms for the h$th$ pattern. This expansion yields

$$W = \sum_{\substack{k=1 \\ k \neq h}}^{n} A_k^T B_k + A_h^T B_h \qquad (5\text{-}94)$$

where the first term corresponds to noise—the "crosstalk" from the other encoded patterns, and the second term represents signal—the actual encoding of the h$th$ pattern pair. Assuming the conditions of eq. 5-92 and eq. 5-93 during encoding, we can rewrite the recall equation as

$$B_h = A_h W = \sum_{\substack{k=1 \\ k \neq h}}^{n} A_h A_k^T B_k + A_h A_h^T B_h \qquad (5\text{-}95)$$

which results in the pattern $B_h$ being perfectly recalled.

### 5.2.4.4. Discussion and Applications

LAM strengths include its real-time response, its fault tolerance (i.e. graceful degradation when the connections are damaged), and its interpolated response. LAM limitations include its inability to store more patterns than the number of $F_A$ PEs, its unpredictable nature when exceeding the storage capacity, and its inability to store nonlinear relationships.

Eich (1982) and Murdock (1982) have used the LAM to explain psychological phenomena such as list learning, short-term memory and prototype formation. Candidate applications include linear pattern matching and control. Possibly the most important aspect of the LAM is that it provides an infrastructure for successively more capable systems like the optimal linear associative memory (see section 5.2.5.) and the Brain-state-in-a-box (see section 5.3.1.) ANS paradigms.

## 5.2.5. Optimal Linear Associative Memory (OLAM)

The optimal linear associative memory (OLAM) ANS—independently introduced by Wee (1968) and Kohonen & Ruohonen (1973)—is an interpolative response, autoassociative pattern encoder, a heteroassociative pattern matcher, or a novelty filter. The OLAM learns off-line, operates in discrete time, and utilizes a synchronous vector-matrix multiplication updating procedure.

As an autoassociative pattern encoder, the OLAM stores arbitrary analog spatial patterns $A_k = (a_1^k, \ldots, a_n^k)$, $k = 1, 2, \ldots, m$. As a novelty filter, the OLAM stores arbitrary analog spatial patterns $A_k = (a_1^k, \ldots, a_n^k)$, $k = 1, 2, \ldots, m$, and determines the difference between the stored patterns and a presented pattern. The autoassociative OLAM and the novelty filter OLAM are both represented by the one-layer feedforward topology shown in Figure 5-18, where the n $F_A$ PEs corresponds to $A_k$'s components.

As a heteroassociative pattern matcher, the OLAM stores arbitrary analog spatial pattern pairs $(A_k, B_k)$, $k = 1, 2, \ldots, m$, using a matrix pseudoinverse encoding scheme, where the $k$th pattern pair is denoted by the vectors $A_k = (a_1^k, \ldots, a_n^k)$ and $B_k = (b_1^k, \ldots, b_p^k)$, and is rep-

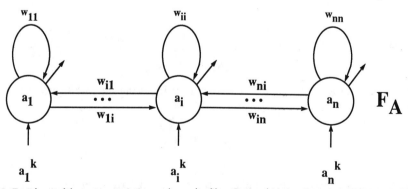

FIGURE 5-18. Topology of the autoassociative and novelty filter Optimal Linear Associative Memory (OLAM) ANS, an unsupervised learning—feedforward recall ANS. This one-layer ANS encodes pattern pairs in the weight matrix W formed from the connections between the $F_A$ PEs. To keep the presentation uncluttered, all connections are not shown—there is actually a connection from each $F_A$ PE to all the other $F_A$ PEs.

resented by the two-layer feedforward topology shown in Figure 5-19, where the n $F_A$ PEs correspond to $a_k$'s components and the p $F_B$ PEs correspond to $B_k$'s components.

### 5.2.5.1. Encoding

Heteroassociative Encoding. The heteroassociative OLAM memory, W, is constructed from two matrices, $\mathcal{A}$ — the m-by-n collection of all $A_k$ — defined as

$$\mathcal{A}^T = [A_1^T | A_2^T | \ldots | A_m^T]$$

and $\mathcal{B}$ — the m-by-p collection of all $B_k$ — defined as

$$\mathcal{B}^T = [B_1^T | B_2^T | \ldots | B_m^T]$$

where | represents vector concatenation, an operation that makes each vector a column of its respective matrix. Using this notation, we note that the Linear Associative Memory (LAM) encoding procedure described by eq. 5-88 (see section 5.2.4.) would be

$$W = \sum_{k=1}^{m} A_k^T B_k = \mathcal{A} \mathcal{B}^T \qquad \text{(5-96)}$$

where W is the memory matrix storing the $(A_k, B_k)$ associations. As noted in the LAM recall analysis section (section 5.2.4.3.), the further the $A_k$ are from orthonormal, the worse the recall. Wee, and later Kohonen & Ruohonen, realized an improved encoding procedure was available by using the pseudoinverse — also called the Moore-Penrose generalized inverse (Albert, 1972) — in place of the tranpose operation used in eq. 5-96. This new encoding equation, yielding the optimal least mean square correlation of A and B, is defined as

$$W = \mathcal{A}^+ \mathcal{B} \qquad \text{(5-97)}$$

where W is the memory matrix and $\mathcal{A}^+$ is the pseudoinverse of $\mathcal{A}$, computed, for example, using Greville's recursive algorithm (Greville, 1960; Kohonen, 1984).

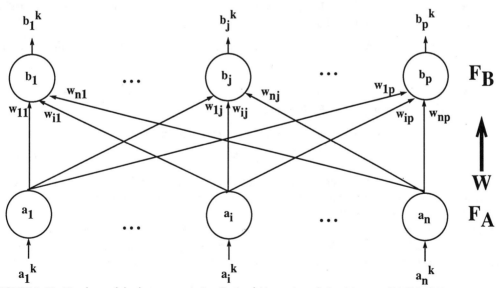

FIGURE 5-19. Topology of the heteroassociative Optimal Linear Associative Memory (OLAM) ANS, an unsupervised learning — feedforward recall ANS. This two-layer ANS encodes pattern pairs in the weight matrix W formed from the connections between the $F_A$ PEs and $F_B$ PEs. To keep the presentation uncluttered, all connections are not shown — there is actually a connection from each $F_A$ PE to each $F_B$ PE.

Autoassociative Encoding. Autoassociative storage, a special case of heteroassociative storage, is performed using the equation

$$V = \mathscr{A}^+ \mathscr{A} \tag{5-98}$$

where V is the autoassociative memory matrix. If all $A_k$ are linearly independent and m = n, then $\mathscr{A}^{-1}$ exists and $\mathscr{A}^+ = (\mathscr{A}^T\mathscr{A})^{-1}\mathscr{A}^T = \mathscr{A}^{-1}$, hence V collapses to the identity matrix. If a subset of the m linearly independent vectors $A_k$ are chosen, there will not be enough vectors to construct the square matrix inverse $\mathscr{A}^{-1}$, and the pseudoinverse is then employed. Conversely, if the number of vectors exceeds their dimensionality (m > n), then the pseudoinverse is also employed.

Novelty Filter Encoding. When V does not collapse to the identity matrix, it is always possible to construct a novelty filter from the pseudoinverse. A novelty filter provides a component-wise measure of the difference between the presented pattern and all the known (stored) patterns. If the presented pattern is similar to those autoassociatively encoded in the novelty filter, it will respond with small values for each component. If the presented pattern is greatly different, large values will result. The novelty filter is computed by taking the difference between the identity matrix and the autoassociative encoding of all the patterns, which is illustrated by the equation

$$N = I - \mathscr{A}^+ \mathscr{A} \tag{5-99}$$

where I is the n-by-n identity matrix.

### 5.2.5.2. Recall

Heteroassociative Recall. Heteroassociative OLAM recall uses simple vector-matrix multiplication

$$B = AW \tag{5-100}$$

where A is a vector of $F_A$ PE values, W is the memory matrix constructed using eq. 5-97, and B is the resultant vector of $F_B$ PE values.

Autoassociative Recall. Autoassociative OLAM recall uses the vector-matrix multiplication

$$A' = AV \tag{5-101}$$

where A is a vector of $F_A$ PE values, V is the memory matrix constructed using eq. 5-98, and A' is the resultant vector of $F_A$ PE values.

Novelty Filter Recall. Novelty filter recall is the vector-matrix multiplication

$$\Delta = AN \tag{5-102}$$

where $\Delta$ is the vector of differences between the known patterns and N is the memory matrix constructed using eq. 5-99. The recall operation can be visualized as shown in Figure 5-20 where the novelty filter operates on the space spanned by $A_1, A_2, \ldots, A_n$, where $A_k \in \mathscr{R}^n$. During novelty filter recall the presented vector A is broken into the projection vector $A_p$, and the error (residual) vector $A_e$. The projection vector $A_p$ is the best linear combination of the $A_k$ in a least squares sense and the residual vector $A_e$ is the novelty (Kohonen, 1984).

### 5.2.5.3. Recall Analysis

The OLAM's recall properties are encompassed by the square-root noise attenuation law

$$\|A_p - A_k\|^{1/2} = (m/n)^{1/2}\|A - A_k\| \tag{5-103}$$

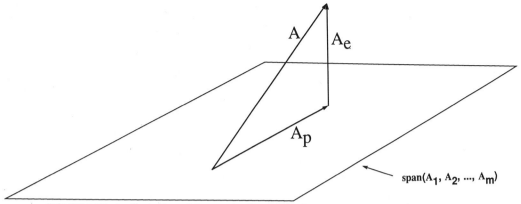

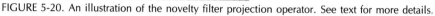

FIGURE 5-20. An illustration of the novelty filter projection operator. See text for more details.

which says if $m < n$, then the distance between the stored vector $A_k$ and the projection vector $A_p$ (i.e. the noise) decreases with m. Restated, noise is attenuated if $m < n$.

### 5.2.5.4. Discussion, Analysis, Applications, and Implementations

The OLAM's strengths include its real-time interpolative response, its least-squares storage degradation when $m > n$, and its well-understood mapping. The OLAM's limitations include the extensive offline computation require to compute the pseudoinverse of a matrix, its linear amplification of signal and noise, and its inability to perform non-linear mappings.

There are several extensions and analyses that are worthy of note. A powerful extension of the OLAM has recently been described by Shepanski (1988) that uses mutliple layers and a clever encoding scheme to capture nonlinear mappings in only a few iterations through the data. Stone (1986) describes the relationship between the OLAM and the Widrow-Hoff LMS algorithm used to encode pattern pairs in the Adaline (see section 5.4.2.). Yeates (1988) has discussed the similarity of the OLAM, the LMS algorithm, Kalman filters, and Karmaker's linear programming algorithm. Wee (1970) has analyzed the performance of the OLAM for pattern classification relative to other techniques. And, Kohonen (1984) has studied the storage capacity and various implementations of the OLAM in great detail and introduced the use of the OLAM as a novelty filter.

The two primary uses of the OLAM are for pattern matching and novelty detection. Application areas where these attributes are useful include image recognition and assembly line quality control. A list of where the OLAM has been applied is found in Table 5-13. In addition, the OLAM has had several optical/electro-optical implementations, especially as a novelty filter (TeKolste & Guest, 1987; Szu & Messner, 1987; D. Anderson, 1987; Anderson, Lininger & Einberg, 1987; Anderson & Erie, 1987).

## 5.2.6. Fuzzy Associative Memory (FAM)

The fuzzy associative memory (FAM) ANS — introduced by Kosko (1987a) as a by-product of his work in fuzzy theory (Kosko, 1986a & 1986b) — is a two-layer, heteroassociative, fuzzy classifier that stores an arbitrary unit-interval valued (fuzzy) spatial pattern pair $(A_k, B_k)$ using fuzzy Hebbian learning, where the $k$th pattern pair is represented by the fuzzy sets $A_k = \{a_1^k, \dots, a_n^k\}$ and $B_k = \{b_1^k, \dots, b_p^k\}$. The FAM learns offline, operates in discrete time, and is represented by the two-layer feedforward topology shown in Figure 5-21, where the n $F_A$ PEs correspond to $A_k$'s members and the p $F_B$ PEs correspond to $B_k$'s members.

| OLAM Applications ||
|---|---|
| **Application** | **Reference** |
| Image Processing | Kadar, 1987<br>Kohonen, 1984<br>Wechsler & Zimmerman, 1988<br>Hurlbert, 1988<br>Kohonen, et al., 1984<br>Oja & Kohonen, 1988<br>Kohonen & Riittinen, 1977 |
| Control | Daunicht, 1988 |
| Pattern Classification | Wee, 1968, 1970 & 1971<br>Kohonen, 1984 |
| Data Fusion | Wechsler & Zimmerman, 1988 |
| Speech Processing | Haltsonen, et al., 1978<br>Homma, Atlas & Marks, 1988<br>Jalanko, et al., 1978<br>Reuhkala, Jalanko & Kohonen, 1979 |
| Character Recognition | Chiueh & Goodman, 1988<br>Wee, 1970 |

TABLE 5-13.

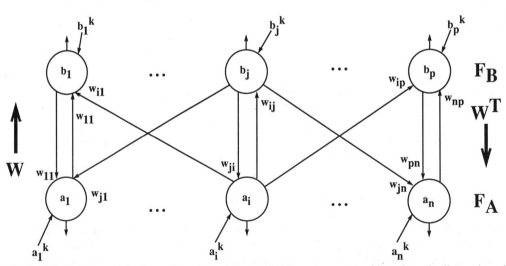

FIGURE 5-21. Topology of the Fuzzy Associative Memory (FAM), an unsupervised learning—feedforward recall ANS. This two-layer ANS stores pattern pairs in the weight matrix W formed from the connections between the $F_A$ and $F_B$ layers. This is a discrete time ANS that stores unit-interval valued (fuzzy) pattern pairs. To keep the presentation uncluttered, all connections are not shown—there is actually a connection from each $F_A$ PE to each $F_B$ PE and vice versa.

*5.2.6.1. Fuzzy Set Terminology*

Before introducing the FAM encoding procedure, a brief introduction to fuzzy set terminology is in order. The values of fuzzy set members range from 0 to 1. The *ith* member's value of the fuzzy set $A_k$ is $M_A(a_i^k)$, and the *jth* member's value of the fuzzy set $B_k$ is $M_B(b_j^k)$. As an example, consider the three-member fuzzy set $A_k = \{.5,.2,.8\}$ and the two-member fuzzy set $B_k = \{.9,.3\}$. The value of $A_k$'s *2nd* element is $M_A(a_2^k) = .2$ and the value of $B_k$'s *1st* element is $M_B(b_1^k) = .9$.

The basic fuzzy set operations are MIN and MAX—the pairwise set equivalents of AND and OR—which represent union and intersection, respectively. Using the fuzzy sets of the previous example, $MIN(M_A(a_1^k),M_A(a_2^k)) = \min(.5,.2) = .2$, and $MAX(M_B(b_1^k),M_B(b_2^k)) = \max(.9,.3) = .9$.

*5.2.6.2. Encoding*

FAM encoding is performed using the fuzzy Hebbian learning equation

$$w_{ij} = MIN(M_A(a_i^k),M_B(b_j^k)) \tag{5-104}$$

where $w_{ij}$ is the symmetric fuzzy connection from the *ith* $F_A$ to the *jth* $F_B$ PE. This encoding procedure only allows the storage of one pattern pair.

*5.2.6.3. Recall*

Although the recall equations are bidirectional, the FAM does not employ feedback—all information flow is purely feedforward. The $F_B$ PE recall equation is

$$b_j = \underset{i=1}{\overset{n}{MAX}} [MIN(a_i,w_{ij})] \tag{5-105}$$

where $a_i$ is the *ith* $F_A$ PE's value, $b_j$ is the *jth* $F_B$ PE's value. The recall equation for the $F_A$ PEs is

$$a_i = \underset{j=1}{\overset{p}{MAX}} [MIN(b_j,w_{ji})] \tag{5-106}$$

This recall process has been proven to map all inputs into subsets of the stored association (Kosko, 1987a). An example of the FAM encoding and recall operations is provided in box 5-4.

*5.2.6.4. Discussion, Applications, and Implementations*

Although the FAM is hindered by its one-pattern pair-storage capacity, work by Togai & Watanabe (1985 & 1986) to make the first fuzzy logic chip will make the FAM a more useful paradigm (Brooks, 1987). Subset recall of a vector of fuzzy values from a presented vector of fuzzy values has many useful applications in control, knowledge processing, and pattern matching that are only now being explored.

## 5.2.7. Learning Vector Quantizer (LVQ)

The Learning Vector Quantizer (LVQ) ANS (an extension of which is referred to as the self-organizing feature map)—introduced by Kohonen (1981)—is an autoassociative, nearest-neighbor classifier that classifies arbitrary analog spatial patterns $A_k = (a_1^k,\ldots,a_n^k)$, k = 1, 2, ..., m, into one of p-many classes using an error-correction encoding procedure. It is clearly related to the competitive learning paradigm (section 3.6.6.). The LVQ ANS learns offline,

# Fuzzy Associative Memory Example

**ENCODING:**

A Fuzzy Associative Memory (FAM) is formed by taking the composite of the fuzzy unit (fit) vectors A and B. Fuzzy composition is defined as:

$$W = A^T \text{o} B$$

or, in pointwise notation as

$$w_{ij} = \min(M_A(a_i), M_B(b_j))$$

Given the two fit vectors A and B, we can construct the FAM matrix W as follows:

$$A = (.2\ 0\ .5\ .7)$$

$$B = (1\ .5\ .6)$$

$$W = \begin{bmatrix} .2 & .2 & .2 \\ 0 & 0 & 0 \\ .5 & .5 & .5 \\ .7 & .5 & .6 \end{bmatrix}$$

**RECALL:**

FAM Recall uses the operators:

$$B = A\text{o}W$$

$$A = B\text{o}W^T$$

which in pointwise notation is the respective operations

$$M_{A\text{o}W}(b_j) = \overset{n}{\underset{i=1}{\text{MAX}}} \{\ \min(a_i, w_{ij})\ \}$$

$$M_{B\text{o}W^T}(a_i) = \overset{p}{\underset{j=1}{\text{MAX}}} \{\ \min(b_j, w_{ij})\ \}$$

Using W and the aforementioned operators, we test the recall of A and B, seeing that A produces a proper subset of B and B produces A.

$$A\text{o}W = (.7\ .5\ .6) = B' \subset B$$

$$B\text{o}W^T = (.2\ 0\ .5\ .7) = A$$

BOX 5-4. An example of how the encoding and recall operations of the Fuzzy Associative Memory (FAM) operate. This example stores a fuzzy pattern pair and then demonstrates how the subset recall property works.

operates in discrete time, and is represented by the two-layer feedforward topology shown in Figure 5-22, where the n $F_A$ PEs correspond to $A_k$'s components, and the p $F_B$ PEs each represent a pattern class. Because each $F_B$ PE represents a class, these PEs are often referred to as grandmother cells.

### 5.2.7.1. Encoding

**Single Winner Unsupervised Learning.** The LVQ encoding procedure automatically determines the p-best reference vectors needed to represent the space spanned by a given set of data vectors. This encoding procedure only allows one $F_B$ PE to be active during the encoding phase, hence only the connections that abut the active $F_B$ PE are adjusted. The encoding procedure is as outlined as follows:

1. Initialize all the $F_A$ to $F_B$ connection strengths to some random value in the range [0,1].
2. The connections that emanate from $F_A$ and abut the *jth* $F_B$ PE form the weight vector $W_j$. For each pattern $A_k$, k = 1, 2, ..., m, do the following:
   a. Find the $W_j$ closest to $A_k$

$$\|A_k - W_g\| = \underset{j=1}{\overset{p}{\text{MIN}}} \|A_k - W_j\|$$ (5-107)

where $W_g$ is the $W_j$ closest to $A_k$ and the Euclidian distance between any two real-valued n-dimensional vectors—X and Y—is defined as

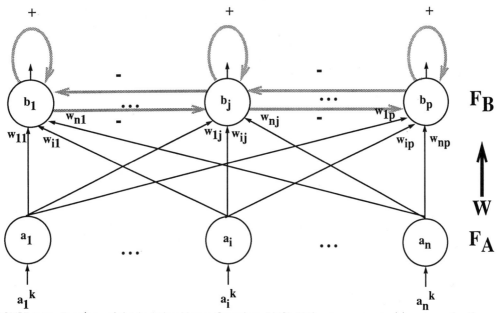

FIGURE 5-22. Topology of the Learning Vector Quantizer (LVQ) ANS, an unsupervised learning—feedforward recall ANS. This two-layer ANS classifies patterns by finding the optimal set of reference vectors (where a reference vector is the set of connections that abut a $F_B$ PE) for a given training set. The reference vectors are stored in the weight matrix W. Each $F_B$ PE (sometimes referred to as a grandmother cell in this context) represents a pattern class. During operation, the $F_B$ PEs employ an invisible on-center/off-surround competition that is used to choose the proper class for the presented input. These lateral interactions are shown in the figure as shaded self-exciting/ neighbor-inhibiting connections to emphasize this point. To keep the presentation uncluttered, all connections are not shown—there is actually a connection from each $F_A$ PE to each $F_B$ PE, a shaded negative lateral connection from each $F_B$ PE to every other $F_B$ PE, and a shaded positive recurrent connection from every $F_B$ PE to itself.

$$\|X - Y\| = \left[ \sum_{i=1}^{n} (x_i - y_i)^2 \right]^{1/2} \tag{5-108}$$

This operation is essentially a competition amongst the $F_B$ PEs with the largest activation (closest reference vector to the data vector) remaining the winner (see section 3.6.6. for a description of competitive learning).

b. Move $W_g$ closer to $A_k$ using the equation

$$\Delta w_{ij} = \alpha(t)[a_i^k - w_{ig}] \tag{5-109}$$

for all $i = 1, 2, \ldots, n$, where $\Delta w_{ig}$ is the connection strength from the $ith$ $F_A$ to the $gth$ $F_B$ PE, and $\alpha(t)$ is the learning rate at time t defined as

$$\alpha(t) = t^{-1} \tag{5-110}$$

or

$$\alpha(t) = .2\left[ 1 - \frac{t}{10000} \right] \tag{5-111}$$

3. Repeat step (2) for $t = 1, 2, \ldots, z$, where $500 \leq z \leq 10,000$.

Multiple Winner Unsupervised Learning. An immediate LVQ encoding extension allows more than one $F_B$ PE to be active during the encoding phase, hence allowing the connections to each active $F_B$ PE to be adjusted during training. To facilitate this extension, we introduce the notion of a set of $F_B$ PEs, $N_c$, of a predetermined size in the physical neighborhood of the winning $F_B$ PE, $W_g$. Instead of only adjusting the connections that abut $b_g$ (i.e. $W_g$), we adjust $W_g$ and all the connections that abut the PEs in the neighborhood of $b_g$. As an example, a set of three around the winner $W_g$ would be $N_g = \{W_{g-1}, W_g, W_{g+1}\}$. Often the $F_B$ PEs are arranged in a two-dimensional topology and the neighborhood is a circle of some predetermined radius around the winning $F_B$ PE. This multiple winner extension places eq. 5-109 with the equation

$$\Delta w_{ig} = \begin{cases} \alpha(t)[a_i^k - w_{ig}] & \text{if } j \in N_g \\ 0 & \text{otherwise} \end{cases} \tag{5-112}$$

where $N_g$ is the neighborhood set of vectors around $W_g$.

Supervised Learning. Another LVQ extension is possible when the proper class for each $A_k$ is known a priori. Although this means the encoding is then supervised, this information accelerates the learning and develops more accurate pattern classifications. The supervision works by rewarding corrections for proper classification and punishing corrections for improper classifications. This supervised learning extension replaces eq. 5-109 with the equation

$$\Delta w_{ig} = \begin{cases} +\alpha(t)[a_i^k - w_{ig}] & \text{if } b_g \text{ is the proper class} \\ -\alpha(t)[a_i^k - w_{ig}] & \text{if } b_g \text{ is not the proper class} \end{cases} \tag{5-113}$$

where $b_g$ is the $F_B$ PE class chosen for $A_k$.

### 5.2.7.2. Recall

LVQ recall determines the class, $b_g$—represented by the weight vector $W_g$—that the input pattern A is most closely associated with. $W_g$ is determined by finding the closest $W_j$—in Euclidian distance—to A. In essence, the $F_B$ PEs all compete with each other and the largest $F_B$ PE activation prevails while all others are quenched. Hence, at the end of the competition, the $F_B$ PE representing the proper class will have a value of 1 and the other $F_B$ PEs will have the value 0. This action is illustrated by the equation

$$b_g = \begin{cases} 1 & \text{if } \|A - W_g\| = \text{MIN } \|A - W_j\| \\ 0 & \text{otherwise} \end{cases} \tag{5-114}$$

where $b_j$ is the $jth$ $F_B$ PE's value and A is the input vector.

### 5.2.7.3. Convergence

LVQ convergence is determined by the learning parameter $\alpha(t)$, where $\alpha(t) \rightarrow 0$ as $t \rightarrow \infty$. In addition, analysis of the LVQ self-organization process — the encoding algorithm — has shown that, after encoding is completed, each $W_j$ represents the centroid of a decision region created in the n-dimensional space of data patterns (Kohonen, 1986b). Moreover, the boundary of each decision region forms a Voronoi tessellation, a tiling of the n-dimensional pattern space with edges that are perpendicular to the lines drawn between the $W_j$ centroids. Grossberg (1976a) proved a similar convergence theorem for the competitive learning law — to which this is closely related — and extended the proof to include multiple $F_B$ winners.

### 5.2.7.4. Discussion, Applications, and Implementations

The LVQ ANS strengths include its ability to perform non-parametric pattern classification and provide real-time nearest-neighbor response. The LVQ's limitations include its extensive offline encoding time and its inability to add new classes without complete retraining.

The LVQ ANS is one of the most useful of all ANS paradigms. The ability to allocate reference vectors to the centroids of decision regions without any *a priori* information concerning the distribution of data makes this a very powerful paradigm. There have been several studies performed to better understand the mechanics of the LVQ ANS, and there have been several extensions developed to further improve its performance. Ritter & Schulten (1986b, 1988a & 1988c) have studied the stationary state, computational abilities and convergence properties of LVQ. Kohonen, Barna & Chrisley (1988) have compared the statistical pattern classification performance of LVQ with that of the Boltzmann Machine ANS (see section 5.4.4.) and classical Bayesian estimation techniques. DeSieno (1988) has extended the LVQ encoding algorithms to allow a conscience mechanism in each $F_B$ PE that limits the number of times that it can win. The conscience mechanism is a simple extension that provides much better pattern classification performance. Durbin & Willshaw (1987) have developed a technique for optimization that uses a network very similar to that of the LVQ, called the elastic net method. Abutaleh (1988) has shown that the LVQ algorithm is a special case of an adaptive time-varying filter. Lutterell (1988b) has extended the LVQ algorithm to allow the growth of the $F_B$ layer to properly perform cluster decomposition problems. Kohonen (1988a) has extended the LVQ algorithm to develop more precise decision boundaries during the self-organization process. And, Nasrabadi & Feng (1988a & 1988b) have compared the LVQ procedure with classical methods of performing vector quantization.

The LVQ ANS is well suited to applications that require data quantization. Examples where this ability is useful include statistical analysis, code book communication, and data compression. Also, through the aforementioned work of Durbin & Willshaw (1987), the LVQ has been successfully applied to combinatorial optimization problems. A listing of specific LVQ applications is shown in Table 5-14.

The LVQ is recognized as one of the primary ANS paradigms because of its relative simplicity and its unsupervised qualities. Because of its many uses, several LVQ implementations have emerged as shown in Table 5-15.

| LVQ Applications | |
|---|---|
| **Application** | **Reference** |
| Image Processing | Nasrabadi & Feng, 1988a & 1988b<br>Egbert & Rhodes, 1988<br>Glover, 1988b<br>Brietkopf & Walker, 1988<br>Kohonen, 1984 |
| Control | Ritter & Schulten, 1986a, 1988b & 1988d<br>Kohonen, 1984 |
| Speech Processing | Lippmann, 1987 & 1988<br>Kohonen, 1984 & 1988b<br>Huang & Lippman, 1988<br>Naylor & Li, 1988a & 1988b<br>Kohonen, Mikisara & Saramaki, 1984 |
| Data Compression | Nasrabai & Feng, 1988a & 1988b<br>Naylor & Li, 1988a & 1988b |
| Combinatorial Optimization | Angeniol, D.L.C.V. Brois & Le Texier, 1988a<br>Durbin & Willshaw, 1988<br>Heuter, 1988<br>Fort, 1988 |

TABLE 5-14.

## 5.2.8. Counterpropagation (CPN)

The counterpropagation (CPN) ANS—introduced by Hecht-Nielsen (1987e)—is a three-layer, heteroassociative, nearest-neighbor pattern matcher that stores arbitrary analog spatial patterns $(A_k, C_k)$, $k = 1, 2, \ldots, m$, using a combination of Hebbian encoding and Kohonen's learning vector quantizer (see section 5.2.7.), where the $k$th pattern pair is represented by the vectors $A_k = (a_1^k, \ldots, a_n^k)$ and $C_k = (c_1^k, \ldots, c_q^k)$. CPN learns offline, operates in discrete

| LVQ Implementations | |
|---|---|
| **Implementation** | **Reference** |
| Coprocessor/Attached Processor | Koikalainen & Oja, 1988<br>HNC, 1987b<br>SAIC, 1988 |
| Integrated Circuit | Mann, et al., 1988 |
| Bus-Oriented Processor · | TRW, 1987 |

TABLE 5-15.

time, and is represented by the three-layer feedforward topology shown in Figure 5-23, where the n $F_A$ PEs correspond to $A_k$'s components, and the q $F_C$ PEs correspond to $C_k$'s components.

### 5.2.8.1. Encoding

CPN encoding works by attaching an outstar to each LVQ $F_B$ PE. The outstar—introduced by Grossberg (1968a) and illustrated in Figure 5-24—encodes a pattern by transferring the normalized values of an output, $C = (c_1,...,c_j,...,c_n)$, onto the connections, $U_i = (u_{i1},...,u_{ij},...,u_{in})$, emanating from some PE, $a_i$, and abutting the set of PEs $B = (b_1,...,b_j,...,b_n)$. Grossberg (1980) has shown that the outstar is the minimal pattern encoding network and has developed an extensive set of dynamics that are able to automatically suppress input noise while contrast enhancing the signal—work that led to the development of the Shunting Grossberg ANS described in section 5.1.2.

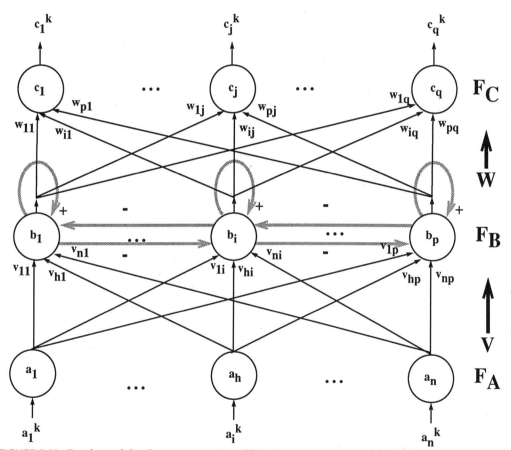

FIGURE 5-23. Topology of the Counterpropagation (CPN) ANS, an unsupervised learning—feedforward recall ANS. This three-layer ANS performs pattern matching by first classifing the input pattern with an $F_B$ PE, and then feeding the winning $F_B$ PE's activation through the attached outstar to produce the output pattern at $F_C$. Each $F_B$ PE (sometimes referred to as a grandmother cell in this context) represents a pattern class. During operation, the $F_B$ PEs employ an invisible on-center/off-surround competition that is used to choose the proper class for the presented input. These lateral interactions are shown in the figure as shaded self-exciting/neighbor-inhibiting connections to emphasize this point. To keep the presentation uncluttered, all connections are not shown—there is actually a connection from each $F_A$ PE to each $F_B$ PE, a shaded negative lateral connection from each $F_B$ PE to every other $F_B$ PE, a shaded positive recurrent connection from every $F_B$ PE to itself, and a connection from each $F_B$ PE to each $F_C$ PE.

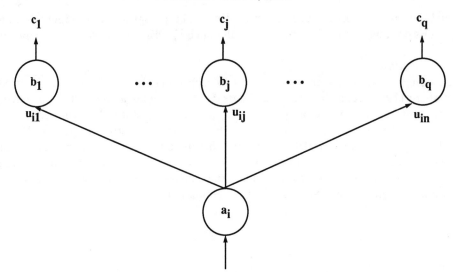

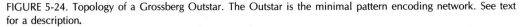

FIGURE 5-24. Topology of a Grossberg Outstar. The Outstar is the minimal pattern encoding network. See text for a description.

The LVQ operation creates a good statistical model of its environment through the automatic creation of decision regions that represent the probability density of the given data patterns using the LVQ encoding algorithm to adjust the $F_A$ to $F_B$ PEs and then encoding the corresponding output pattern to the outstar of the winning PE. The CPN encoding procedure is outlined as follows:

1. Normalize all $A_k$ to unit length

$$a_h^k = \frac{a_h^k}{\|A_k\|} \tag{5-115}$$

    for all h = 1, 2, ..., n, and all k = 1, 2, ..., m.

2. Randomize each $F_A$ to $F_B$ connection strength to some random value in the range [0,1].

3. The connections that emanate from $F_A$ and abut the *i*th $F_B$ PE form the weight vector $V_i = (v_{1i}, \ldots, v_{hi}, \ldots, v_{hp})$ and are normalized to unit length

$$v_{hi} = \frac{v_{hi}}{\|V_i\|} \tag{5-116}$$

    for all h = 1, 2, ..., n, and all i = 1, 2, ..., p.

4. For each pattern $A_k$, k = 1, 2, ..., m, do the following:
   a. Find the $V_i$ closest to $A_k$:

$$\|A_k - V_g\| = \underset{i=1}{\overset{p}{\text{MIN}}} \|A_k - V_i\| \tag{5-117}$$

   b. Move $V_g$ closer to $A_k$

$$\Delta v_{hg} = \alpha(t)[a_h^k - v_{hg}] \tag{5-118}$$

    for all h = 1, 2, ..., n, where $\Delta v_{hg}$ is the connection strength from the h*th* $F_A$ to the g*th* $F_B$ PE, and $\alpha(t)$ is the learning rate at time t defined by either eq. 5.110 or eq. 5-111.

c. Renormalize $V_g$ to unit length

$$v_{hg} = \frac{v_{hg}}{\|V_g\|} \tag{5-119}$$

for all $h = 1, 2, \ldots, n$.

d. Encode $C_k$'s pattern onto the outstar from $b_g$ to $F_C$

$$\Delta w_{gj} = -\beta w_{gj} + \gamma b_g c_j^k \tag{5-120}$$

for all $j = 1, 2, \ldots, q$, where $\Delta w_{gj}$ is the amount of change to make to the connection strength from the $gth$ $F_B$ and $jth$ $F_C$ PEs, $\beta$ is a positive constant controlling decay rate, $\gamma$ is a positive constant controlling encoding rate, and $b_g$ is the $F_B$ PE value corresponding to $V_g$ calculated by

$$b_g = \sum_{h=1}^{n} v_{hg} a_h^k \tag{5-121}$$

5. Repeat step (4) for $t = 1, 2, \ldots, z$, where $500 \leq z \leq 10,000$.

It is also possible to extend the learning equations by incorporating multiple winner learning and supervised learning as described by eq. 5-112 and eq. 5-113 in section 5.2.7.1., respectively (Hecht-Nielsen, 1987e & 1987f). Like the LVQ (see section 5.2.7.), an immediate CPN extension allows the s closest (in Euclidian distance) $V_i$ to excite their corresponding $F_B$ PEs, allowing s outstars to adapt from $F_B$ to $F_C$.

### 5.2.8.2. Recall
CPN recall filters inputs activation values from $F_A$ through V to $F_B$

$$b_i = \sum_{h=1}^{n} v_{hi} a_h \tag{5-122}$$

for all $i = 1, 2, \ldots, p$. The recall process is completed by filtering the maximum $F_B$ PE activation through its outstar with the equation

$$c_j = w_{gj} b_g \tag{5-123}$$

for all $j = 1, 2, \ldots, q$, where $b_g$ is the $F_B$ PE with the maximum activation, determined by

$$b_j = \begin{cases} 1 & \text{if } b_j = \underset{s=1}{\overset{p}{\text{MAX}}} \left[ \sum_{h=1}^{n} v_{hs} a_h \right] \\ 0 & \text{otherwise} \end{cases} \tag{5-124}$$

### 5.2.8.3. Discussion, Applications, and Implementations
The $F_A$ to $F_B$ mapping is identical to that performed by the LVQ. The data vectors self-organize according to the probability density of the presented data, and each $V_i$ represents the centroid of the $ith$ decision region. CPN strengths include its ability to perform nearest-neighbor mappings for an arbitrary set of pattern pairs in a self-programming look-up table fashion. Another strength of the CPN ANS is its ability to learn nonlinear mappings. CPN limitations include the need for a $F_B$ PE for each $F_C$ output pattern (i.e. a $F_B$ PE is needed for each pattern pair). It is possible to improve this pattern matching performance by allowing multiple winners and adjusting the outstars of each $F_B$ PE to slowly become adjusted in a fashion similar to that done by the slow learning version of ART1 (see section 5.1.3.) and

ART2 (see section 5.1.4.), although the dynamics of these types of interactions are poorly understood.

The CPN ANS provides an alternative to other pattern matchers, an area that has been investigated by Woods (1988) and Caudill (1988) in comparisons of CPN performance to that of the backpropagation ANS (see section 5.4.3). Areas where the CPN is well suited include statistical analysis, function approximation and pattern recognition (Hecht-Nielsen, 1987c & 1988b). The CPN has recently been applied to image processing (Glover, 1988a & 1988b) and it has been implemented on coprocessors/attached processors (HNC, 1987b & SAIC, 1988).

# 5.3. SUPERVISED LEARNING AND FEEDBACK RECALL ARTIFICIAL NEURAL SYSTEMS

## 5.3.1. Brain-State-in-a-Box (BSB)

The Brain-state-in-a-box (BSB) ANS—introduced by Anderson, Silverstein, Ritz, & Jones (1977)—is a one-layer, autoassociative, nearest-neighbor classifier that stores arbitrary analog spatial patterns, $A_k = (a_1^k, \ldots, a_n^k)$, using error-correction learning. The BSB learns off-line, operates in discrete time, and displays the one-layer feedback topology shown in Figure 5-25, where the n $F_A$ PEs correspond to $A_k$'s components. The BSB represents an alternative to the previous pattern storage algorithms in that it incorporates the feedback recall dynamics of the models presented in section 5.1. while using the supervised learning procedure common to the ANSs presented in section 5.4. This alternative typically yields improved storage capacity over the unsupervised learning routines at the expense of increased encoding time.

### 5.3.1.1. Encoding
The BSB encoding procedure uses the error-correction encoding equation

$$\Delta w_{ij} = \alpha a_i^k d_j \qquad \textbf{(5-125)}$$

where $\Delta w_{ij}$ is the change in the connection strength from the $i$th to the $j$th $F_A$ PE, $\alpha$ is a positive constant controlling the learning rate, and

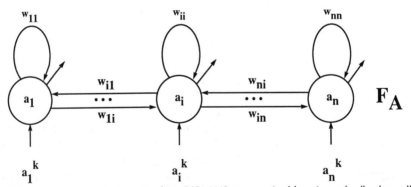

FIGURE 5-25. Topology of the Brain-state-in-a-box (BSB) ANS, a supervised learning—feedback recall ANS. This single-layered ANS paradigm has lateral and recurrent connections. The input vectors's components $A_k = (a_1^k, a_2^k, \ldots, a_n^k)$ feed directly into the $F_A$ layer, and outputs can be read from the $F_A$ layer at any time. This is a discrete time ANS that stores analog patterns. To keep the presentation uncluttered, all connections are not shown— there is actually a lateral connection from each $F_A$ PE to every other $F_A$ PE, and a recurrent connection from every $F_A$ PE to itself.

$$d_j = a_j^k - \sum_{i=1}^{n} w_{ij} a_i \qquad (5\text{-}126)$$

The first term of eq. 5-126 is the desired value of the $jth$ $F_A$ PE and the second term is the computed value of the same PE. During the encoding process, eq. 5-125 is employed repeatedly for each pattern until the amount of error $d_j$ produced by each output is sufficiently low.

### 5.3.1.2. Recall

BSB recall utilizes a threshold-linear ramp function (see section 3.2.) in an intra-layer feedback operation. When an input is presented to $F_A$ it is processed until all $F_A$ PEs cease to change, typically meaning that they have saturated to either the high or low end of the ramp function using the equation

$$a_i(t + 1) = f\left( a_i(t) + \beta \sum_{j=1}^{n} w_{ij} a_j(t) \right) \qquad (5\text{-}127)$$

where $a_i(t)$ and $a_j(t)$ are the activation values of the $ith$ and $jth$ $F_A$ PEs at time t, $\beta$ is a positive constant controlling the amount of intra-layer feedback, and $f()$ is the ramp threshold function

$$f(x) = \begin{cases} +\gamma & \text{if } x \geq \gamma \\ x & \text{if } |x| < \gamma \\ -\gamma & \text{if } x \leq \gamma \end{cases} \qquad (5\text{-}128)$$

Identifying terms in 5-127 the first term in $f()$ is the positive feedback term, and the second term is the lateral feedback term from the other $F_A$ PEs. Eq. 5-127 can be rewritten in matrix-vector form as

$$A(t + 1) = f((I + W)A(t)) \qquad (5\text{-}129)$$

where $A(t)$ and $A(t + 1)$ are the vectors representing the $F_A$ PE activations at time t and $t + 1$, respectively, I is the identity matrix, and W is the matrix of connection strengths between all the $F_A$ PEs.

### 5.3.1.3. Stability

Grossberg (1988a), inspired by the work of Golden (1986a), has shown that the BSB ANS is stable by translating the discrete time equations to continuous time and performing a signal-sum exchange. Once the BSB is in the translated form, stability can be proven using any one of the three global stability theorems presented in section 3.7.2. We will prevail upon the Cohen-Grossberg Theorem as it yields the result with the least amount of mathematical difficulty. Translation begins by creating a matrix V from the two terms inside the threshold function of eq. 5-129 using the equation

$$v_{ij} = \delta_{ij} + w_{ij} \qquad (5\text{-}130)$$

where each connection $v_{ij}$ in V is the sum of W's components and the Kronecker delta, $w_{ij}$ and $\delta_{ij}$, respectively. Now, eq. 5-130 can be rewritten as

$$a_i(t + 1) = f\left( \sum_{j=1}^{n} v_{ji} a_j(t) \right) \qquad (5\text{-}131)$$

Converting eq. 5-131 from discrete to continuous time and adding the decay term ubiquitous to all continuous time interactions yields

$$\dot{a}_i = -a_i + f\left(\sum_{j=1}^n v_{ji} a_j\right) \qquad (5\text{-}132)$$

Identifying terms in eq. 5-132, the first term is passive decay and the second is the ramp threshold lateral feedback term. Conversion is completed by translating the ramp threshold feedback from a threshold of sums to a sum of thresholds, a conversion Grossberg calls the signal-sum (S$\Sigma$) exchange. The S$\Sigma$ translation begins with the assignment

$$c_i = \sum_{j=1}^n v_{ji} a_j \qquad (5\text{-}133)$$

where $c_i$ is the total activation value for the $i$th $F_A$ PE. The translation is completed by rewriting eq. 5-132, the continuous time recall equation, as

$$\dot{c}_i = -c_i + \sum_{j=1}^n v_{ji} S(c_j) \qquad (5\text{-}134)$$

where $S()$ is a sigmoid function (see section 3.2. for a description of the sigmoid threshold function)—an approximation of the ramp threshold function.

Using the notation described in section 3.7.2.1., we need only make algebraic identifications with eq. 5-134 that do not violate the five listed restrictions and the BSB ANS is automatically proven stable. Referring to eq. 3-40, we substitute the Cohen-Grossberg terms (left hand side) with the BSB ANS terms (right hand side) as follows:

$$\alpha_i(x_i) = 1$$

$$\beta_i(x_i) = -c_i$$

$$m_{ij} = -v_{ij}$$

$$S_j(x_j) = S(c_j)$$

and

$$x_i = c_i$$

### 5.3.1.4. Discussion, Applications, and Implementations

BSB strengths include its fault and noise tolerance, its ability to store as many patterns (m) as $A_k$'s dimensions (n) (possible only when all $A_k$ are orthogonal), and its real-time nearest-neighbor categorization performance for arbitrary inputs. BSB limitations are the encoding supervision required, the lengthy encoding time, and the inability to learn online.

Recent work by Greenburg (1988) has studied the stability of the BSB ANS at points that are between the saturation levels of the ramp function. Also, Golden (1986a) has mathematically analyzed the gradient descent learning/feedback recall dynamics of the BSB. Applications of the BSB are primarily of a pattern completion nature. Table 5-16 lists several applications that make use of this processing capability. In addition, Stoll & Lee (1988) have discussed an all-optical BSB implementation.

## 5.3.2. Fuzzy Cognitive Map (FCM)

The fuzzy cognitive map (FCM)—introduced by Kosko (1985) and inspired by Axelrod's (1976) work with cognitive maps—is a one-layer inference engine that encodes arbitrary unit-valued (fuzzy) inference patterns $A_k = (a_1^k, \ldots, a_n^k)$, $k = 1, 2, \ldots, m$, using either hard-

## BSB Applications

| Application | Reference |
| --- | --- |
| Pattern Classification | J. Anderson, et al., 1988 |
| Diagnostics | J. Anderson, 1987 |
| Knowledge Processing | Anderson & Mozer, 1981 |
| Image Processing | J. Anderson, 1987 |
| Psychological Experiments | Anderson, et al., 1977<br>Anderson & Mozer, 1981<br>Wood, 1978<br>Anderson & Murphy, 1986<br>Anderson, Golden & Murphy, 1986<br>Kawamoto & Anderson, 1984 & 1985<br>Golden, 1986a |

TABLE 5-16.

wired (supervised) learning or differential Hebbian (unsupervised) learning. Although the FCM could be considered an unsupervised learning/feedback recall ANS, it is almost explicitly used in a supervised fashion. Both FCM versions display the one-layer topology shown in Figure 5-26, where the n $F_A$ PEs correspond to $A_k$'s components.

### 5.3.2.1. Encoding

Hardwired (Supervised) Encoding. Each FCM PE (or more generally a set of PEs) represents a concept. The hardwired version of this paradigm assigns causal signed values in the range $[-1,1]$ to each lateral connection. Each positive fuzzy value represents causal increase, each negative fuzzy value represents causal decrease, and each 0 represents no causal connection (Kosko, 1986b & 1986c). An example of this approach is shown in Figure 5-27 where a six-concept FCM captures the relationships between objects on a California freeway at rush hour. These connections are easily stored in the weight matrix

$$
W = \begin{bmatrix}
0 & 1 & 0 & 0 & 0 & .6 \\
0 & 0 & -.9 & 0 & 0 & .4 \\
0 & 0 & 0 & 0 & 0 & .4 \\
0 & 0 & -.5 & 0 & 0 & -.2 \\
0 & 0 & 0 & 1 & 0 & 0 \\
0 & .8 & 0 & .1 & -.9 & 0
\end{bmatrix}
$$

where each $w_{ij}$ is the causal connection value from $a_i$ to $a_j$. From this example, it is easy to see that knowledge combination is easily performed by collecting all the FCMs that might be gathered during knowledge collection, creating a super-matrix that contains an entry for each concept in the union of the FCMs, and cumulatively encoding all the knowledge in the super-matrix.

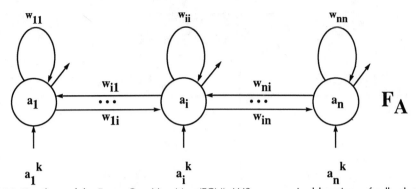

FIGURE 5-26. Topology of the Fuzzy Cognitive Map (FCM) ANS, a supervised learning—feedback recall ANS. This single-layered ANS paradigm has lateral and recurrent connections. The input vector's components $A_k = (a_1^k, a_2^k, \ldots, a_n^k)$ feed directly into the $F_A$ layer and outputs can be read from the $F_A$ layer at any time. This is a discrete time ANS that stores fuzzy causal relationships (connections) between concepts (PEs). To keep the presentation uncluttered, all connections are not shown—there is actually a lateral connection from each $F_A$ PE to every other $F_A$ PE, and a recurrent connection from every $F_A$ PE to itself.

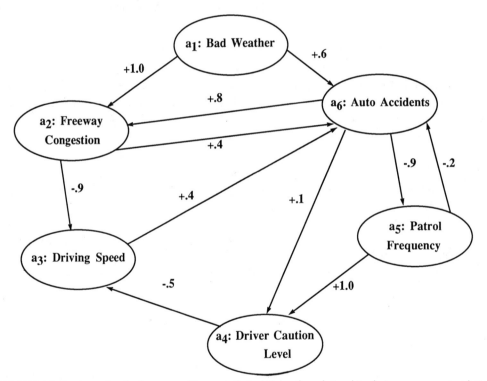

FIGURE 5-27. An example of a fuzzy cognitive map that captures the relationships between concepts relating to a California freeway at rush hour. The fuzzy valued causal connections are intepreted as follows:

- An increase in Bad Weather ($a_1$) causes a .6 increase in Auto Accidents ($a_6$) and a 1.0 increase in Freeway Congestion ($a_2$).
- An increase in Freeway Congestion ($a_2$) causes a .4 increase in Auto Accidents ($a_6$) and a .9 decrease in Driving Speed ($a_3$).
- An increase in Driving Speed causes a .4 increase in Auto Accidents ($a_6$).
- An increase in Driver Caution Level ($a_4$) causes a .5 decrease in Driver Speed ($a_3$).
- And so on.

Adaptive (Unsupervised) Encoding. The adaptive version automatically infers the connection values between concepts (PEs) using differential Hebbian learning (Kosko, 1987b & 1988a). Differential Hebbian learning was chosen because it correlates changes in PE activations; hence, only changes in the same direction — either both increasing or both decreasing — will positively affect the connections of an FCM, an activity appropriately called concomitant variation. The FCM encoding equation is

$$\dot{w}_{ij} = -w_{ij} + \dot{S}(a_i^k)\dot{S}(a_j^k) \tag{5-135}$$

where $w_{ij}$ is the connection strength from the $ith$ to the $jth$ $F_A$ PE, $a_i^k$ and $a_j^k$ are the $ith$ and $jth$ components of the $kth$ inference vector $A_k$, and $dS()/dt$ is the time derivative of a sigmoid function (see section 3.2. for a discussion of threshold functions). Identifying terms in eq. 5-135, the first term is passive decay and the second term is the differential Hebbian correlation term.

### 5.3.2.2. Recall

FCM recall is described by either the general additive recall equation

$$\dot{a}_i = -\alpha_i(a_i)\left[\beta_i(a_i) - \sum_{j=1}^{P} w_{ji}S_j(a_j)\right] \tag{5-136}$$

where $a_i$ and $a_j$ are the $ith$ and $jth$ $F_A$ PE activations, $\alpha_i()$ is a non-decreasing function, $\beta_i()$ is an arbitrary bounded function, and $S()$ is a sigmoid function with possibly negative derivatives. The more familiar FCM recall equation is the additive STM equation

$$\dot{a}_i = -a_i + \sum_{j=1}^{n} S(a_j)w_{ji} + I_i \tag{5-137}$$

where $I_i$ is the $ith$ component of some initial input state. Identifying terms in eq. 5-137, the first term is passive decay, the second term is lateral feedback, and the last term is external input.

### 5.3.2.3. Stability

Like the temporal associative memory (section 5.1.9.), the FCM does not exhibit stable point behavior, rather it exhibits oscillatory, or limit cycle, behavior. Limit cycles are described as two or more unique sets of $F_A$ PE activations being repeatedly visited. The dynamics of the FCM are amenable to the limit cycle stability analysis performed in section 5.1.9., with the primary difference between the temporal associative memory's limit cycles and those of the FCM being that the temporal associative memory's are known *a priori* and the FCM's are not.

### 5.3.2.4. Discussion, Applications, and Implementations

The FCM's strengths include its ability to perform online adaption and its real-time recall ability. FCM drawbacks are that limit cycles are not easily decipherable and knowledge processing systems, in general, require extensive data collection (i.e. determination of relevant concepts and performing expedient knowledge collection for those concepts).

Recent work by Taber & Siegel (1987) describes a method of assigning the credibility to an arbitrary set of experts without *a priori* knowledge of each expert's fidelity. Kosko (1986b, 1987b & 1988a) has discussed how the knowledge from a large number of experts can be easily and reliably combined. The extension to higher order causal connections and the use of time-lagged variations is discussed in an Air Force Wright Aeronautical Laboratories Re-

| FCM Applications | |
|---|---|
| **Application** | **Reference** |
| Knowledge Processing | Kosko, 1986b, 1986c, 1987b & 1988b<br>Taber & Siegel, 1987<br>Edson, et al., 1988<br>Myers, et al., 1988 |
| Signal Flow Graph Analysis | Styblinski & Meyer, 1988 |
| Requirements Analysis | Mentazemi & Conrath, 1986 |

TABLE 5-17.

port (Myers, et al., 1988). Zhang & Chen (1988) and Zhang, Bezdak & Pettus (1988) have developed a three-valued logical calculus for cognitive maps that has ties to the FCM ANS. Styblinski & Meyer (1988) have analyzed the similarities of FCMs and signal flow graphs.

The FCM is an excellent example of how to produce a parallel expert system. The primary application of an FCM is any situation that requires a response (or a set of responses) when given a set of initial conditions. Areas where the FCM has been applied can be found in Table 5-17. In addition, Kosko & Limm (1985) have discussed an optical implementation of the FCM.

## 5.4. SUPERVISED LEARNING AND FEEDFORWARD RECALL ARTIFICIAL NEURAL SYSTEMS

### 5.4.1. Perceptron

The perceptron ANS — introduced by Rosenblatt (1957) and extensively studied by him (Rosenblatt, 1958a, 1958b, 1959, 1960 & 1962) — is a significant body of work that will be presented here only in its simplest form. There are actually several ANS topologies that have been used within the framework of the perceptron. Figure 5-28 illustrates the *elementary perceptron* that will be discussed here. Figure 5-29 illustrates the *series-coupled perceptron*, a multilayered perceptron that has static randomly preset $F_A$ to $F_B$ PE connection strengths and adaptable $F_B$ to $F_C$ PE connection strengths. Figure 5-30 illustrates the *cross-coupled perceptron*, a multilayered perceptron that has the same connection configuration as the series-coupled perceptron with additional hardwired lateral $F_B$ connections. Figure 5-31 illustrates the *back-coupled perceptron*, a multilayered perceptron that has static randomly preset connection strengths from the $F_A$ to the $F_B$ PEs and adaptable inter-layer feedback connections from the $F_B$ to the $F_C$ PEs. For a description of the wide variety of encoding algorithms and accompanying analysis, refer to Rosenblatt's (1962) book *Principles of Neurodynamics*.

The elementary perceptron is a two-layer, heteroassociative, nearest-neighbor pattern matcher that stores the pattern pairs $(A_k, B_k)$, k = 1, 2, ..., m, using the perceptron error-correction procedure, where the k*th* pattern pair is represented by the analog valued vector $A_k = (a_1^k, ..., a_n^k)$ and the bipolar $\{-1, +1\}$ valued vector $B_k = (b_1^k, ..., b_p^k)$. The perceptron learns offline, operates in discrete time, and is represented by the two-layer feedforward topology

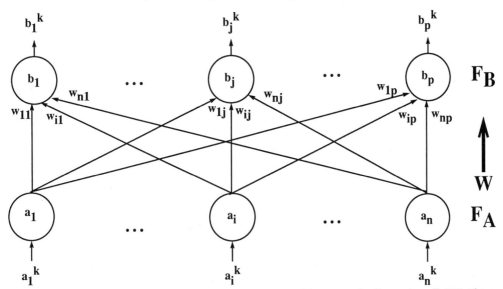

FIGURE 5-28. Topology of the elementary perceptron, a supervised learning—feedforward recall ANS. This two-layer ANS stores pattern pairs in the weight matrix W formed from the connections between the $F_A$ and $F_B$ layers. This is a discrete time ANS that stores the mapping between analog valued inputs and bipolar valued outputs. To keep the presentation uncluttered, all connections are not shown—there is actually a connection from each $F_A$ PE to each $F_B$ PE.

shown in Figure 5-28, where the n $F_A$ PEs correspond to $A_k$'s components and the p $F_B$ PEs correspond to $B_k$'s components.

### 5.4.1. Encoding

First Order Learning. Each component of $B_k$, $b_j^k$, has one of two possible values ($+1$ or $-1$) where each value represents one of two possible classes. At the beginning of the encoding procedure a hyperplane, determined by the connection strengths from the $F_A$ to the $F_B$ PEs, is randomly placed into the n-dimensional $A_k$ pattern space. During the perceptron's error-correction procedure, the hyperplane is moved until it is properly positioned between the two classes of data. The encoding algorithm that performs this hyperplane adjustment is described as follows:

1. *Initial hyperplane placement:* Assign random values in the range $[+1,-1]$ to all the $F_A$ to $F_B$ inter-layer connections, $w_{ij}$, and to each $F_B$ PE threshold, $\Theta_j$.

2. *Hyperplane adjustment:* For each pattern pair $(A_k, B_k)$, $k = 1, 2, \ldots, m$, do the following:

    a. Transfer $A_k$'s values to the $F_A$ PEs, filter the $F_A$ PE activations through W and calculate the new $F_B$ PE activation values using the equation

$$b_j = f\left(\sum_{i=1}^{n} w_{ij}a_i - \Theta_j\right) \tag{5-138}$$

for each $j = 1, 2, \ldots, p$, where the bipolar step function, f(), defined as

$$f(x) = \begin{cases} 1 & \text{if } x > 0 \\ -1 & \text{otherwise} \end{cases} \tag{5-139}$$

    b. Compute the discrepancy (error) between the computed and desired $F_B$ PE values using the equation

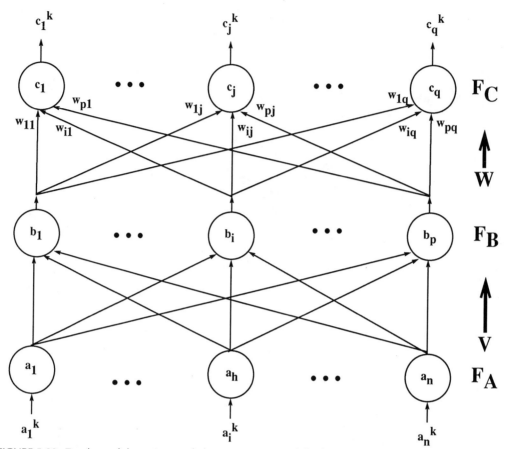

FIGURE 5-29. Topology of the series-coupled perceptron, one of the four primary perceptron topologies. This three-layer ANS has randomly preset feedforward connections between the $F_A$ and $F_B$ layers and adaptable connections between the $F_B$ and $F_C$ layers. To keep the presentation uncluttered, all connections are not shown—there is actually a connection from each $F_A$ PE to each $F_B$ PE and from each $F_B$ PE to each $F_C$ PE.

$$d_j = b_j^k - b_j \qquad \text{(5-140)}$$

for each $j = 1, 2, \ldots, p$, where $d_j$ is the $j$th $F_B$ PE's computed error.

c. Adjust the connection strengths between $F_A$ and $F_B$ PEs using the equation

$$\Delta w_{ij} = \alpha a_i d_j \qquad \text{(5-141)}$$

for each $i = 1, 2, \ldots, n$, and each $j = 1, 2, \ldots, p$, where $\alpha$ is a positive constant controlling the learning rate.

3. Test: Repeat step (2) until the error-correction value $d_j$, $j = 1, 2, \ldots, p$, and $k = 1, 2, \ldots, m$, is either sufficiently low or zero.

Higher Order Learning. There is an immediate encoding extension that can improve the capabilities of the perceptron at the cost of higher connectivity. Maxwell, Giles & Lee (1986) have shown that higher order correlations can be effectively added to the encoding algorithm. Second-order connections (see section 5.1.5. and section 5.1.8. for a more thorough description of these correlations) are stored in the n-by-n-by-p matrix V and adjusted using the equation

$$\Delta v_{hij} = \alpha a_h^k a_i^k d_j \qquad \text{(5-142)}$$

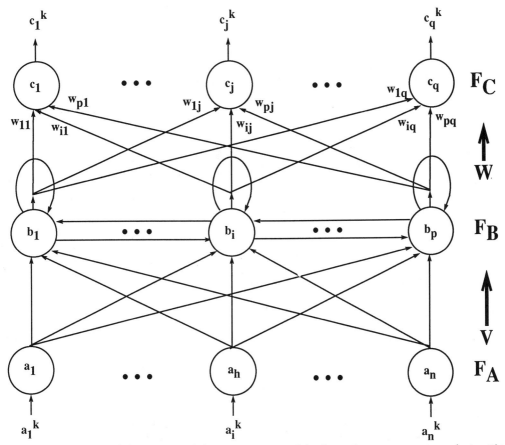

FIGURE 5-30. Topology of the cross-coupled perceptron, one of the four primary perceptron topologies. This three-layer ANS has randomly preset feedforward connections between the $F_A$ and $F_B$ layers, hardwired $F_B$ lateral connections, and adaptable feedforward connections between the $F_B$ and $F_C$ layers. To keep the presentation uncluttered, all connections are not shown—there is actually a connection from each $F_A$ PE to each $F_B$ PE, a connection from each $F_B$ PE to each $F_C$ PE, a lateral connection from each $F_B$ PE to every other $F_B$ PE, a recurrent connection from every $F_B$ PE to itself, a connection from each $F_B$ PE to each $F_C$ PE.

where $\Delta v_{hij}$ is the amount of change to the connection strength from the $hth$ and $ith$ $F_A$ PEs to the $jth$ $F_B$ PE. These second-order correlations are incorporated into the above encoding algorithm by adding eq. 5-142 as step (2)–(d) and replacing eq. 5-138 with the equation

$$b_j = f\left( \sum_{i=1}^{n} w_{ij}a_i + \sum_{h=1}^{n}\sum_{i=1}^{n} v_{hij}a_h a_i - \Theta_j \right) \tag{5-143}$$

Second-order correlations can be extended to include $3rd$-order ($u_{ghij}$) correlations and higher. Higher-order correlations like eq. 5-142 allow important nonlinear mappings to be captured, an attribute that significantly improves the pattern classification power of the perceptron.

The First Backpropagation Algorithm. Rosenblatt created a heuristic algorithm for adapting the $F_A$ to $F_B$ connections of the series-coupled perceptron shown in Figure 5-29 entitled the back-propagating error correction procedure which is described in *Principles of Neurodynamics* (Rosenblatt, 1962, p. 292) as follows:

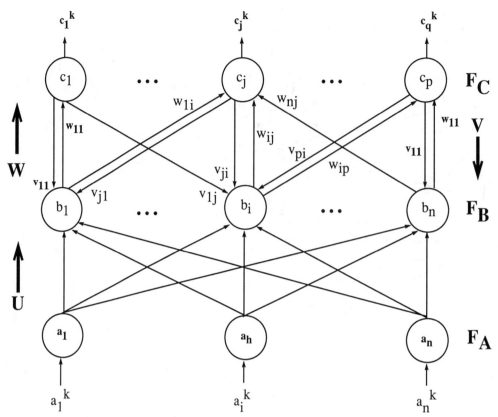

FIGURE 5-31. Topology of the back-coupled perceptron, one of the four primary perceptron topologies. This three-layer ANS has randomly preset feedforward connections between the $F_A$ and $F_B$ layers, and adaptable feedback connections between the $F_B$ and $F_C$ layers. To keep the presentation uncluttered, all connections are not shown — there is actually a connection from each $F_A$ PE to each $F_B$ PE, a connection from each $F_B$ PE to each $F_C$ PE, and a connection from each $F_C$ PE to each $F_B$ PE.

The procedure to be described here is called the "back-propagating error correction procedure" since it takes its cue from the error of the R-units [output PEs], propagating corrections back towards the sensory end of the network [the input PEs] if it fails to make a satisfactory correction quickly at the response end [output PEs]. The actual correction procedure for the connections to a given unit, whether it is an A-unit [hidden PE] or an R-unit [output PE], is perfectly identical to the correction procedure employed for an elementary perceptron, based on the error-indication assigned to the terminal unit.

As this paragraph explains, Rosenblatt came very close to discovering the key to training a multiple-layered ANS. Not surprisingly, the title of this algorithm has been applied to a currently popular multilayer learning algorithm independently discovered by several researchers (see section 5.4.3.).

### 5.4.1.2. Recall
Perceptron recall employs the feedforward equation 5-138

$$b_j = f\left(\sum_{i=1}^{n} w_{ij}a_i - \Theta_j\right) \qquad \textbf{(5-138)}$$

if only first order correlations are used and it uses the equation 5-143

$$b_j = f\left( \sum_{i=1}^{n} w_{ij}a_i + \sum_{h=1}^{n} \sum_{i=1}^{n} v_{hij}a_h a_i - \Theta_j \right) \tag{5-143}$$

if both first and second-order correlations are employed.

### 5.4.1.3. Convergence

The perceptron convergence theorem proves that the above encoding algorithm will find a solution for any linearly separable configuration in finite time. This result was first stated in the context of linear systems by Agmon (1954) who solved a set of linear inequalities by successive adjustments similar to those of eq. 5-141. The perceptron convergence theorem was first proven in the ANS community by Rosenblatt (1960 & 1962), and later by Papert (1961), Block (1962), Joseph (1960b), Nilsson (1965), and Minsky and Papert (1969).

### 5.4.1.4. Discussion, Analysis, Applications, and Implementations

As a paradigm, the perceptron is limited by its linear separability condition. As a foundational building block toward successively more powerful models, the perceptron has been a huge success. This is evidenced by the triumph of more sophisticated paradigms, such as the adaline and backpropagation ANSs. The perceptron's strengths are its well understood behavior, its adequate storage capacity, and its immediate recall. Perceptron limitations have been explored in detail by Rosenblatt (1962) where he points out that the perceptron is poor at generalization, it requires lengthy supervised offline learning, and it cannot encode nonlinearly separable classifications.

The perceptron has enjoyed an immense amount of study and has had several extensions proposed to its existing architecture and dynamics. Keller & Hunt (1985) have incorporated fuzzy membership functions into the perceptron's algorithm to improve the classification performance for nonseparable data sets. Singleton (1962) developed a test for linear separability that allows pretesting of candidate perceptron problems. Maxwell, Giles & Lee (1986) have studied the capabilities of higher ordered correlations in the learning procedure with respect to translation and rotation invariances of images and the capture of some complex inference structures. Minsky & Papert (1969) developed an extensive argument against the perceptron in their book *Perceptrons* that had a devastating effect on ANS research in the early 1970's (see Minsky in the Appendix). Block (1974) wrote a beautiful review of *Perceptrons* that clarified many misconceptions that were attached to the book. Joseph (1960a & 1960b) studied the predictability of the perceptron's performance. There have been several researchers who have analyzed the extension of the perceptron to allow multiple thresholds, including Bentor & Huang (1988), Takiyama (1978 & 1985), Haring (1966), Olafson & Abu-Mostafa (1988) and Winder (1963). Pemberton & Vidal (1988) have compared the performance of the perceptron and the adaline (section 5.4.2.) with respect to noise immunity. Ahmad (1988) has studied the scaling and generalization abilities of the perceptron. And, R. Levine (1988) has compared the perceptron to the backpropagation ANS (section 5.4.3.) within the framework of detecting variance transitions in Gaussian noise.

The perceptron is ideally suited to pattern matching applications that are inherently linear and only require a two-class response. Areas where the perceptron has been applied are found in Table 5-18. Also, the implementations that have been developed for the perceptron are found in Table 5-19.

## Perceptron Applications

| Application | Reference |
|---|---|
| Knowledge Processing | Gallant & Balachandra, 1986<br>Gallant, 1987b |
| Pattern Recognition | Roberts, 1960<br>Rosenblatt, 1962<br>Block, Nilsson & Duda, 1964 |
| Speech Processing | Rosenblatt, 1962<br>Burr, 1988a<br>Kammerer & Kuppu, 1988 |
| Sequence Recognition | Gallant, 1987a<br>Rosenblatt, 1962 |
| Image Processing | Kollias & Anastassiou, 1988a<br>Rosenblatt, 1962 |
| Control | Eberlein, 1988 |

TABLE 5-18.

## Perceptron Implementations

| Implementation | Reference |
|---|---|
| Optical/Electro-Optical | Hsu, Brady & Psaltis, 1988 |
| Magnetic Core Components | Hawkins, 1960 |
| Electronic Components | Hay, Martin & Wightman, 1960 |

TABLE 5-19.

### 5.4.2. Adaline/Madaline

The adaptive linear element (adaline) ANS — introduced by Widrow & Hoff (1960) and inspired by the work of Widrow (1959) — is a two-layer feedforward (perceptron) ANS with n $F_A$ PEs and one $F_B$ PE as shown in Figure 5-32. The multiple adaline (madaline) ANS is a configuration of several adalines placed in the familiar two-layer feedforward topology shown in Figure 5-33. The madaline is a heteroassociative, nearest-neighbor pattern matcher that stores the pattern pairs $(A_k, B_k)$, k = 1, 2, ..., m, using the least mean-square (LMS)

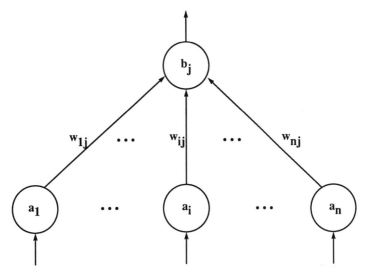

FIGURE 5-32. Topology of the adaline ANS. The adaline is described as a combinatorial logic circuit that accepts several inputs and produces one output. Using the terminology adopted in this book, the adaline is a two-layer ANS with a single output PE. Grossberg (1968a) has described an identical topology with different dynamics called the instar—the dual of the outstar shown in Figure 5-24—and shown that it is the minimal structure capable of recognizing a spatial pattern.

error-correction encoding procedure, where the k*th* pattern pair is represented by the analog valued vector $A_k = (a_1^k, \ldots, a_n^k)$ and the bipolar $\{-1, +1\}$ valued vector $B_k = (b_1^k, \ldots, b_p^k)$. The madaline learns offline, operates in discrete time, and is represented by the two-layer feedforward topology shown in Figure 5-33, where the n $F_A$ PEs correspond to $A_k$'s components and the p $F_B$ PEs correspond to $B_k$'s components.

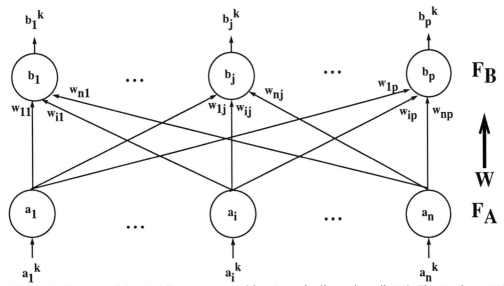

FIGURE 5-33. Topology of the Madaline, a supervised learning—feedforward recall ANS. This two-layer ANS stores pattern pairs in the weight matrix W formed from the connections between the $F_A$ and $F_B$ layers. This is a discrete-time ANS that stores the mapping between analog valued inputs and bipolar valued outputs. To keep the presentation uncluttered, all connections are not shown—there is actually a connection from each $F_A$ PE to each $F_B$ PE.

*5.4.2.1. Encoding*

Least Mean Square (LMS) Algorithm. The madaline encodes patterns by minimizing the least mean-square error between the computed and desired outputs of each $F_B$ PE. The mean-squared error is minimized by changing the $F_A$ to $F_B$ connections, $w_{ij}$, in a way that follows the error gradient to its minimum. This encoding procedure, commonly referred to as the LMS algorithm, is as follows:

1. Assign random values in the range $[-1,+1]$ to all the $F_A$ to $F_B$ inter-layer connections, $w_{ij}$, and to each $F_B$ PE threshold, $\Theta_j$.
2. For each pattern pair $(A_k, B_k)$, $k = 1, 2, \ldots, m$, do the following:
   a. Transfer $A_k$'s values to the $F_A$ PEs, filter the $F_A$ PE activations through W and calculate the new $F_B$ PE activation values using the equation

   $$b_j = \sum_{i=1}^{n} w_{ij} a_i + \Theta_j \tag{5-144}$$

   for each $j = 1, 2, \ldots, p$.
   b. Compute the discrepancy (error) between the computed and desired $F_B$ PE values using the equation

   $$d_j = b_j^k - b_j \tag{5-145}$$

   for each $j = 1, 2, \ldots, p$, where $d_j$ is the $j$th $F_B$ PE's computed error.
   c. Adjust the $F_A$ to $F_B$ PE connection strengths using equation

   $$\Delta w_{ij} = \alpha a_i d_j \tag{5-146}$$

   for each $i = 1, 2, \ldots, n$, and each $j = 1, 2, \ldots, p$. The parameter $\alpha$ is a positive scalar, $0 < \alpha < 1$, that is used to control the learning rate. This correction procedure does gradient descent on the n-dimensional mean-squared error surface and was found by calculating the gradient of the error with respect to the weights.
3. Repeat step (2) until the error correction value $d_j$, for each $j = 1, 2, \ldots, p$, and $k = 1, 2, \ldots, m$, is either sufficiently low or zero.

A comparison of this encoding procedure with that of the perceptron's (section 5.4.1.) shows that they are identical, with the exception of the sign of the threshold and the omission of the threshold function in eq. 5-144. Yet they are each associated with different mathematical foundations; the perceptron encoding algorithm is based upon the placement of a hyperplane, and the madaline encoding algorithm is based upon the minimization of the mean-squared error between desired and computed outputs.

Madaline Rule II Multi-Layer Learning Rule. Extensions have been made to the LMS encoding procedure. This new encoding procedure employs the three-layer feedforward topology shown in Figure 5-34 to encode the pattern pairs $(A_k, C_k)$, $k = 1, 2, \ldots, m$. This algorithm—first presented by Widrow (1962) as an extension of the work of Ridgway (1962) and later refined by Widrow (1987), Widrow & Winter (1988) and Widrow, Winter & Baxter (1988)—is described as follows:

1. Find the $F_B$ PE closest to zero and adjust its $F_A$ to $F_B$ connections just enough to switch the sign of its output.
2. If the $F_C$ PEs have less computed error after these changes, accept the change; otherwise reject it and try the next closest.

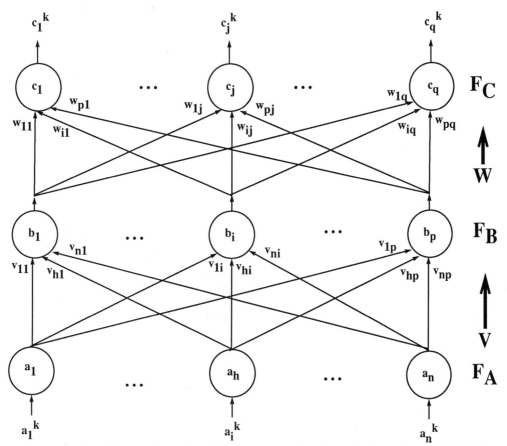

FIGURE 5-34. Toplogy of the Multilayered Madaline, a supervised learning—feedforward recall ANS. This three-layer ANS uses a heuristic-based algorithm to adjust the connections between the $F_A$ and $F_B$ layers and later the connections between the $F_B$ and $F_C$ layers. To keep the presentation uncluttered, all connections are not shown—there is actually a connection from each $F_A$ PE to each $F_B$ PE and from each $F_B$ PE to each $F_C$ PE.

3. Continue until all $F_B$ PEs have been processed singly, then use combinations of all the pairs that are closest to zero, then do all the triples closest to zero, and so on, until some predetermined number of combinations is achieved.

4. Once the $F_A$ to $F_B$ PEs have been adapted as much as possible, repeat steps (1) to (3) with the $F_C$ PEs to further improve the mapping.

Mixed Logic Multilayer Learning Rule. Another multilayer madaline encoding extension—primarily the work of Ridgway (1962)—adapts the $F_A$ to $F_B$ connections and combines the $F_B$ PE values into logical combinations to produce the $F_C$ PE values. As an example, Figure 5-35 shows two $F_B$ PEs combined by the AND operator to produce one $F_C$ PE value, and three other PEs combined by the OR operator to produce another $F_C$ PE value.

### 5.4.2.2. Recall
The madaline recall equation is a thresholded version of eq. 5-144 that produces bipolar values, expressed as

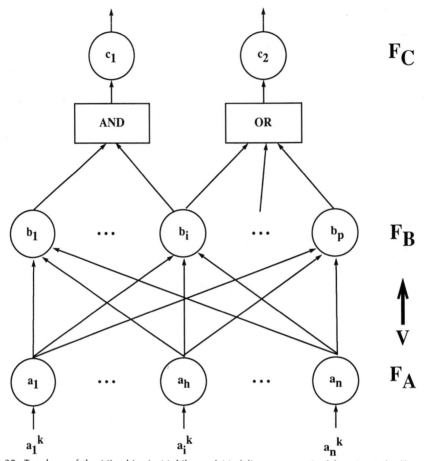

FIGURE 5-35. Topology of the Mixed-Logic Multilayered Madaline, a supervised learning—feedforward recall ANS. This three-layer ANS uses the LMS algorithm to adjust the connections between the $F_A$ and $F_B$ layers and then combines the outputs of the $F_B$ PEs and processes them through a logic operator to create $F_C$ PE activations. To keep the presentation uncluttered, all connections are not shown—there is actually a connection from each $F_A$ PE to each $F_B$ PE and a predetermined set of hardwired connections from the $F_B$ PEs to the $F_C$ PEs.

$$b_j = f\left(\sum_{i=1}^{n} w_{ij}a_i + \Theta_j\right) \qquad \textbf{(5-147)}$$

for all $j = 1, 2, \ldots, p$, where the bipolar step function, $f()$, is defined as

$$f(x) = \begin{cases} 1 & \text{if } x > 0 \\ -1 & \text{otherwise} \end{cases} \qquad \textbf{(5-148)}$$

### 5.4.2.3. Convergence

The LMS encoding procedure is proven to converge to the global error minimum through an analysis of its mean-squared error. The error, defined as the difference between the computed and desired values for each $F_B$ PE, is found using the equation

$$d_j = b_j^k - b_j = b_j^k - \sum_{i=1}^{n} w_{ij}a_i - \Theta_j \qquad \textbf{(5-149)}$$

Without any loss in generality, we can replace each $\Theta_j$ with the product $w_{0j}a_0$, resulting in the equation

$$d_j = b_j^k - \sum_{i=0}^{n} w_{ij}a_i \tag{5-150}$$

which is rewritten in vector notation as

$$d_j = b_j^k - A_k W_j^T \tag{5-151}$$

where $W_j$ is the vector of weights abutting the $jth$ $F_B$ PE. Continuing, the squared error is defined as

$$d_j^2 = (b_j^k)^2 - 2b_j^k A_k W_j^T + [A_k W_j^T]^2 \tag{5-152}$$

$$= (b_j^k)^2 - 2b_j^k A_k W_j^T + W_j A_k^T A_k W_j^T$$

Assuming a stationary input environment, we replace the $F_A$ and $F_B$ variables with their means, yielding the mean-squared error equation

$$E\{(d_j)^2\} = E\{(b_j^k)^2\} - 2E\{b_j^k A_k\}W_j^T + W_j E\{A_k^T A_k\}W_j^T \tag{5-153}$$

where $E\{*\}$ represents the estimated mean operator. Eq. 5-153 is simplified by making the substitutions

$$P = E\{b_j^k A_k\} \tag{5-154}$$

where P is the input-correlation vector of $F_A$ PE values and the $F_B$ desired response, and

$$R = E\{A_k^T A_k\} \tag{5-155}$$

where R is the autocorrelation matrix of $F_A$ PEs. Substituting P and R in eq. 5-153 yields the simplified equation

$$E\{(d_j)^2\} = E\{(b_j^k)^2\} - 2PW_j^T + W_j R W_j^T \tag{5-156}$$

Minimizing the mean-squared error is performed by calculating the change in the estimated mean-squared error with respect to the change in the weight vector $W_j$ calculated using the equation

$$\frac{\partial}{\partial W_j} E\{(d_j)^2\} = 0 - 2P + 2W_j R \tag{5-157}$$

Setting the result equal to 0, and solving for $W_j$, results in

$$W_j = PR^{-1} \tag{5-158}$$

which is the matrix form of the Wiener-Hopf equation (Widrow, Mantey & Griffiths, 1967; Widrow, 1968). This result proves that the LMS algorithm will find the optimal weight vector, in the least-squares sense, providing the inverse of R exists. Interestingly, eq. 5-158 is the same equation used to encode pattern pairs in the optimal linear associative memory's heteroassociative encoding equation (eq. 5-97, section 5.2.5.). As a final note, madaline convergence is guaranteed only if the learning rate, $\alpha$, used in eq. 5-146 is not greater than the inverse of the largest eigenvalue of the autocorrelation matrix R. Mathematically this relationship is expressed as

$$0 < \alpha < (\lambda_{max})^{-1} \tag{5-159}$$

where $\lambda_{max}$ is the largest eigenvalue of the autocorrelation matrix.

*5.4.2.4. Discussion, Analysis, Applications, and Implementations*

Adaline/madaline strengths include its capacity to hold twice as many patterns as there are $A_k$ dimensions (m = 2n), and its well understood mathematics. Limitations of this paradigm include the lengthy encoding time, the inability to learn online, and the restriction to linear $(A_k, B_k)$ mappings.

The LMS algorithm is the most pervasive of all ANS encoding algorithms. The number of researchers who have analyzed, altered and extended this algorithm is large. Widrow, Gupta & Maitra (1973) developed an encoding procedure called bootstrap adaptation that is similar to stochastic learning automata (Narendra & Thathachar, 1974) in that it makes adjustments based solely on two signals returned by the environment—reward and punishment. This type of learning—now commonly referred to as reinforcement learning—has since been explored by Barto, Sutton & Anderson (1983), Barto & Anandan, (1985), and Williams (1986 & 1987). Parker (1987a & 1987b) has developed an extension of the LMS algorithm that uses second-order calculations of the gradient to make weight adjustments. Widrow & McCool (1976) compared the LMS algorithm with two other methods of adjusting the weights in an adaptive system. Steinbuch & Widrow (1965) have compared the performance of the Learning Matrix (section 5.2.1.) with the LMS algorithm. Nguyen & Lee (1988) have developed an LMS adaptation method that uses two sets of weights for two-class problems, an approach that significantly improves the training time. Sethares (1988) has applied a continuous threshold function to the $F_B$ PE value produced during encoding and has shown that there is still convergence. Fong & Jensen (1988) have modified the LMS algorithm correction procedure to make adjustments only after all the patterns have been presented instead of after each pattern presentation. Pemberton & Vidal (1988a) have compared the effects of noise on the performance of the perceptron and the adaline (section 5.4.2.). Wolf (1988) has extended the LMS encoding algorithm to include higher ordered correlations. Stone (1986) and Homma, Atlas & Marks (1988) have compared the encoding operation of the LMS algorithm to that employed by the optimal linear associative memory (section 5.2.4.).

The adaline was introduced within the framework of a neuron analogy (Widrow & Hoff, 1960), but quickly the engineering community learned of its capabilities and spawned an entire field—adaptive signal processing (Widrow & Stearns, 1985)—based almost entirely upon the LMS algorithm. The application areas of adaptive signal processing include system modeling, statistical prediction, noise cancelling, adaptive echo cancelling, inverse modeling and channel equalization (Widrow & Winter, 1988). The ANS related work with the LMS algorithm is primarily focused upon adaptive pattern matching and control. Table 5-20 lists the wide variety of application areas where the LMS algorithm/adaline/madaline have been employed. Widrow has developed an electro-chemical device called the memistor (Widrow, 1960) that he used in an implementation called the KNOBBY ADALINE (Widrow, 1962). Also, Simmes (1987) and O'Callaghan & Anderson (1988) have discussed optical/electro-optical implementations of the adaline/madaline.

## 5.4.3. Backpropagation

The elementary backpropagation is a three-layer (perceptron) ANS with feedforward connections from the $F_A$ PEs to the $F_B$ PEs and feedforward connections from the $F_B$ PEs to the $F_C$ PEs. In general, it is possible to have several hidden layers, connections that skip over layers, recurrent connections, and lateral connections. Although these advanced topologies are important, they tend to obfuscate the simplicity of this algorithm. Hence, the primary description of the backpropagation algorithm assumes the elementary backpropagation topology.

The elementary backpropagation ANS is a heteroassociative, function-estimating ANS that

| Adaline/LMS Applications | |
|---|---|
| **Application** | **Reference** |
| Control | Widrow & Smith, 1964<br>Tolat, 1988<br>Tolat & Widrow, 1988<br>Waxman, et al., 1988<br>Widrow, 1988 |
| Pattern Recognition | Widrow, 1962<br>Widrow, et al., 1963<br>Widrow & Winter, 1987 & 1988<br>Widrow, Winter & Baxter, 1988 |
| Temporal Processing | Ferrara & Widrow, 1981<br>Wolf, 1988 |
| Image Processing | Waxman, et al., 1988<br>Lee, Nguyen & Lin, 1988 |
| Noise Cancellation | Widrow, et al., 1975<br>Hassoun & Spitzer, 1988<br>Widrow & Stearns, 1985<br>Jablon, 1986 |
| Antenna Systems | Widrow, Mantey & Griffiths, 1967<br>Jablon, 1986<br>Widrow & Stearns, 1985 |

TABLE 5-20.

stores arbitrary analog spatial pattern pairs $(A_k, C_k)$, $k = 1, 2, \ldots, m$, using a multilayer gradient descent error-correction encoding algorithm, where the $k$th pattern pair is represented by the vectors $A_k = (a_1^k, \ldots, a_n^k)$ and $C_k = (c_1^k, \ldots, c_q^k)$. Backpropagation learns offline, operates in discrete time, and is represented by the three-layer feedforward topology shown in Figure 5-36, where the n $F_A$ PEs correspond to $A_k$'s components and the q $F_C$ PEs correspond to $C_k$'s components.

### 5.4.3.1. A Brief History

The backpropagation ANS has been independently derived by several people from wide-ranging disciplines. The first gradient descent approach to training multilayered ANSs came from mathematics and was developed by Amari (1967), who introduced a single hidden layer PE to perform nonlinear classification. Amari's approach was in the right direction, but it still was not a complete description of how to develop a multilayered mapping. Bryson & Ho (1969) developed an algorithm very similar to that of backpropagation for nonlinear adaptive control. Werbos (1974) independently discovered the backpropagation algorithm and several variants — calling the algorithm dynamic feedback — while working on his doctoral thesis in statistics. Parker (1982) rediscovered the backpropagation algorithm — calling the

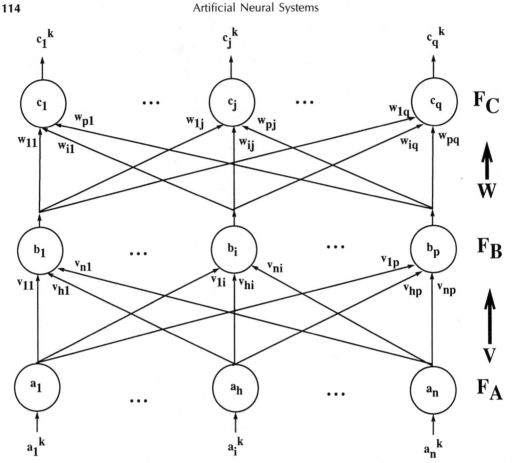

FIGURE 5-36. Topology of elementary backpropagation, a supervised learning—feedforward recall ANS. This three-layer ANS uses the backpropagation encoding algorithm to adjust the connections between the $F_A$ and $F_B$ layers and the $F_B$ and $F_C$ layers. To keep the presentation uncluttered, all connections are not shown—there is actually a connection from each $F_A$ PE to each $F_B$ PE and from each $F_B$ PE to each $F_C$ PE.

algorithm learning logic—and even took preliminary steps to patent his work while doing graduate work at Stanford. When Rumelhart, Hinton & Williams (1986)—a group of cognitive and computer scientists—exploited the power and potential of backpropagation, the scientific community became excited about this ANS paradigm. Although this was not the first successful multilayered learning algorithm—the Boltzmann Machine (section 5.4.4.) was—it has had the immediate effect of answering the key argument that led to the demise of ANS research in the late 1960's and 1970's (see Minksy and Rosenblatt in Appendix).

### 5.4.3.2. Encoding
The backpropagation encoding algorithm performs the input to output mapping by minimizing a cost function. The cost function is minimized by making weight connection adjustments according to the error between the computed and desired output ($F_C$) PE values. The cost function that is typically minimized is the squared error—the squared difference between the computed output value and the desired output value for each $F_C$ PE across all patterns in the data set. This is not the only cost function that can be minimized. White (1988) and Baum & Wilczek (1988) have discussed the use of an entropic cost function. Alstyne (1988) has used a linear error instead of a squared error cost function. And, Hanson & Burr (1988) have used r*th* power of the absolute value of the error.

Regardless of the cost function, the weight adjustment procedure is derived by computing the change in the cost function with respect to the change in each weight. The element that makes the backpropagation algorithm so powerful is that this derivation is extended to find the equation for adapting the connections between the input ($F_A$) and hidden ($F_B$) layers of a multilayer ANS, as well as the penultimate layer to output layer adjustments. The key element of the extension to the hidden layer adjustments is the realization that each $F_B$ PE's error is a proportionally weighted sum of the errors produced at the $F_C$ layer.

The *vanilla backpropagation algorithm* is the encoding algorithm that minimizes the squared error cost function and uses the three-layer elementary backpropagation topology shown in Figure 5-36. The algorithm is outlined as follows:

1. Assign random values in the range $[+1, -1]$ to all the $F_A$ to $F_B$ inter-layer connections, $v_{hi}$, all the $F_B$ to $F_C$ inter-layer connections, $w_{ij}$, to each $F_B$ PE threshold, $\Theta_i$, and to each $F_C$ PE threshold, $\Gamma_j$.

2. For each pattern pair $(A_k, C_k)$, $k = 1, 2, \ldots, m$, do the following:

   a. Transfer $A_k$'s values to the $F_A$ PEs, filter the $F_A$ PE activations through V and calculate the new $F_B$ PE values (activations) using the equation

   $$b_i = f\left(\sum_{h=1}^{n} a_h v_{hi} + \Theta_i\right) \tag{5-160}$$

   for all $i = 1, 2, \ldots, p$, where $b_i$ is the activation value of the $i$th $F_B$ PE, $\Theta_i$ is the $i$th $F_B$ PE's threshold value, and $f()$ is the logistic sigmoid threshold function $f(x) = (1 + e^{-x})^{-1}$.

   b. Filter the $F_B$ activations through W to $F_C$ using the equation

   $$c_j = f\left(\sum_{i=1}^{n} b_i w_{ij} + \Gamma_j\right) \tag{5-161}$$

   for all $j = 1, 2, \ldots, q$, where $c_j$ is the activation value of the $j$th $F_C$ PE and $\Gamma_j$ is the $j$th $F_B$ PE's threshold value.

   c. Compute the discrepancy (error) between the computed and desired $F_C$ PE values using the equation

   $$d_j = c_j(1 - c_j)(c_j^k - c_j) \tag{5-162}$$

   for all $j = 1, 2, \ldots, q$, where $d_j$ is the $j$th $F_C$ PE's computed error.

   d. Calculate the error of each $F_B$ PE relative to each $d_j$ with the equation

   $$e_i = b_i(1 - b_i)\sum_{j=1}^{q} w_{ij} d_j \tag{5-163}$$

   for all $i = 1, 2, \ldots, p$, where $e_i$ is the $i$th $F_B$ PE's computed error.

   e. Adjust the $F_B$ to $F_C$ connections

   $$\Delta w_{ij} = \alpha b_i d_j \tag{5-164}$$

   for all $i = 1, 2, \ldots, p$, and all $j = 1, 2, \ldots, q$, where $\Delta w_{ij}$ is the amount of change made to the connection from the $i$th $F_B$ to the $j$th $F_C$ PE, and $\alpha$ is a positive constant controlling the learning rate.

   f. Adjust the $F_C$ thresholds

   $$\Delta\Gamma_j = \alpha d_j \tag{5-165}$$

   for all $j = 1, 2, \ldots, q$, where $\Delta\Gamma_j$ is the amount of change to the $j$th $F_C$ PE's threshold value.

g. Adjust the $F_A$ to $F_B$ connections

$$\Delta v_{hi} = \beta a_h e_i \tag{5-166}$$

for all h = 1, 2, ..., n, and all i = 1, 2, ..., p, where $\Delta v_{hi}$ is the amount of change made to the connection from the h*th* $F_A$ and i*th* $F_B$ PE, and $\beta$ is a positive constant controlling the learning rate.

h. Adjust the $F_B$ thresholds

$$\Delta \Theta_i = \beta e_i \tag{5-167}$$

for all i = 1, 2, ..., n, where $\Delta \Theta_i$ is the amount of change to the i*th* $F_C$ PE's threshold value.

3. Repeat step (2) until the error correction value $d_j$, for each j = 1, 2, ..., p, and each k = 1, 2, ..., m, is either sufficiently low or zero.

### 5.4.3.3. Recall

Backpropagation recall accepts an input at the $F_A$ PEs and feeds it through the V and W matrices to produce a response at the $F_C$ PEs. This feedforward operation creates $F_B$ PE values (activations) using eq. 5-160

$$b_i = f\left(\sum_{h=1}^{n} a_h v_{hi} + \Theta_i\right) \tag{5-160}$$

for all i = 1, 2, ..., p. Once the $F_B$ PE values have been all calculated they are then used to create new $F_C$ PE values using eq. 5-161

$$c_j = f\left(\sum_{i=1}^{n} b_i w_{ij} + \Gamma_j\right) \tag{5-161}$$

for all j = 1, 2, ..., q.

### 5.4.3.4. Convergence

Backpropagation is not guaranteed to find the global error minimum during training, only the local error minimum. This situation often leads to severe oscillations in the weight changes during training and abandonment of the training at that point. The key to solving this problem is multifaceted. Several questions must be answered concerning the proper selection of the number of hidden layer PEs, the size of the learning rate parameters, and the amount of data necessary to create the proper mapping.

Theoretical results have recently been emerging that are moving towards answering these questions. Several studies have independently found that a three-layer ANS using the backpropagation algorithm can approximate a wide range of functions to any desired degree of accuracy (Le Cunn, 1987; Irie & Miyake, 1988; Moore & Poggio, 1988; Hornick, Stinchcombe & White, 1988; White, 1988; Hecht-Nielsen, 1988c). The primary result of this work states only that a mapping exists that backpropagation can find; it does not state how to find that mapping.

### 5.4.3.5. Discussion and Analysis

Backpropagation strengths include its ability to store many more patterns than the number of $F_A$ dimensions (m $\gg$ n) and its ability to acquire arbitrarily complex nonlinear mappings. Backpropagation limitations are its extremely long training time, its offline encoding requiremem, and the inability to know how to precisely generate any arbitrary mapping procedure (knowing, as we do, that one does exist).

The number of studies and applications of backpropagation is quickly becoming too numerous to count. Extensive analysis has centered in six areas: (1) optimizing the number of PEs in the hidden layer(s), (2) improving the rate of learning, (3) extending the topology to any arbitrary connection topology, (4) analyzing the scaling, generalization and fault tolerance properties, (5) employing higher-order correlations and arbitrary threshold functions, and (6) other research and comparisons. The analysis in each of these areas is summarized in the following six sections.

Hidden Layer Size Optimization. Rumelhart (1988) has added cost functions that will minimize the number of connections and the number of hidden PEs as well as the overall squared error during training. The preliminary results with this are encouraging, but the training time is greatly increased. Sietsma & Dow (1988) and Yu & Teh (1988) have proposed some heuristics for pruning away hidden layer PEs during the training. Surkan & Chen (1988) have used a code generation approach to optimize the number of hidden layer PEs. Ash (1988) has developed a technique entitled dynamic node creation that grows hidden layer PEs as they are needed.

Learning Rate Improvement. It is possible to make precise changes in weights by employing Newton's method to adjust the weights, hence eliminating the guesswork of deciding how large the learning parameters should be during encoding. Newton's method gives the gradient that will move from the current point on a curve (in this case the n-dimensional error surface) in a straight line to the intersection on the curve as shown in Figure 5-37. The unfortunate

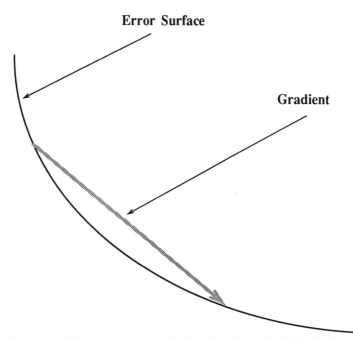

FIGURE 5-37. Illustration of the how Newton's method works. The product of the gradient and the pseudoinverse of the Hessian gives the vector that intersects the curve. Using this method for updating the connection weights in the backpropagation can eliminate some of the local minima traps and facilitate a more efficient adaption process.

drawback to using Newton's method is it requires computing the pseudoinverse of the Hessian. Those that have studied the use of Newton's method in the backpropagation include Sutton (1986), Watrous (1987), Parker (1987a, 1987b & 1987c), Kollias & Anastassiou (1988b), Ricotti, Ragazzinni & Martinelli (1988), Le Cunn (1987 & 1988), Hecht-Nielsen (1988c), and McInerny, et al. (1989).

There have been several other methods and heuristics employed to decrease the training time of the backpropagation algorithm. Rumelhart, Hinton & Williams (1986) have added a portion of the last gradient (weight change) — entitled the momentum — to the current weight to speed the learning time. Hush & Salas (1988) have extended this idea to reusing the gradient several times in succession. Cater (1987) has used 10 to 30 times the size of the calculated gradient (weight change) to speed the learning rate. Watrous (1987) has employed line search routines on the calculated gradient in order to make the optimal size change during each training iteration. Pemberton & Vidal (1988b) have performed *a priori* weight and threshold computations, before applying the gradient descent training procedure, to improve the training time. Sandon & Uhr (1988) have developed a set of heuristics for escaping local error minima during training. Lehman, et al. (1988) have studied the effects of adding noise to decrease the training time and found that it helped for small problems. Vogl, et al. (1988) have proposed a set of heuristics to improve the training time that adjusts the learning rates for the current and past gradients during encoding. Stornetta & Huberman (1987) have been able to improve the training time by using a sigmoid threshold function that had a range of $[-1, +1]$. Wittner & Denker (1988), C. Anderson (1987), Dahl (1987a), Jacobs (1988) and Samad (1988) have contributed similar heuristics for improving the training time. Wang (1988) has employed the notion of trust regions to improve the encoding precision. Weiland & Leighton (1988) have discussed the use of shaping schedules — a training procedure that starts with the easier-to-learn mappings and gradually works to the more difficult. Kung & Huang (1988b) have employed algebraic projection analysis to analyze the discrimination and convergence speed during training. And, Caillon, Angeniol & Markade (1988) have constrained the weights during training to prevent oscillations.

Alternate Connection Topologies. The elementary backpropagation topology has been extended in many ways. In Werbos' (1974) description of dynamic feedback (backpropagation), he allowed any parameter to be adjusted by any previous set of parameters. In the ANS framework, every PE would be ordered and each PE would be connected to every preceding PE in the order. Jordan (1986b) used a backpropagation topology that employed the last set of output PE activations to augment the current set of input activations. Elman (1988) has done something similar in that he uses the last set of hidden PE activations to augment the current set of input PE activations. And, Waibel, et al. (1987) have developed a backpropagation for recognizing time-varying signals that replace each connection in the elementary backpropagation ANS with several time-stamped connections.

The most general backpropagation topology possible is one that allows any PE to connect to any other PE. These topologies introduce feedback into the recall dynamics and are suitably called recurrent backpropagation ANSs. These paradigms have been studied by Almeida (1987 & 1988), Rohwer & Forrest (1987), Samad & Harper (1987), Shimohar, Uchiyama & Tokunuga (1988), Atiya (1988), Pineda (1987 & 1988), and Williams & Zipser (1988).

Scaling, Generalization, and Fault-Tolerance Properties. One of the most important areas of backpropagation research has been the analysis of the backpropagation performance as the size of the problem begins to scale up. Those that have looked at this issue include Tesauro (1987) and Richards (1988).

A topic that is also of great importance, especially with regard to the application of backpropagation to real-world problems, is its ability to generalize from the given data. Those that have studied this issue include Baum (1986a), Denker (1987), Gallinari, et al. (1987), Psaltis & Neifield (1988), Musari, et al. (1988), and Smieja (1988).

A final performance issue of great importance to backpropagation's application viability is its fault-tolerance—its ability to withstand damage to connections and nodes and still process properly. Bookman & Zhang (1988) have directly addressed this issue.

Higher Order Correlations and Alternate Threshold Functions. Several efforts have been made to incorporate higher order connections into this already inherently nonlinear function optimizing ANS. Rumelhart, Hinton & Williams (Rumelhart & McClelland, 1986) proposed the use of higher order correlations, calling the PEs that used higher order correlations sigma-pi units. Others who have worked with higher order correlations in the backpropagation algorithm include Klassen, Pao & Chen (1988), and Pineda (1988).

In addition to incorporating higher order correlations, several researchers have studied the effects of using threshold functions other than the sigmoid. Klassen, Pao and Chen (1988) have applied the sine and cosine functions to the input layer PE activations and used the result to augment the input layer. Lapedes & Farber (1988a & 1988b) and Gallant & White (1988) have used a clipped cosine function for thresholding PE values and found that backpropagation was able to construct a Fourier series approximation to a given function as its output.

Other Research and Comparisons. Tillery & Combs (1987), Cottrell, Munro & Zipser (1987), Elman & Zipser (1987), Watson (1987), Smieja (1988), and Gorman & Sejnowski (1988a) have studied the hidden layer PEs in an effort to understand what representation was being created in the mapping. Sutton (1987) has developed a variant of backpropagation that uses temporal differences to adjust the weights. Longstaff & Cross (1987) have analyzed the backpropagation ANS from a pattern recognition approach. Plaut, Nowlan & Hinton (1986) have conducted several basic experiments with the elementary backpropagation architecture which has provided valuable benchmark tests. Kuczewski, Myers & Crawford (1987) have explored the self-organization properties of backpropagation. Brady & Ragharan (1988) have done work that shows there are problems that are linearly separable—a task guaranteed solvable by the perceptron—yet backpropagation could not perform the task. Kuh (1988) has developed a backpropagation algorithm with decay terms that can train and recall at the same time. McInerny, et al. (1989) have extensively studied the error topology of several backpropagation solutions to nonlinear mapping problems and verified that local minima do exist. Lehar (1988b) has developed a graphics tool that is used to explore the dynamics of backpropagation networks.

Several comparisons have been made between backpropagation and other ANSs. Gallinari et al. (1988) have compared the performance of backpropagation against that of the optimal linear associative memory (see section 5.2.4.) for linear classification tasks. Woods (1988) and Caudill (1988) have compared the performance of backpropagation with that of counterpropagation (see section 5.2.8.). Bernasconi (1988) has compared the performance of the backpropagation with that of the Boltzmann machine (see section 5.4.4.) for pattern matching problems. Lippmann (1987 & 1988) and Huang & Lippmann (1988) have compared backpropagation against learning vector quantization (see section 5.2.7.) and other conventional classifiers for speech classification problems. And, R. Levine (1988) has compared the performance of backpropagation with that of the perceptron (see section 5.4.1.) within the framework of detecting variance transitions in Gaussian noise.

### 5.4.3.6. Applications and Implementations

The primary application of the backpropagation ANS is any situation that requires the acquisition of a complex nonlinear mapping, provided that the system can wait long enough for the ANS to learn the mapping. Table 5-21 lists several of the application areas where backpropagation has been employed.

Because backpropagation takes so long to train, several researchers, engineers and entrepreneurs have designed hardware specific to the task to help speed things along. Table 5-22 lists the implementations of the backpropagation ANS.

## 5.4.4. Boltzmann Machine (BM)

The Boltzmann machine (BM) ANS — introduced by Hinton, Ackley and Sejnowski (1984) — is a heteroassociative, nearest-neighbor pattern matcher that stores arbitrary binary spatial patterns $(A_k, C_k)$, $k = 1, 2, \ldots, m$, using a combination of Hebbian encoding and simulated annealing (i.e. stochastic learning), where the $k$th pattern pair is represented by the vectors $A_k = (a_1^k, \ldots, a_n^k)$ and $C_k = (c_1^k, \ldots, c_q^k)$. The BM learns offline, operates in discrete time, and is represented by the three-layer feedforward topology shown in Figure 5-38, where the n $F_A$ PEs correspond to $A_k$'s components, and the q $F_C$ PEs correspond to $C_k$'s components.

### 5.4.4.1. Encoding

The BM encoding procedure incorporates an internal $(F_B)$ layer of binary valued PE activations that are probabilistically adjusted using gradually decreasing amounts of noise to escape local energy minima in favor of the global minimum. The use of noise to escape local minima is called simulated annealing (Kirkpatrick, Gelatt & Vecchi, 1983), and the combination of simulated annealing and the probabilistic assignment of internal layer $(F_B)$ PE activations is called stochastic learning. The BM encoding algorithm is the following:

1. Assign random values in the range $[+1, -1]$ to all the $F_A$ to $F_B$ inter-layer connections, $v_{hi}$, and all the $F_B$ to $F_C$ inter-layer connections, $w_{ij}$.

2. Starting at time $t = 1$, and for each pattern pair $(A_k, C_k)$, $k = 1, 2, \ldots, m$, do the following:
   a. Transfer $A_k$'s values to the $F_A$ PEs and transfer $C_k$'s values to the $F_C$ PEs.
   b. Randomly select an $F_B$ PE and switch its state (binary value) as follows

   $$b_i = \begin{cases} 1 & \text{if } b_i = 0 \\ 0 & \text{otherwise} \end{cases} \qquad \text{(5-168)}$$

   where $b_i$ is the randomly chosen $F_B$ PE.
   c. Calculate the change in global energy with respect to the $i$th $F_B$ PE, $\Delta E_i$, created by the switched state

   $$\Delta E_i = \sum_{h=1}^{n} v_{hi} b_i + \sum_{j=1}^{q} w_{ji} b_i \qquad \text{(5-169)}$$

   d. If $\Delta E_i < 0$, keep the change. If $\Delta E_i > 0$, accept the change if $P_i > r$, where r is a number randomly chosen from $P_i$, the Boltzmann distribution given $\Delta E_i$, computed using the equation

   $$P_i = e^{-(\Delta E_i / T(t))} \qquad \text{(5-170)}$$

   where $T(t)$ is the positive valued temperature at time t that regulates the search granularity for the system's global minimum (larger T means courser search). If $\Delta E_i > 0$ and $P_i < r$, then return $b_i$ to its original state prior to step (b).

# Backpropagation Applications

| Application | Reference |
|---|---|
| Image Processing | Troxel, Rogers & Kabrisky, 1988<br>Dayhoff & Dayhoff, 1988<br>Moya, Fogler & Hostetler, 1988<br>Fogler, Williams & Hostetler, 1988<br>Lehar, 1988a<br>Roberts, 1988<br>Weiland, Leighton & Jacyna, 1988<br>Cottrell & Willen, 1988<br>Hurlbert, 1988 | Castelaz, 1988<br>Glover, 1988a & 1988b<br>Modorikawa, 1988<br>Wright, 1988<br>Scaletter & Zee, 1988<br>Cottrell, Munrop & Zipser, 1987<br>Dodd, 1987<br>Yang & Guest, 1987<br>Kuczewski, 1987 |
| Speech Processing | Ricotti, Ragazzini & Martinelli, 1988<br>Robinson & Fallside, 1988<br>Tishby, 1988<br>Anderson, Merril & Port, 1988<br>Bourlard & Wellekens, 1987 & 1988<br>Kammerer & Kuppu, 1988<br>Landauer, Kamm & Singhal, 1987<br>Treurniet, et al., 1988<br>Burr, 1988a & 1988b | Tenorio, Tom & Schwartz, 1988<br>Lippmann, 1987 & 1988<br>Rosenberg & Sejnowski, 1986<br>Sejnowski & Rosenberg, 1987<br>Elman & Zipser, 1987<br>Luse, et al., 1988<br>Watson, 1987<br>Waibel, et al., 1987 |
| Temporal Processing | Shimohara, Uchiyama & Tokinuga, 1988<br>Graupe & Uth, 1988<br>Elman, 1988 | Lewis, 1988<br>Robinson & Fallside, 1988<br>Tam, Perkel & Tucker, 1988 |
| Prediction/Optimization | Werbos, 1974 & 1988<br>Castelaz, 1988<br>Moody & Denker, 1988<br>Madey & Denton, 1988<br>Smith, 1988 | Dutta & Shekha, 1988<br>Lapedes & Farber, 1988a & 1988b<br>Tishby, 1988<br>Karsai, et al., 1988<br>Quian & Sejnowski, 1988<br>Baum, 1986a & 1986b |

TABLE 5-21.

# Backpropagation Applications (cont'd)

| Application | Reference |
|---|---|
| Diagnostics | Bounds, et al., 1988<br>Guha, 1988 |
| Control | Suddarth, Sutton & Holden, 1988<br>Tolat & Widrow, 1988<br>Means & Caid, 1988<br>Ransil & Siegal, 1988<br>Rock, et al., 1988<br>Ahmad, 1988<br>Josin, 1988<br>Miyata, 1987<br>Dietz, Kiech & Ali, 1988<br>Baum & Wilczek, 1988<br>Psaltis, Sideris & Yamamura, 1988<br>Liu, Iberall & Bekey, 1988<br>Elsley, 1988<br>Josin, Charney & White, 1988<br>Sobajic, Lu & Pao, 1988<br>Guez & Selinsky, 1988<br>Karsai, et al., 1988<br>Tarrel & Thakoor, 1988<br>Grajski, 1988 |
| Character Recognition | Pawlicki, et al., 1988<br>Shirvaiker & Musari, 1988<br>Burr, 1986 & 1988b<br>Khotanzad & Lu, 1988<br>Shimohara, et al., 1988<br>Rasure & Salas, 1988 |
| Knowledge Processing | Charney, 1988<br>Munro, 1988<br>Hinton, 1986<br>Hanson, 1987<br>Kaplan & Johnson, 1988<br>Pollack, 1988<br>Levy & Stenning, 1988<br>Tesauro & Sejnowski, 1988 |
| Text & Sentence Processing | Allen, 1987<br>Kwasny, 1988<br>Kukich, 1988<br>Miikkulainen & Dyer, 1987 |
| Signal Processing | Gorman & Sejnowski, 1988a & 1988b<br>Sejnowski, 1987<br>Lapedes & Farber, 1988a & 1988b<br>Ramamoorthy, Gouird & Iyer, 1988 |

TABLE 5-21. *Continued*

| Backpropagation Implementations ||
| :--- | :--- |
| **Implementation** | **Reference** |
| Integrated Circuit | Akers & Walker, 1988<br>Kung & Huang, 1988<br>Fiesler, Chandry & Caulfied, 1988<br>Furman, White & Abidi, 1988<br>Paulos & Hollis, 1988<br>Rasure & Salas, 1988 |
| Coprocessor/Attached Processor | Works, 1988<br>Savely, 1987<br>SAIC, 1988<br>HNC, 1987b |
| Optical/Electro-Optical | Owechko, Soffer & Dunning, 1988<br>Owechko, 1987<br>Soffer, 1987<br>Wagner, 1987<br>Wagner & Psaltis, 1987a |
| Bus-Oriented Processor | TRW, 1987 |

TABLE 5-22.

e. Select a new $F_B$ PE and repeat steps (b)–(d).

f. Increment the time t by 1 and calculate a new value for the temperature T(t), using the equation

$$T(t) = \frac{T_0}{1 + \log t} \qquad (5\text{-}171)$$

where $T_0$ is the initial temperature, an equation referred to as the cooling schedule.

g. Repeat steps (b)–(f) until all $\Delta E_i = 0$. At this point the system is in equilibrium and the global energy minimum has been reached.

h. Save the activation values of all the $F_B$ PEs as a vector $D_k$ (for later statistical analysis of the equilibrium states) using the equation

$$d_i^k = b_i \qquad (5\text{-}172)$$

for all i = 1, 2, ..., p, where $d_i^k$ is the value of $D_k$'s *ith* component.

3. Using the collected equilibrium states $D_k$, compute the symmetric probability $Q_{hi}$ of finding both the h*th* $F_A$ and i*th* $F_B$ PEs in the same state with the equation

$$O_{hi} = \frac{1}{m}\left[\sum_{k=1}^{m} \Phi(a_h^k, d_i^k)\right] \qquad (5\text{-}173)$$

for all h = 1, 2, ..., n, and all i = 1, 2, ..., p, where the correlation function $\Phi()$ is defined as

$$\Phi(x,y) = \begin{cases} 1 & \text{if } x = y \\ 0 & \text{otherwise} \end{cases} \qquad (5\text{-}174)$$

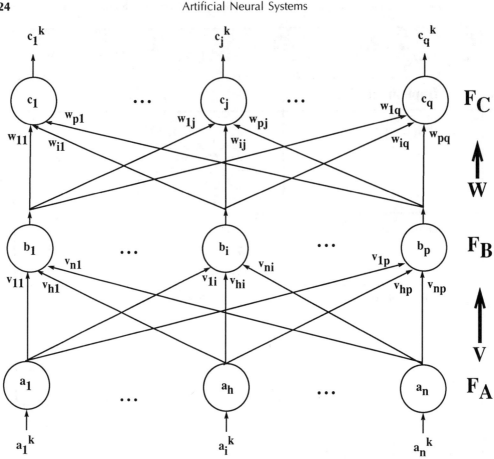

FIGURE 5-38. Topology of the Boltzmann and Cauchy Machines (BM and CM), supervised learning—feedforward recall ANSs. These three-layer ANSs uses stochastic learning algorithms to adjust the connections between the $F_A$ and $F_B$ layers and the $F_B$ and $F_C$ layers. To keep the presentation uncluttered, all connections are not shown— there is actually a symmetric connection from each $F_A$ PE to each $F_B$ PE and a symmetric connection from each $F_B$ PE to each $F_C$ PE.

where x and y are binary valued scalars. In a similar fashion, compute the symmetric probability $R_{ij}$ of finding both the $jth$ $F_C$ and $ith$ $F_B$ PEs in the same state

$$R_{ij} = \frac{1}{m} \left[ \sum_{k=1}^{m} \Phi(c_j^k, d_i^k) \right] \tag{5-175}$$

for all $j = 1, 2, \ldots, q$, and all $i = 1, 2, \ldots, p$.

4. Starting again at time $t = 1$, and for each pattern $A_k$, $k = 1, 2, \ldots, m$, do the following:
   a. Transfer $A_k$'s values to the $F_A$ PEs
   b. Randomly select an $F_B$ PE and switch its state (binary value) using eq. 5-168.
   c. Calculate the change in global energy with respect to the $ith$ $F_B$ PE, $\Delta E_i$, created by the switched state using the equation

$$\Delta E_i = \sum_{h=1}^{n} v_{hi} b_i \tag{5-176}$$

   d. If $\Delta E_i < 0$, keep the change. If $\Delta E_i > 0$, keep the change if $P_i > r$, where r is a number randomly chosen from the Boltzmann probability $P_i$, given $\Delta E_i$ is computed using eq. 5-170. If $\Delta E_i > 0$ and $P_i < r$, then return $b_i$ to its original state prior to the switch in step (c).

e. Repeat steps (b)–(d) once more.

f. Increment the time t and calculate a new value for the temperature T(t) using eq. 5-171.

g. Repeat steps (b)–(f) until all $\Delta E_i = 0$. At this point the system is in equilibrium and the global energy minimum has been reached.

h. Save the activation values of all the $F_B$ PEs as a vector $D_k$ using eq. 5-172.

5. Using the collected equilibrium states $D_k$, compute the symmetric probability $Q'_{hi}$ of finding both the $h$th $F_A$ and $i$th $F_B$ PEs in the same state using the equation

$$Q'_{hi} = \frac{1}{m}\left[\sum_{k=1}^{m} \Phi(a_h^k, d_i^k)\right] \tag{5-177}$$

for all $h = 1, 2, \ldots, n$, and all $i = 1, 2, \ldots, p$. In a similar fashion, compute the symmetric probability $R'_{ij}$ of finding both the $j$th $F_C$ and $i$th $F_B$ PEs in the same state using the equation

$$R'_{ij} = \frac{1}{m}\left[\sum_{k=1}^{m} \Phi(c_j^k, d_i^k)\right] \tag{5-178}$$

for all $j = 1, 2, \ldots, q$, and all $i = 1, 2, \ldots, p$.

6. Adjust the memory matrices V and W using the collected statistics from the equilibrium states as follows:

a. Adjust the $F_A$ to $F_B$ connections using the equation

$$\Delta v_{hi} = \alpha[Q_{hi} - Q'_{hi}] \tag{5-179}$$

where $\Delta v_{hi}$ is the change in the symmetric connection strength from the $h$th $F_A$ to the $i$th $F_B$ PE, and $\alpha$ is a positive constant controlling the learning rate.

b. Adjust the $F_B$ to $F_C$ connections using the equation

$$\Delta w_{ij} = \alpha[R_{ij} - R'_{ij}] \tag{5-180}$$

where $\Delta w_{ij}$ is the change in the symmetric connection strength from the $i$th $F_B$ to the $j$th $F_C$ PE.

7. Repeat steps (2)–(6) until $\Delta v_{hi}$ and $\Delta w_{ij}$ become sufficiently small or 0 for all $h = 1, \ldots,$ n, all $i = 1, \ldots, p$, and all $j = 1, \ldots, q$.

### 5.4.4.2. Recall
BM recall filters an input pattern A from $F_A$, through $F_B$, to $F_C$. The $F_A$ to $F_B$ operation is

$$b_i = f\left(\sum_{h=1}^{n} v_{hi} a_h\right) \tag{5-181}$$

where f() is the step function (3). The $F_B$ to $F_C$ operation is

$$c_j = f\left(\sum_{i=1}^{p} w_{ij} b_i\right) \tag{5-182}$$

### 5.4.4.3. Convergence
The BM learning rules, eq. 5-179 and eq. 5-180, minimize an entropic measure $G_h$ that describes the difference between the $F_B$ (internal) states and the $F_A$ and $F_C$ (external) states

during the presentation of the h*th* pattern pair (Ackley, Hinton & Sejnowski, 1985). This entropic cost function is defined as

$$G_h = \sum_{i=1}^{n} Q_{hi} \ln(Q_{hi}/Q'_{hi}) + \sum_{j=1}^{p} R_{hj} \ln(R_{hj}/R'_{hj}) \qquad (5\text{-}183)$$

In essence, the encoding procedure attempts to capture, as well as possible, the regularities in the environment (input-output pairs) via a set of connection strengths that properly perform the input-output mapping. Geman and Geman (1984) have proved that simulated annealing will find the global minimum of a given cost function (here it is eq. 5-183) using the cooling schedule of eq. 5-171.

### 5.4.4.4. *Discussion, Analysis, Applications, and Implementations*

BM strengths include its ability to perform nonlinear mappings between arbitrary sets of patterns and its natural fit with combinatorial optimization problems. BM limitations include its prohibitively long training time, its ability to get stuck in local minima, and its extensive offline encoding time.

There have been several studies and extensions of the BM ANS. Derthick (1984) has proposed several variations of the original BM ANS. Lutterell (1985) has analyzed the relationship between BMs and Markov random fields. Sejnowski (1986) introduced the use of higher-order correlations. Derthick & Tebelskis (1988) have developed a representation scheme that uses ensembles of PEs to encode analog valued pattern pairs. Gutzmann (1987) and Lutterell (1988a) have developed a continuous time BM that inherently handles analog valued pattern pairs. Bounds (1986) has conducted an extensive suite of simulations with the BM and has provided some important benchmark comparisons. Mazaika (1987) has studied the BM from the perspective of Markov chains and developed some techniques for allowing several PEs to synchronously update. Parks (1987) has performed an extensive study of the BM's learning rate. Cattaneo & Casa-Bianchi (1988) have employed microcanonical annealing (Cruetz, 1983) instead of simulated annealing in the BM algorithm to reduce the computational complexity of the algorithm. And, Eggers (1988) has compiled a very thorough survey of work done with the BM and has discussed some extensions and generalizations to the weight update rule.

The BM has also been compared to several other ANS paradigms. Kohonen, Barna & Chrisley (1988) have compared the BM's pattern classification ability with the optimal Bayes classifier and learning vector quantization (see section 5.2.7.) and found that the BM performed well. Bernasconi (1988) has compared the BM with that of backpropagation (see section 5.4.3.) for pattern matching problems.

The BM is primarily a pattern matching device, although it has been used for combinatorial optimization as well (see Table 5-23). In addition, there have been several BM implementation efforts (see Table 5-24). Of particular interest is the use of magnetic films, a natural fit with the BM algorithm.

## 5.4.5. Cauchy Machine (CM)

The Cauchy machine (CM) ANS—introduced by Szu (1986a)—is a heteroassociative, nearest-neighbor pattern matcher that stores arbitrary binary spatial patterns $(A_k, C_k)$, $k = 1, 2, \ldots, m$, using a combination of Hebbian encoding and fast simulated annealing (i.e. stochastic learning), where the k*th* pattern pair is represented by the vectors $A_k = (a_1^k, \ldots, a_n^k)$ and $C_k = (c_1^k, \ldots, c_q^k)$. The CM learns offline, operates in discrete time, and is represented by the three-layer feedforward topology shown in Figure 5-38, where the n $F_A$ PEs correspond to $A_k$'s components, and the q $F_C$ PEs correspond to $C_k$'s components.

| Boltzmann Machine Applications | |
|---|---|
| **Application** | **Reference** |
| Image Processing | Lutterell, 1985, 1988a, 1988b & 1988c<br>Lin, et al., 1988<br>Sejnowski & Hinton, 1986<br>Randall & Caelli, 1988<br>Kienker, et al., 1986<br>Koch, 1987<br>Gardner, 1986 |
| Knowledge Processing | Touretzky & Hinton, 1988<br>Touretzky, 1986a & 1986b<br>Touretzky & Derthick, 1987 |
| Speech Processing | Prager, Harrison & Fallside, 1986 |
| Pattern Recognition | Pawlicki, et al., 1988<br>Sejnowski, Kienker & Hinton, 1986 |
| Graph Search & Optimization | Mei & Lin, 1988<br>Eggers, 1988<br>Gutzmann, 1987 |

TABLE 5-23.

| Boltzmann Machine Implementations | |
|---|---|
| **Implementation** | **Reference** |
| Optical/Electro-Optical | Farhat & Shae, 1987 & 1988<br>Farhat, 1987a & 1987b<br>Ticknor & Barrett, 1987 |
| Integrated Circuit | Alspector & Allen, 1986<br>Alspector, 1987<br>Alspector, et al., 1988 |
| Magnetic Processor | Goodwin, Rosen & Vidal, 1988a & 1988b |
| Attached Processor/Coprocessor | SAIC, 1988 |

TABLE 5-24.

### 5.4.5.1. Encoding, Recall, and Convergence

The CM encoding and recall procedures are identical to the Boltzmann machine's (see section 5.4.4.), with the following two exceptions:

1. Replace the Boltzmann probability density function, eq. 5-170, with the Cauchy probability density function

$$P_i = \frac{T(t)}{T(t) + (\Delta E_i)^2} \qquad (5\text{-}184)$$

2. Replace the simulated annealing cooling schedule, eq. 5-171, with the fast simulated annealing cooling schedule

$$T(t) = \frac{T_0}{1 + t} \qquad (5\text{-}185)$$

where all variables are as described for eq. 5-171.

These changes reflect a switch from simulated annealing to fast simulated annealing, a method that allows the acceptance of higher energy states more often and yields a significantly quicker annealing schedule. Moreover, Szu (1986a & 1986b) has shown that the fast simulated annealing cooling schedule, eq. 5-185, will find the global cost function minimum with probability equal to 1 when used in conjunction with the Cauchy distribution.

### 5.4.5.2. Discussion, Applications, and Implementations
CM strengths include its ability to perform arbitrary heteroassociative mappings. CM limitations include its encoding time (albeit significantly faster than the Boltzmann Machine) and its offline learning restriction.

The CM ANS has been applied to the areas of image processing (Szu, 1987) and combinatorial optimization problems (Szu, 1986a, 1986b; Szu & Hartley, 1987). Wasserman (1988) has discussed a combined backpropagation/Cauchy machine. And, the CM has been implemented in optics/electro-optics (Scheff & Szu, 1987; Szu, 1987).

## 5.4.6. Adaptive Heuristic Critic (AHC)

The adaptive heuristic critic (AHC) ANS — introduced by Barto, Sutton, and Anderson (1983) — is a heteroassociative, nearest-neighbor performance optimizer that stores a mapping from an arbitrary analog spatial pattern $A_k$, to an arbitrary bipolar valued spatial pattern $C_s$, s = 1, 2, ..., m, using a temporally adjusted reinforcement learning procedure, where the k*th* pattern pair is represented by the vectors $A_s = (a_1^s, ..., a_n^s)$ and $C_s = (c_1^s, ..., c_p^s)$. The AHC learns online, operates in discrete time, incorporates an extra field of PEs used for internal reinforcement, and is represented by the three-layer feedforward topology shown in Figure 5-39, where the n $F_A$ PEs correspond to $A_k$'s components, the p $F_B$ PEs each provide an internal reinforcement value that is delivered to its respective $F_C$ PE, the p $F_C$ PEs correspond to $C_k$'s components, and r(t) corresponds to the external reinforcement at time t. The AHC plays a role analogous to the Drive Representation in Grossberg's (1972a & 1982b) theory of reinforcement learning.

### 5.4.6.1. Encoding
Reinforcement adaptation differs from the previously described error-correction procedures in that each output PE does not receive a component-by-component evaluation of its error; rather, all components receive the same value (reward/punish) and corrections are made from that limited amount of information. Also, there are two types of corrections that must be delineated, temporal correction and structural correction. The feedforward encoding procedures previously described are concerned with *where* corrections must be made to improve ANS performance; this is called structural correction. The paradigm presented here is concerned with *when* corrections must be made to improve ANS performance; this is called

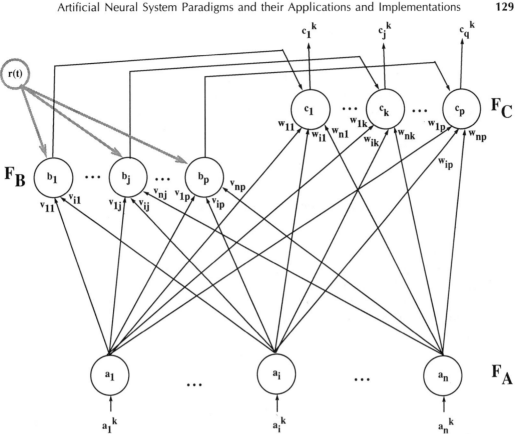

FIGURE 5-39. Topology of the Adaptive Heuristic Critic (AHC), a supervised learning—feedforward recall ANS. This three-layer ANS uses a reinforcement learning algorithm to adjust the connections between the $F_A$ and $F_B$ layers and the $F_A$ and $F_C$ layers. The reinforcement is illustrated with the shaded lines emanating from the external reinforcement signal. To keep the presentation uncluttered, all connections are not shown—there is actually a connection from each $F_A$ PE to each $F_B$ PE and a connection from each $F_A$ PE to each $F_C$ PE.

temporal correction. The AHC uses a reinforcement encoding procedure that makes temporal corrections to improve its responses. The $F_B$ PEs act as critics that provide a heuristically derived correction value to each $F_C$ PE, hence the name adaptive heuristic critic. The encoding procedure is as follows:

1. Assign random values in the range [0,1] to all the $F_A$ to $F_B$ inter-layer connections, $v_{hi}$, and all the $F_A$ to $F_C$ inter-layer connections, $w_{ij}$.

2. For each pattern s = 1, 2, ..., m, do the following:
   a. Filter $A_s$ through $W$ and produce $c_k$ at time t using the equation

$$c_k(t) = f\left(\sum_{i=1}^{n} a_i^s w_{ik}(t) + \gamma(t)\right) \qquad \textbf{(5-186)}$$

where $\gamma(t)$ is a random value in the range [0,1] chosen from the distribution D, and f() is the bipolar step function defined as

$$f(x) = \begin{cases} +1 & \text{if } x > 0 \\ -1 & \text{otherwise} \end{cases} \qquad \textbf{(5-187)}$$

b. Adjust the $F_A$ to $F_C$ connections using the equation

$$\Delta w_{ik} = \alpha b_k(t)e_{ik}(t) \qquad (5\text{-}188)$$

where $\alpha$ is a positive constant controlling the learning rate, $\Delta w_{ik}$ is the change in the connection strength from the $ith$ $F_A$ to the $kth$ $F_C$ PEs, $e_{ik}(t)$ is the eligibility of $w_{ik}$'s change at time t, and $b_k(t)$ is the value of the $kth$ $F_B$ PE at time t, also referred to as the $kth$ $F_C$ PE's internal reinforcement signal. The eligibility of $w_{ik}$'s change at time t, $e_{ik}(t)$, is defined as

$$e_{ik}(t + 1) = \delta e_{ik}(t) + (1 - \delta)a_i^s c_k^s \qquad (5\text{-}189)$$

where $\delta$ is a positive constant in the range [0,1] controlling the eligibility's decay rate. The internal reinforcement signal for the $jth$ $F_B$ PE at time t, $b_j(t)$, is defined as

$$b_j(t) = r(t) + \mu p_j(t) - p_j(t - 1) \qquad (5\text{-}190)$$

where $\mu$ is a positive constant in the range [0,1] controlling the amount of internal reinforcement, r(t) is the analog valued external reinforcement, and $p_j(t)$ is the prediction of the $b_j(t)$ at time t. The external reinforcement r(t) provides a graded performance value that describes how well it performed ($-1$ = poor performance and $+1$ = good performance). The prediction of $b_j(t)$ at time t, $p_j(t)$, is calculated using the equation

$$p_j(t) = \sum_{i=1}^{n} v_{ij}a_i^s \qquad (5\text{-}191)$$

c. Adjust the $F_A$ to $F_B$ connections

$$\Delta v_{ij} = \beta b_j(t)x_i(t) \qquad (5\text{-}192)$$

where $\Delta v_{ij}$ is the change in the connection strength from the $ith$ $F_A$ to the $jth$ $F_B$ PEs, $\beta$ is a positive constant controlling the learning rate, and $x_i(t)$ is the weighted average of the $ith$ $F_A$ PE's values found by the equation

$$x_i(t + 1) = \epsilon x_i(t) + (1 - \epsilon)a_i^s \qquad (5\text{-}193)$$

where $\epsilon$ is a positive constant controlling the decay rate.

d. Increment t and return to (a) until there are no poor performances (i.e. until r(t) = $+1$ for a sufficient period of time t).

### 5.4.6.2. Recall
The AHC ANS learns online, it provides a constantly updated output value throughout the encoding process. AHC recall is governed by the $F_A$ to $F_C$ weight matrix and eq. 5-186

$$c_k(t) = f\left( \sum_{i=1}^{n} a_i^s w_{ik}(t) + \gamma(t) \right) \qquad (5\text{-}186)$$

### 5.4.6.3. Discussion, Applications, and Implementations
The AHC strength is its ability to continuously learn and improve its performance for a specific control task with a limited amount of performance information. The AHC limitations include its restriction to bipolar responses and its tendency to become trapped in local error minima.

The AHC is an extension of a previous ANS—the associative search ANS—that was successful at modeling classical conditioning phenomena (Sutton & Barto, 1981a) and landmark learning simulations (Barto & Sutton, 1981a; Barto, 1984). Extensions by Sutton (1984) have improved the AHC's predictive quality. And, Williams (1987) has analyzed the AHC in the more general framework of reinforcement learning algorithms.

Candidate AHC applications include time-series prediction and control. Raibert (1988) and Collins & Helferty (1988) have used the AHC to control a one-legged hopping machine. Barto, Sutton & Anderson (1983) have used the AHC to control a one-dimensional broom balancer simulation. HNC (1988) has demonstrated a two-dimensional broom balancer that uses a variation of the AHC.

### 5.4.7. Associative Reward-Penalty (ARP)

The associative reward-penalty (ARP) ANS—introduced by Barto (1985) and Barto & Anandan (1985)—is a heteroassociative, nearest-neighbor pattern matcher that stores a mapping from an analog spatial pattern $A_k$, to a bipolar valued spatial pattern $B_k$, $k = 1, 2, \ldots, m$, using a stochastic reinforcement learning procedure, where the $k$th pattern pair is represented by the vectors $A_k = (a_1^k, \ldots, a_n^k)$ and $B_k = (b_1^k, \ldots, b_p^k)$. The ARP learns online, operates in discrete time, and is represented by the two-layer feedforward topology shown in Figure 5-40, where the n $F_A$ PEs correspond to $A_k$'s components, the p $F_B$ PEs correspond to $B_k$'s components, and r(t) corresponds to the external reinforcement at time t.

*5.4.7.1. Encoding*
The ARP encoding procedure adjusts the $F_A$ to $F_B$ connections using the equation

$$\Delta w_{ij} = \begin{cases} \alpha x_j(t)a_i^k & \text{if } r(t) = +1 \\ \alpha\beta x_j(t)a_i^k & \text{if } r(t) = -1 \end{cases} \qquad \textbf{(5-194)}$$

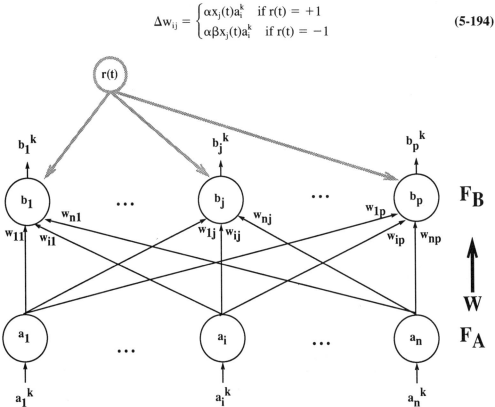

FIGURE 5-40. Topology of the Associative Reward-Penalty (ARP) ANS, a supervised learning—feedforward recall paradigm. This two-layer ANS uses a reinforcement learning algorithim to adjust the connections between the $F_A$ and $F_B$ layers. The reinforcement is illustrated with the shaded lines emanating from the external reinforcement signal. To keep the presentation uncluttered, all connections are not shown—there is actually a connection from each $F_A$ PE to each $F_B$ PE.

where $\Delta w_{ij}$ is the change to the connection strength from the $ith$ $F_A$ to the $jth$ $F_B$ PE, $\alpha$ and $\beta$ are positive constants that control the encoding rate, and $x_j(t)$ is the reinforcement encoding factor defined as

$$x_j(t) = r(t)b_j^k - E\{b_j(t)|y_j(t)\} \tag{5-195}$$

where $E\{b_j(t)|y_j(t)\}$ is the expected value of the $jth$ $F_B$ PE, $b_j(t)$, at time t, given the input sum $y_j(t)$. The $jth$ $F_B$ PE's value is found using the equation

$$b_j(t) = f(y_j(t) + \mu(t)) \tag{5-196}$$

where $\mu(t)$ is a randomly chosen threshold in the range $[0,1]$, $f()$ is the bipolar step function (see previous section, eq. 5-187), and

$$y_j(t) = \sum_{i=1}^{u} a_i^k w_{ij} \tag{5-197}$$

Using the logistic probability distribution function when choosing the random threshold at time t, $\mu(t)$, the expected value of $b_j(t)$ given $y_j(t)$ can be expressed as

$$E\{b_j(t)|y_j(t)\} = \frac{-1 + e^{-(y_j(t)/T)}}{1 + e^{-(y_j(t)/T)}} \tag{5-198}$$

where T is a positive constant representing the temperature of the system, and the logistic distribution, $\Psi$, is defined as

$$\Psi(y_j(t)) = [1 + e^{-(y_j(t)/T)}]^{-1} \tag{5-199}$$

### 5.4.7.2. Recall
ARP recall uses eq. 5-196

$$b_j(t) = f(y_j(t) + \mu(t))$$

and eq. 5-197

$$y_j(t) = \sum_{i=1}^{n} a_i^k w_{ij}$$

that were introduced in the encoding procedure.

### 5.4.7.3. Convergence
ARP convergence is proven for a single component of $B_k$, $b_j^k$, under the following assumptions:

1. $\{A_1,\ldots,A_m\}$ are linearly independent,

2. $P(A_k$ being presented on trial q$) > 0 \ \forall \ q$

3. $\mu(t)$ is selected from a continuous and strictly monotonically increasing distribution, and

4. the learning rate decreases to zero in time, i.e. $\alpha \rightarrow 0$ as $t \rightarrow \infty$.

Under the above conditions, ARP convergence is guaranteed to converge from any set of initial weights $w_{ij}$ and any $\beta$, to the set of weights that will produce the proper response with probability greater than 0.5. This convergence will occur in every infinite sequence of trials (i.e. as $t \rightarrow \infty$). Moreover, as $\beta \rightarrow 0$, the probability of a proper response approaches 1.

### 5.4.7.4. Discussion and Applications
The ARP strength is its ability to learn online when provided only bipolar valued external reinforcement. ARP limitations include extensive training time, the restriction to linearly independent $A_k$ for guaranteed convergence, and its inability to provide analog valued responses.

Barto & Jordan (1987) have recently extended the ARP ANS to include internal layers of PEs that will allow nonlinear mappings to occur. Also, theoretical analysis by Williams (1986 & 1987) has shown that the expected change to any of the ARP's connection strengths is proportional to the partial derivative of the expected reinforcement with respect to the weight.

Candidate ARP applications are in pattern matching and control systems. Barto (1986) and Barto, Anandan & Anderson (1986) have used the ARP to learn how to win at games. Also, Yeung & Bekey (1988) have used a network similar to ARP to optimize the allocation of robots in a manufacturing domain.

## 5.4.8. Avalanche Matched Filter (AMF)

The Avalanche Matched Filter (AMF) ANS—an extension of the Grossberg (1969d & 1970b) Avalanche introduced by Hecht-Nielsen (1982 & 1987b)—is a nearest-neighbor spatiotemporal pattern classifier that stores an arbitrary sequence of analog spatial patterns $A_1, \ldots, A_p$ using a Hebbian correlation procedure, where the $kth$ spatial pattern in the sequence is represented by the vector $A_k = (a_1^k, \ldots, a_n^k)$. The AMF learns offline, operates in discrete time, and is represented by the two-layer feedforward topology shown in Figure 5-41, where the n $F_A$ PEs correspond to $A_k$'s components, the p $F_B$ PEs correspond to successive time slices of the spatiotemporal pattern.

### 5.4.8.1. Encoding

The AMF encoding procedure commits successive $F_B$ PEs to one spatial pattern in a sequence. This operation requires that both the vector of connections from all the $F_A$ PEs to the $jth$ $F_B$ PE be normalized and each input pattern $A_k$ be normalized to unit length, i.e.

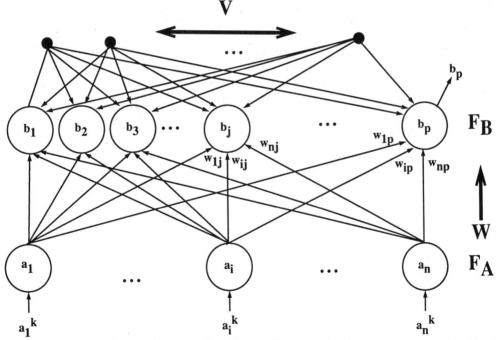

FIGURE 5-41. Topology of the Avalanche Matched Filter (AMF), a supervised learning—feedforward recall ANS. This two-layer ANS stores spatiotemporal patterns by encoding spatial patterns for successive time slices onto the connections that abut each $F_B$ PE (which create the matrix W) and by encoding the temporal relationships between the spatial patterns in the intra-layer connections stored in the matrix V. To keep the presentation uncluttered, all connections are not shown—there is actually a connection from each $F_A$ PE to each $F_B$ PE and a connection from each $F_B$ PE to every other $F_B$ PE.

$$\|W_j\| = \|A_k\| = 1 \tag{5-200}$$

where $W_j$ is the vector of connections from $F_A$ that abut the $j$th $F_B$ PE. The $k$th pattern in the sequence of p patterns is encoded onto $W_k$ using the equation

$$\Delta w_{ik} = -\alpha w_{ik} + \beta a_i^k b_k \tag{5-201}$$

for all $i = 1, 2, \ldots, n$, where $\alpha$ is a positive constant controlling the decay rate, $\beta$ is a positive constant controlling the encoding rate, $w_{ik}$ is the connection strength from the $i$th $F_A$ to the $k$th $F_B$ PE, and the value of the $k$th $F_B$ PE, $b_k$, is set to 1 to represent the $k$th pattern of the sequence. The $F_B$ to $F_B$ connections are fed forward from $b_k$ to each successive $F_B$ PE remaining in the sequence. Because the length of the sequence is known *a priori,* this is possible. These feedforward connections, $v_{hj}$, are preset to some constant value

$$v_{hj} = \gamma \tag{5-202}$$

where $v_{hj}$ is the connection strength from the $h$th to the $j$th $F_B$ PEs and $\gamma$ is a positive constant. It is important to note that the AMF does not support a distributed representation, rather it encodes only one spatiotemporal pattern per AMF. Additional spatiotemporal patterns require additional AMFs.

### 5.4.8.2. Recall

AMF recall works by presenting a sequence of patterns, $C_1, \ldots, C_p$, and recording the value of the final $F_B$ PE, $b_p$. If $b_p$ has a sufficiently large activation, then the presented sequence has matched the encoded sequence. The matching operation is a cooperative effort between the $F_A$ to $F_B$ inter-layer activations and the $F_B$ to $F_B$ feedforward lateral activations. If the current input matches the stored pattern during the current time slice, a large value will be fed forward on the $F_B$ lateral connections. If the input continues to match the stored pattern for each time slice, the final $F_B$ PE will have a very large value indicating a good match had occurred. If the input does not match the stored pattern well at each time slice, the final $F_B$ PE will have a small value indicating a poor match. When there is a small portion of the presented sequence that does not match the encoded sequence, the $F_B$ lateral feedforward activations can compensate, hence a window for these minor phase differences is inherent to the network.

The $F_B$ PE activations are calculated using the equation

$$b_j = g\left(-\mu b_j + f\left(\sum_{i=1}^{n} c_i^k w_{ij} + \sum_{h=1}^{p} b_h v_{hj} - \Theta_j\right)\right) \tag{5-203}$$

for all $k = 1, 2, \ldots, p$, where $\mu$ is a positive constant controlling the activation decay rate, $c_i^k$ is the $C_k$'s $i$th component being fed through the $i$th $F_A$ PE, $b_h$ and $b_j$ are the activation values for the $h$th and $j$th PEs, $\Theta_j$ is the $j$th $F_B$ PE's threshold value, f() is the ramp function

$$f(x) = \begin{cases} 0 & \text{if } x \leq 0 \\ x & \text{otherwise} \end{cases} \tag{5-204}$$

and g() is the attack function

$$g(y) = \begin{cases} y & \text{if } y > 0 \\ \epsilon y & \text{otherwise} \end{cases} \tag{5-205}$$

where $\epsilon$ is a positive constant controlling the activation decay. The attack function, eq. 5-205, has an activation decay of $1/(\alpha\mu)$ when the activation function, eq. 5-204, becomes 0. This determines the size of the window for phase differences.

### 5.4.8.3. Discussion, Applications, and Implementations

AMF strengths include the ability to store and nearest-neighbor classify arbitrary analog spatiotemporal patterns with a minimum amount of preprocessing, and the ability to perform these classifications in real-time. AMF limitations include the need for a separate AMF for each sequence, the lack of a distributed representation, the intolerance to severe phase distortion and time-warping, and the offline encoding requirement.

Hecht-Nielsen (1987b) has shown that the AMF has an error rate of misclassification equivalent to that of the best possible performing classifier, and that it is extremely noise tolerant to a wide range of noise types. Work by Taber, Siegel & Deich (1988), and Taber & Deich (1988), has employed a third layer of PEs that use fuzzy theoretical interactions to determine the degree of classification of each spatiotemporal pattern. Myers (1986) has compared the AMF to more traditional spatiotemporal pattern classifiers. And, Lippmann & Gold (1987) have developed an extension of the AMF called the Viterbi Net, that uses transition probabilities assigned as lateral $F_B$ connections, that has been used for classifying speech (Lippman, 1988).

Because of context requirements of many pattern recognition tasks such as speech and image recognition, the spatiotemporal capabilities of the AMF offer some appealing qualities over many spatial pattern recognizers. The AMF has been applied to the recognition of sonar signals (Taber, Siegel & Deich, 1988; Taber & Deich, 1988), whale calls (Taber, et al., 1988), speech (Hudak, 1988), battlefield acoustic signals (Simpson & Deich, 1988), and radar signals (Myers, 1987). The AMF has also been proposed as an actual neuronal mechanism for spatiotemporal pattern classification (Cohen & Grossberg, 1986; Grossberg, 1986c).

# APPENDIX

# History of Artificial Neural Systems

ANS research dates back to the 1800's with some of the initial work being done by Freud (Strachey, 1966) in his pre-psychoanalysis period. The first implementation of an ANS was a hydraulic device described by Russell (1913). The primary ANS thrust was first witnessed in the early 1940's. This work has enjoyed periods of great enthusiasm alternating with periods of obscurity or even disfavor. The recent re-emergence of interest in ANS is attributable to complex social and historical forces, as well as to the work of several brilliant scientists and the incredible advances in hardware (Darpa, 1988). Thousands of individuals have poured their life's blood into ANS research over the years. Listed, in chronological order, are some of the leading scientists, engineers and entrepreneurs who have brought ANS technology to where it is today.

## MCCULLOCH AND PITTS—1943

Warren McCulloch & Walter Pitts (1943) made the first mathematical model of an ANS. The McCulloch-Pitts model was based on the idea that neurons operated in an all-or-none fashion. Using this digital basis, McCulloch & Pitts showed that any arbitrary logical function could be configured by an ANS of interconnected digital neurons. This model introduced the idea of the step threshold function used in many ANS models such as the discrete Hopfield ANS (Hopfield, 1982) and the discrete bidirectional associative memory (Kosko, 1988b). Although this model created great excitement by showing that an ANS could generate rather sophisticated behavior from simple computations, it lacked a key factor, the ability to learn. This work, and many other fascinating experiments, are described in McCulloch's book *Embodiments of Mind* (1965).

## HEBB—1949

Donald Hebb described a concept that evolved into a mathematical procedure for learning. From Hebb's studies of the neuron and his observations of learning and classical conditioning, described in his book *Organizaton of Behavior* (1949), he developed a learning paradigm that now bears his name—Hebbian learning. The Hebbian learning rule states the efficacy (efficiency) of a synapse increases if there is a presynaptic activity followed closely in time with a postsynaptic activity. Later versions of Hebbian learning are described as an increase in the efficacy (strength) of the synaptic connections in proportion to the correlation of presynaptic and postsynaptic potentials. To explain, if a synapse has a positive presynaptic potential and a positive postsynaptic potential, the synaptic conductance is increased. Conversely, if the presynaptic potential is negative (positive) and the postsynaptic potential is positive (negative), then synaptic conductance is decreased. This simple synaptic modification paradigm has led to significant strides in ANS, but only the original idea of increasing synaptic efficacy when presynaptic activity is closely followed by postsynaptic activity was Hebb's; the extensions made to correlate the synaptic changes with pre/postsynaptic potentials were done by others and the Hebb name remained attached.

136

## MINSKY — 1951

Marvin Minsky is responsible for some of the first results using ANSs. While working toward his Ph.D. at Princeton in the summer of 1951, Minsky teamed with Dean Edmonds to create a learning machine (Bernstein, 1981). Inspired by McCulloch & Pitts' work, Minsky and Edmonds designed a 40-neuron machine with synapses that adjusted their conductances according to the success of performing a specified task (Hebbian learning). The machine was built of tubes, motors, and clutches, and it successfully modeled the behavior of a rat in a maze searching for food. Minsky (1954) explored other ideas on how the nervous system might learn, and ultimately combined them into his doctoral thesis.

In the mid-1960's, Minsky began to study a learning model developed by Frank Rosenblatt (1957) called the perceptron. Minsky felt that Rosenblatt was making claims that could not be substantiated, so he and Seymour Papert began to study the limitations of the perceptron. Minsky & Papert's (1969) studies were collected into the extremely influential book *Perceptrons* that showed the two-layer perceptron to be severely limited by exploiting the fact that perceptrons would only work for problems with linearly separable solution spaces. Minsky & Papert then empirically extended their results to multilayered perceptrons and made the following statement (pp. 231–232):

> The perceptron has shown itself to be worthy of study despite (and even because of!) its severe limitations. It has many features to attract attention: its linearity; its intriguing learning theorem; its clear paradigmatic simplicity as a kind of parallel computation. There is no reason to suppose that any of these virtues carry over to the many-layered version. Nevertheless, we consider it an important research problem to elucidate (or reject) out intuitive judgement that the extension is sterile. Perhaps some powerful convergence theorem will be discovered, or some profound reason for the failure to produce an interesting 'learning theorem' for the multilayered machine will be found.

By showing all the limitations of the two-layer perceptron, and because of no available solution to the credit-assignment problem (Minsky, 1961), Minsky & Papert successfully convinced enough people that further ANS study was futile which, in turn, had the effect of reallocating the majority of ANS funding into AI programs. ANS funding has only recently enjoyed the status it had prior to *Perceptrons*.

## UTTLEY — 1956

Albert Uttley (1956a & 1956b) began developing ANS paradigms in the late 1950's. Uttley created a theoretical machine that consisted of informons (processing elements). The informon was a linear separator that adjusted its input parameters using Shannon's entropic measure — the natural logarithm of the ratio of input/output probabilities. These machines have been used to simulate operant and classical conditioning phenomena (Uttley, 1966 & 1976b), they have been applied to adaptive pattern recognition (Uttley, 1975 & 1976a), and they have been proposed as actual nervous system mechanisms (Uttley, 1976c). A complete discussion of Uttley's work can be found in his book *Information Transmission in the Nervous System* (1979).

## ROSENBLATT — 1957

Frank Rosenblatt (1957, 1958a & 1958b) generalized the McCulloch-Pitts model by adding learning, calling his hybrid creation a perceptron. Rosenblatt studied both two-layer and three-layer perceptrons, but he was only able to prove that his two-layer perceptron could separate inputs into two classes if the two classes were linearly separable (i.e. a hyperplane could divide the input space). Rosenblatt's two-layer result, called the perceptron convergence theorem, adjusts the weights between the input and output layers in proportion to the error between the desired and computed outputs. Rosenblatt's attempts to extend his learning procedure to three-layer perceptrons were encouraging, but he could not find a solid mathematical method to train the hidden PEs. Most of the work that Rosenblatt had done with the perceptron is documented in his book *Principles of Neurodynamics* (1962). The credit-assignment problem was not solved and the popularity of *Perceptrons* (Minsky & Papert, 1969) led to a suspension of interest in the perceptron.

## WIDROW — 1959

Bernard Widrow created an ANS similar to the perceptron called the adaptive linear element, or adaline (1959 & 1960). The two-layer adaline, like the perceptron, adjusts its weights between the input and output layers in response to the error between the computed and desired outputs. The difference between the two ANS models is slight, but the applications are very different. In 1960, Widrow and a young graduate student, Marcian Hoff, mathematically proved that the error between the desired and computed response would find a global minimum under certain conditions (Widrow & Hoff, 1960), the most important being that the inputs are linearly separable. Because the adaline shared the perceptron's problem of linear separability of input classes, three-layer adalines were also attempted, but these attempts also lacked a mathematical solution to the credit assignment problem. The adaline is being successfully used for adaptive signal processing (Widrow, 1969, 1973; Widrow, et al., 1963; Widrow & Stearns, 1985; Widrow, et al., 1975), control systems (Widrow & Smith, 1964; Widrow, 1988), and adaptive antenna systems (Widrow, Mantey & Griffiths, 1967). Later Widrow, et al. (1973) extended the adaline's learning ability by developing a form of reinforcement learning called selective bootstrap adaptation and Widrow & Winters (Widrow & Winter, 1988; Widrow, Winter & Baxter, 1988) developed a multilayer learning algorithm based upon the earlier work of Widrow (1962).

## STEINBUCH — 1961

Steinbuch (1961) was one of the first researchers to develop a method of encoding information in a crossbar ANS. Steinbuch's ANS — the Learning Matrix — was applied to problems such as recognizing highly distorted handwritten characters, diagnosing mechanical failures to reduce downtime of machines, and controlling higher processes in production (Steinbuch & Piske, 1963; Steinbuch & Zendeh, 1963).

## GROSSBERG AND THE CENTER FOR ADAPTIVE SYSTEMS — 1964

Stephen Grossberg is the most influential and thorough of all ANS researchers. Grossberg extensively studies the psychological (mind) and biological (brain) processes and phenomena of human information processing and ties the two (mind and brain) together into unified theories (Grossberg, 1964). Grossberg's work includes strict mathematical analysis and emphasizes producing ANS paradigms that are self-organizing, self-stabilizing, and self-scaling, that allow direct access to information while operating in real-time. Grossberg's initial studies led to the development of minimal ANS constructs called the instar, outstar, and avalanche for learning spatial patterns, recalling spatial patterns and processing temporal patterns, respectively (Grossberg 1968a, 1968b, 1968c & 1982a). Grossberg's ANS paradigms and associated constructs include competitive-cooperative learning (Grossberg, 1970a, 1972b, 1973, 1978a & 1987a), adaptive resonance theory (ART) (Grossberg, 1976b), the binary ART implementation (Carpenter & Grossberg, 1986a & 1987b), the analog ART implementation (Carpenter & Grossberg, 1987a, 1987c, 1987d & 1988), gated dipoles (Grossberg, 1972a & 1986a), masking fields (Grossberg, 1987b; Cohen & Grossberg, 1987), and serial learning (Grossberg, 1968c).

Grossberg has also formed a research group at Boston University entitled the Center for Adaptive Systems. With his group, Grossberg is investigating all facets of human information processing. Research performed by Grossberg and his colleagues covers all areas of the ANS spectrum. Cohen & Grossberg (1983) have studied the dynamical properties of ANSs, proving a theorem of global convergence for many classes of ANS models. Cohen & Grossberg have also studied vision (1982), speech (1986), and masking fields (1987). Carpenter & Grossberg have extensively characterized binary adaptive resonance theory — ART1 (Carpenter & Grossberg, 1986a, 1986b, 1986c & 1987b) and have extended the model to include analog inputs — ART2 (Carpenter & Grossberg, 1987a, 1987c, 1987d & 1988). Carpenter & Grossberg have also studied circadian (24-hour) rhythms (1983, 1984, 1985a & 1985b) and the relationship between chaos and nerve assemblies (1983). Other researchers who have worked with or currently reside at the Center include Ennio Mingolla — vision (Grossberg & Mingolla, 1985, 1986a & 1986b), Michael Kuperstein — eye movement motor control (Grossberg & Kuperstein, 1989), Daniel Levine — short term memory, conditioning and reinforcement (Grossberg & Levine, 1975 & 1987), David Stork — speech (Cohen, Grossberg & Stork, 1987), Gregory Stone — word recognition and short term memory (Grossberg & Stone, 1986a & 1986b), and Daniel Bullock — arm movement motor control (Bullock & Grossberg, 1986).

It is important to note Grossberg's approach to dissolving the human information processing barrier. Each ANS model created for speech, vision or motor control is a synergistic approach that includes all elements of human information processing. One example is the ANS model being designed for speech, that includes both vision and motor control subsystems (Bullock & Grossberg, 1986). Grossberg is a prolific author who has published five books on his work. Grossberg's early work can be found in *Studies of Mind and Brain* (1982a), his later work in *The Adaptive Brain: Volumes I and II* (1986b), his work with motor-control (co-authored with Kuperstein) in *Neural Dynamics of Adapative Sensory-Motor Control: Ballistic Eye Movements* (Grossberg & Kuperstein, 1989), and his most recent work in *Neural Networks and Natural Intelligence* (1988). Papers by Hestenes (1986) and Hecht-Nielsen (1983) serve as excellent introductions to Grossberg's work.

## AMARI — 1967

Shun-Ichi Amari is one of the most substantial researchers of ANS theory. Amari has been combining biological neural network activity and rigorous mathematical expertise in his studies of ANS since the late 1960's. One of Amari's earliest results included a mathematical solution to the credit assignment problem that largely went unnoticed (Amari, 1967). Had Amari's solution to the credit assignment problem been widely known, Minsky's and Papert's (1969) book, *Perceptrons,* would assuredly not had the impact it did.

Other research that Amari has done in ANS includes the treatment of the dynamics of randomly connected ANSs and its rigorous mathematical foundation (Amari, 1971, 1972a, 1972b & 1974; Amari, Yoshida & Kanatani, 1977), studies of competitive learning (Amari,

1977a & 1983; Amari & Arbib, 1977; Amari & Takeuchi, 1978), and the mathematical analysis of associative memory (Amari, 1972b, 1977b & 1982). Amari has produced outstanding results in his studies of the stability of symmetrically connected ANS models (Amari, 1971), the stability of recalling temporal pattern sequences in asymmetrically connected ANS models (Kishimoto & Amari, 1979), and the dynamics of pattern formation in ANSs (Amari, 1982; Amari, 1983). In addition to the mathematical theory, Amari has also extended his results to the biological aspects of self-organization and topographic feature representation (Amari & Takeuchi, 1978; Amari, 1980 & 1983; Takeuchi & Amari, 1979).

## ANDERSON — 1968

James Anderson began working with ANS models with a memory model based upon the associations of the activations of the synapses of a neuron (Anderson, 1968). Anderson's model used the linear threshold function on the dot product of the input vector and output vector, calling each of these dot products a trace (Anderson, 1968, 1970 & 1972). By adding together all the traces for all patterns (the superimposition of multiple patterns on the same memory), a linear associative memory (LAM) was formed. Anderson (1973 & 1977) applied the LAM to such problems as recognition, reconstruction and association of arbitrary visual patterns. In the Hebbian spirit, Anderson (1968 & 1970) also used the LAM to explain the possible associations between activations and synaptic connections or memory matrix.

A significant advance in Anderson's LAM was made in the late 1970's (Anderson, Silverstein, Ritz & Jones, 1977). By adding positive lateral feedback, employing error correction learning, and replacing the linear threshold function with the ramp threshold function, a new model called the Brain-state-in-a-box (BSB) was created. The BSB ANS stores information at the corners of an n-dimensional cube. Recall is performed by entering a point within the cube and allowing the ANS to equilibrate to a corner of the cube. The BSB ANS has been used to explain concept formation (Anderson & Murphy, 1986a & 1986b; Anderson, Golden & Murphy, 1986), categorization (Anderson & Mozer, 1981; Anderson, 1983), and knowledge processing (Anderson, 1983 & 1986).

## LONGUET-HIGGINS, WILLSHAW, AND BUNEMAN — 1968

Researchers from the Department of Machine Intelligence at the University of Edinburgh were among the first to see the natural relationship between a hologram and an associative memory. Both holograms and associative memory are able to recall a complete pattern from a partial cue. Longuet-Higgins (1968) examined the temporal dimension of this relationship by creating a system of encoding equations for storing and retrieving a sequence of signals. Later, Willshaw and Buneman joined Longuet-Higgins in a continued effort to exploit holographic principles as possible mechanisms in human memory (Willshaw, Buneman & Longuet-Higgins, 1969; Willshaw & Longuet-Higgins, 1969 & 1970). This work at the University of Edinburgh resulted in a temporal ANS model called the holophone (Willshaw & Longuet-Higgins, 1970) — a paradigm that stores input signals and can retrieve a complete signal given only a portion. Even more significantly, the work at University of Edinburgh laid the foundations for the use of optics for ANS paradigm implementations, a concept that shows great promise in the future of ANS. Later work by Willshaw (1971 & 1972) has been toward the analysis of the self-organization and generalization properties of ANSs, and joint work with Christoph von der Malsburg (Willshaw & Malsburg, 1976) rigorously analyzes the biological neural system and strives to develop accurate mathematical analogies.

## FUKUSHIMA—1969

Kunihiko Fukushima began working with ANS in the late 1960's (Fukushima, 1969) by studying spatial and spatiotemporal ANS models of the visual system (Fukushima, 1970) and the brain (Fukushima, 1973). Fukushima's most notable work has been the creation of a multilayered ANS paradigm for vision that has enjoyed several refinements in the past years. Fukushima called his first effort the cognitron (1975, 1979), and his later improved version the neocognitron (Fukushima, 1980, 1984, 1986 & 1987; Fukushima & Miyake, 1982; Fukushima, Miyake & Takayuki, 1983). Fukushima's neocognitron has several layers—as many as nine. Each layer does an abstraction of features from the previous layer, cascading connections and layers from the input space through hidden layers, to the eventual classification of the object being recognized. Fukushima has successfully demonstrated his model for recognizing handwritten numerals that were distorted, shifted, rotated and scaled in many different configurations.

## KLOPF—1969

A. Harry Klopf has been studying the relationship between the psychology of the mind and the biology of the brain since 1969 (Klopf & Gose, 1969). Klopf (1972, 1979 & 1982) has theorized that the neuron is a hedonistic component of the brain, a goal seeking, adaptive system that increases the efficacy of its excitatory synapses when it fires and is depolarized (pleasure), and increases the efficacy of its inhibitory synapses when it is hyperpolarized (pain). Klopf's theory is supported by the fundamental notion of heterostasis (1982). Heterostasis is the maximization of an internal variable theorized to be the mechanism for learning in the somatic nervous system (the system used for human information processing), while homeostasis, the equilibrium of all internal variables, is thought to be the mechanism for learning in the autonomic nervous system (the system used to control the heart and lungs). Klopf's heterostatic theory is developed in his book (p. 13), *The Hedonistic Neuron* (1982), where he summarizes

> The overall conclusion is that intelligent brain function can be understood in terms if nested hierarchies of heterostatic goal-seeking adaptive loops, beginning at the level of the single neuron and extending upward to the level of the whole brain.

Recently Klopf (1986, 1987a, 1987b & 1987c) has extended his theory and embodied it in a new model called drive-reinforcement learning, which accounts for a wide range of classical conditioning phenomena by exploiting the causality of activations. The drive-reinforcement model is based upon the signal levels between neurons—drives—and the changes in signal levels between neurons—reinforcers. This idea of correlating the changes in signal levels was independently discovered by Klopf (1986) and Kosko (1985), and is commonly referred to as differential Hebbian learning.

## KOHONEN—1971

Tuevo Kohonen began his ANS research with randomly connected paradigms in 1971. Kohonen's work (Kohonen, 1972b, 1974 & 1977) quickly focused upon associative memories—correlation matrices—similar to those of Anderson (1968, 1970 & 1972) and Steinbuch (Steinbuch, 1961; Steinbuch & Piske, 1963). Later, Kohonen & Ruohonen (1973) extended the linear associative memory—which requires linearly independent vectors for good performance—to an associative memory that would find the optimal mapping for vectors being stored that were not linearly independent, and called the optimal linear associative memory (OLAM). The OLAM is useful not only as a storage medium, but it can also be used as a novelty filter that provides a dimension-by-dimension comparison of a given input vector to all the stored vectors. Kohonen's later research (1981, 1982, 1984) led to the development of an application of the competitive learning system into an ANS paradigm—called learning vector quantization (LVQ)—that automatically (unsupervised learning) determines the k-best reference vectors from a sufficiently large set of data points in n-dimensions. Kohonen has also called this ANS the self-organizing feature map because of its early success in accurately organizing sounds into a phonotopic map (Kohonen, Mikisara & Saramaki, 1984) and motor commands into a motor-control map (Kohonen, 1984 & 1986a). Recently, Kohonen has applied LVQ to speech recognition (Kohonen, Riittinen, Reuhkala & Haltsonen, 1984), pattern recognition (Kohonen, 1986b), and image recognition (Kohonen, 1984). Kohonen's work has been collected into three monographs entitled *Associative Memory—A System Theoretic Approach* (1977), *Content-Addressable Memories* (1980), and *Self-Organization and Associative Memory* (1984).

## COOPER, ELBAUM, AND NESTOR ASSOCIATES—1973

Brown University Physicists Leon Cooper (a Nobel laureate) and Charles Elbaum have been involved with ANS modeling since the early 1970's (Cooper, 1973; Cooper, et al, 1979). In 1975, Cooper and Elbaum began a limited partner venture called Nestor Associates with the intent of developing, patenting and exploiting the potential of ANSs (Nestor, 1987a). This small group represents the first ANS-based commercial attempt, an attempt that prospered. In 1983, Cooper and Elbaum joined with an early collaborator, Doug Reilly, and formed Nestor, Inc. Nestor has developed an ANS called the Reduced Coulomb Energy (RCE) Network (Reilly, Cooper & Elbaum, 1982) that is the core of their Nestor Learning System (Nestor, 1987b). Since 1982, Nestor has been awarded several neural network application patents based upon the RCE Network (Cooper & Elbaum, 1982; Cooper, Elbaum & Reilly, 1982). In addition, Nestor has applied their NLS to character recognition, quality control diagnostics, signal classification, target recognition, and signature verification (Nestor, 1988).

## SEJNOWSKI—1976

Terrence Sejnowski began working with ANSs in 1976. Sejnowski is among the few researchers that has both a strong mathematics background and a strong biology background. Sejnowski's first work was focused upon finding neurological evidence for his covariance leaning rule (Sejnowski, 1976, 1977a & 1977b). Later, Sejnowski (1981) developed the notion of skeleton filters in brain and studied the visual systems (Ballard, Hinton & Sejnowski, 1983).

One of the most prominent contributions Sejnowski has made to ANS theory has been the co-discovery (with Geoff Hinton) of the Boltzmann Machine algorithm (Hinton, Ackley & Sejnowski, 1984; Ackley, Hinton & Sejnowski, 1985) and its higher ordered extensions (Sejnowski, 1986), the first ANS to be recognized as a true multilayer learning algorithm. Sejnowski and others applied the Boltzmann Machine mainly to the areas of vision (Kienker, et al., 1986; Sejnowski & Hinton, 1986).

More recently, Sejnowski made three significant contributions to ANS in his application of the backpropagation algorithm. In 1986, Sejnowski & Rosenberg (1986 & 1987) used the backpropagation algorithm to map text to its phonemic representation. This work received a tremendous amount of attention and is responsible for much of the excitement of this period. Later, Gorman & Sejnowski (1988a & 1988b) used the backpropagation algorithm to classify sonar signals better than the best human to date. Most recently Quian & Sejnowski (1988) have used backpropagation to predict the structure of globular proteins and found that it had outperformed all methods previously known.

## MCCLELLAND, RUMELHART, AND THE PDP GROUP—1977

McClelland and Rumelhart are cognitive psychologists who are primarily interested in using ANS models to help understand the psychological functions of the mind. David Rumelhart (1977) became interested in ANSs through his work with the HEARSAY model of speech understanding, a semi-parallel interactive model of reading. James McClelland (1979), inspired by James Anderson's (1968) work, began investigating ANSs by formulating a semi-parallel model of mental processes. Later, Rumelhart and McClelland combined efforts and designed their first ANS paradigm, entitled the interactive activation model—a paradigm used to explain word recognition (McClelland & Rumelhart, 1981; Rumelhart & McClelland, 1982). McClelland & Rumelhart extended their research to other ANS architectures and used the moniker parallel distributed processing (PDP) to describe their work. As interest in McClelland and Rumelhart's work grew, they attracted the attention of other researchers, eventually forming the PDP Research Group, a group dedicated to studying the "microstructure of cognition." The culmination of the PDP Research group's efforts is embodied in a two-volume set of books entitled *Parallel Distributed Processing: Explorations in the Microstructures of Cognition* (1986). The first volume of this set introduces PDP (ANS) theory and outlines four of the ANS paradigms that dominated their research. The second volume describes the applications of ANSs in psychological and neurobiological modeling. Studies by the PDP Research Group of particular note include the construction of a speech model by McClelland and Jeffrey Elman (Elman & McClelland, 1984 & 1986; McClelland & Elman, 1986), research of the correspondence between PDP architectures and the physiology of the brain by Francis Crick (1979) and David Zipser (1984a, 1984b & 1985), and mathematical analysis performed by Michael Jordan (1986a & 1986b) and Ronald Williams (1983, 1985a, 1985b & 1986).

## SUTTON AND BARTO—1978

Richard Sutton and Andrew Barto began working with ANSs in 1978 (Sutton, 1978, Barto & Sutton, 1981a & 1981b, Sutton & Barto, 1981a & 1981b) when they developed an ANS model of classical conditioning inspired by Klopf's heterostatic theory (Klopf, 1982). In later experiments Sutton, Barto and Charles Anderson further developed the theory of reinforcement learning (Barto, 1984, 1985 & 1986; Barto, Sutton & Anderson, 1983; Barto & Anandan, 1985). Reinforcement learning is similar to error-correction learning, with the differences described by Barto (1984) as follows:

> In the first case [error-correction learning], the learning system need only remember what it is told, whereas in the second case [reinforcement learning], the system must somehow discover what actions have consequences that lead to improving performance.

The reinforcement learning model has been used for control applications and classical conditioning models (Barto & Sutton, 1982; Barto, Anderson & Sutton, 1982; Barto, Sutton & Anderson, 1983). More recently, Sutton (1984 & 1986) has been working with a behavior prediction model that correlates differences averaged over time—called the temporal difference model—and Barto has been working with a new model of reinforcement learning called the associative reward-penalty model (Barto & Anandan, 1985; Barto 1985, 1986; Barto & Jordan, 1987).

## FELDMAN, BALLARD, AND THE CONNECTIONIST GROUP—1980

Jerome Feldman and Dana Ballard were two of the first ANS researchers at the University of Rochester. These researchers and their fellow associates, called the Connectionist Group, have developed many different ANSs. Feldman and Ballard's early work was with vision— Feldman (1980, 1981a & 1981b) working on an ANS model of visual memory and Ballard (1981) studying visual Gestalts. Other areas of research by the Connectionist Group include work in computer vision by Ballard & Brown (1982), natural language by Cottrell & Small (1984 & 1985), semantic networks by Shastri (1987), logical inference by Ballard & Hayes (1984 & 1985), concept representation by Feldman (1986) and Feldman & Shastri (1986), ANS surveys by Feldman & Ballard (1982) and Feldman (1985), and ANS simulators by Fanty (1986a).

## HECHT-NIELSEN—1982

Robert Hecht-Nielsen founded the neurocomputing research and development program at Motorola in 1979. Later, in 1983, Hecht-Nielsen (1981 & 1982) founded the neurocomputing program at TRW. Hecht-Nielsen has had a significant impact on ANS from several perspectives: engineering; research; instruction; and commercialization. As an engineer, Hecht-Nielsen was a principal designer of one of the first modern electronic neurocomputers—a computer dedicated to the processing of ANS paradigms. This neurocomputer, the TRW Mark III, is hosted by a VAX computer and was made commercially available in 1986 (TRW, 1987). Hecht-Nielsen has since started his own company (co-founded with Todd Gutschow)—entitled Hecht-Nielsen Neurocomputer Corporation—and has developed a PC-based neurocomputer called the ANZA (HNC, 1987b). As a researcher, Hecht-Nielsen has developed an extension of Grossberg's avalanche entitled the neural network spatiotemporal nearest matched-filter (1987b), a multilayer pattern recognition ANS called the counterpropagation network (1987e, 1987f & 1988b), extended a theorem by A. N. Kolmogorov that proves there exists a three layer ANS that will perform any continuous mapping defined on a compact set (1987d), and independently derived a theorem that proves the convergence of the backpropagation algorithm for a wide range of mappings (1988c). In addition, Hecht-Nielsen has also presented many applications where ANS technology can prosper (1986a, 1987c & 1988a). As an instructor, Hecht-Nielsen was one of the first to offer a course that succinctly presents this divergent field (1985, 1986b & 1987a). As an entrepreneur, Hecht-Nielsen and Gutschow formed their own company dedicated to applying ANSs to real-world applications (HNC, 1987a & 1987b).

## HOPFIELD AND TANK—1982

In 1982 John Hopfield concisely described a method of analyzing the stable point within a crossbar ANS (1982). Hopfield's method is based on an energy argument called Lyapunov energy, a short cut to studying the global dynamics of a system of nonlinear equations. Hopfield showed that an energy equation could be constructed which described the activities of a single-layer discrete-time ANS and, for all possible inputs to the ANS, the energy dissipated and the system converged to a local minimum and remained there indefinitely. The inception of global analysis by Hopfield created a great resurgence of interest in applying ANS paradigms to difficult problems that conventional computers were not able to solve. Hopfield later extended his original model from discrete to continuous time (1984).

Hopfield and his associate, David Tank, also discovered a significant application of ANS models. By creating an energy function that describes a specific combinatorial optimization problem — for example the traveling salesman problem — and working backward by constructing an ANS model from the energy function, Tank and Hopfield (Hopfield & Tank, 1985 & 1986; Tank & Hopfield, 1986, 1987a, & 1987c) found a way to get nearly optimum solutions to NP-complete problems (i.e. problems unsolvable in real-time). Most recently, Hopfield and Tank have extended the Lyapunov energy argument to spatiotemporal (space-time) pattern storage, and are currently experimenting with an ANS model that recognizes time varying patterns of speech (Tank & Hopfield, 1987b).

## MEAD — 1985

Carver Mead is a pioneer in VLSI systems (Mead & Conway, 1980) who has focused his talents on the replication of animal nervous systems in electronic circuitry. Mead's first efforts resulted in the development of a silicon retina (Mead, 1985; Mead & Mahowald, 1988) — a VLSI chip that contains 2,304 photosensitive cells in a square array and connected in the same manner as the cones of the human retina. Later work by Mead has yielded a silicon cochlea. Eventually, Mead hopes to build an entire nervous system of silicon — a goal that is described in his recent book *Analog VLSI and Neural Systems* (Mead, 1989).

## KOSKO — 1985

Bart Kosko has offered three significant contributions to the field of ANS: bidirectional associative memories; fuzzy cognitive maps; and the incorporation of fuzzy logic and ANSs.

Kosko (1987c, 1987d & 1988b) has created a family of ANS paradigms — called bidirectional associative memories (BAMs) — that extend the one-layer autoassociative Hebbian correlators to two-layer pattern matching heteroassociators. BAMs are unsupervised learning ANSs that are able to learn and recall patterns in real-time and — because of their feedback architecture and the nature of the dynamical equations that describe their two-layer interactions — BAMs are able to converge to a minimum solution given any arbitrary matrix. The most recent work with the BAM has led to the development of a globally stable dynamical system that can learn and recall at the same time, a result that led to the extension of the Cohen-Grossberg (1983) absolute stability theorem.

Another architecture devised by Kosko (1986a, 1986b, 1986c, 1987b & 1988a) is the fuzzy cognitive map (FCM) — an ANS-like knowledge processing paradigm that captures the causal relationships between an arbitrary number of variably valued experts. The FCM utilizes differential Hebbian learning, a learning rule independently discovered by both Kosko (1985 & 1986d) and Klopf (1986) that correlates the rate of change of nodes in its digraph of causally weighted edges.

Kosko (1986a & 1987a) has discovered a link between fuzzy logic and ANS, showing that the minimization of fuzzy entropy, or the motion of a point from within the n-dimensional unit cube to one of its corners, is the exact operation many ANS paradigms perform. This link to fuzzy logic is joined by a pure fuzzy logic ANS paradigm called the fuzzy associative memory (Kosko, 1987a), an ANS model that uses fuzzy correlations to form a memory matrix.

# Bibliography

Abu-Mostafa, Y., & St. Jacques, J. (1985). Information capacity of the Hopfield model, *IEEE Transactions on Information Theory, IT-31*, 461–464.

Abutaleh, A. (1988). Self-organization as a special case of the time-varying adaptive filters, *Neural Networks Supplement: INNS Abstracts, 1*, 65.

Ackely, D., Hinton, G., & Sejnowski, T. (1985). A learning algorithm for Boltzmann machines, *Cognitive Science, 9*, 147–169.

Agmon, S. (1954). The relaxation method for linear inequalities, *Canadian Journal of Mathematics, 3*, 382–392.

Agranat, A. (1987). Semiparallel microelectronic implementation of neural networks model using CCD technology, *Workshop on Neural Network Devices and Applications*, Jet Propulsion Laboratory, 197–201.

Ahmad, S. (1988). A study of scaling and generalization in neural networks, University of Illinois at Urbana-Champaign, Department of Computer Science Technical Report UIUCDCS-R-88-1454.

Ajmera, R., Newcomb, R., Chitale, S. & Nilsson, A. (1983). VLSI brightness module for robot retinas, *Proceedings of the 26th Midwest Symposium on Circuits and Systems*, 70–73.

Akers, L. & Walker, M. (1988). A limited-interconnect synthetic neural IC, *Proceedings of the IEEE International Conference on Neural Networks: Vol. II*, (pp. 151–158). San Diego: IEEE.

Albert, A. (1972). *Regression and the Moore-Penrose Pseudoinverse*, New York: Academic Press.

Allanson, J. (1956). Some properties of a randomly connected neural network, In C. Cherry (Ed.), *Proceedings of the Third London Symposium on Information Theory*, London: Butterworths.

Allen, R. (1987). Several studies on natural language and back-propagation, *Proceedings of the IEEE First International Conference on Neural Networks, II*, (p. 335–342). San Diego: IEEE.

Almeida, L. (1987). A learning rule for asynchronous perceptrons with feedback in a combinatorial environment, *Proceedings of the IEEE First International Conference on Neural Networks: Vol. II*, (pp. 609–618). San Diego: IEEE.

Almeida, L. (1988). Backpropagation in perceptrons with feedback, In R. Eckmiller & C. v. d. Malsburg (Eds.), *NATO ISI Series, Vol. F41: Neural Computers*, (pp. 199–208). Berlin: Springer-Verlag.

Alspector, J. (1987). A neuromorphic VLSI learning system, *Workshop on Neural Network Devices and Applications*, Jet Propulsion Laboratory, 53–71.

Alspector, J. & Allen, R. (1986). A VLSI model of neural nets, Bellcore Technical Memorandum, TM ARH002688.

Alspector, J., Allen, R., Hu, V. & Satyanarayana, S. (1988). Stochastic learning networks and their electronic implementation, In D. Anderson (Ed.), *Proceedings of the 1987 IEEE Conference on Neural Information Processing Systems—Natural and Synthetic*, (pp. 9–21). New York: American Institute of Physics.

Alstyne, M. v. (1988). Remaking the neural net: A perceptron logic unit, *Neural Networks Supplement: INNS Abstracts, 1*, 143.

Altes, R. (1988). Unconstrained minimum variance mean-squared error parameter estimation with Hopfield nets, *Proceedings of the IEEE International Conference on Neural Networks: Vol. II*, (pp. 541–548). San Diego: IEEE.

Amari, S-I. (1967). A theory of adaptive pattern classifiers, *IEEE Transactions on Electronic Computers, EC-16*, 299–307.

Amari, S-I. (1971). Characteristics of randomly connected threshold-element networks and network systems, *Proceedings of the IEEE, 59*, 1, 35–47.

Amari, S-I. (1972a). Characteristics of random nets of analog neuron-like elements, *IEEE Transactions on Systems, Man and Cybernetics, SMC-2*, 643–657.

Amari, S-I. (1972b). Learning patterns and pattern sequences by self-organizing nets of threshold elements, *IEEE Transactions on Computers, C-21*, 1197–1206.

Amari, S-I. (1974). A method of statistical neurodynamics, *Kybernetik, 14*, 201–215.

Amari, S-I. (1977a). Dynamics of pattern formation in lateral-inhibition type neural fields, *Biological Cybernetics, 27*, 77–87.

Amari, S-I. (1977b). Neural theory of association and concept formation, *Biological Cybernetics, 26*, 175–185.

Amari, S-I. (1980). Topographic organization of nerve fields, *Bulletin of Mathematical Biology, 42*, 339–364.

Amari, S-I. (1982). A mathematical theory of self-organizing nerve systems, In J. Metzler & M. Arbib (Eds.), *Biomathematics: Current Status and Perspectives*, (pp. 159–197). Amsterdam: North-Holland.

Amari, S-I. (1983). Field theory of self-organizing neural nets, *IEEE Transactions on Systems, Man, and Cybernetics, SMC-13*, 741–748.

Amari, S-I. (1988). Statistical neurodynamics of various versions of correlation associative memory, *Proceedings of the IEEE International Conference on Neural Networks: Vol. I*, (pp. 633–640). San Diego: IEEE.

Amari, S-I. & Arbib, M. (1977). Competition and cooperation in neural nets, In J. Metzler & M. Arbib (Eds.), *Systems Neuroscience*, (pp. 119–165). New York: Academic Press.

Amari, S-I. & Arbib, M. (Eds.), (1982). *Lecture Notes in Biomathematics 45: Competition and Cooperation in neural nets*, Berlin: Springer-Verlag.

Amari, S-I. & Maginu, K. (1988). Statistical neurodynamics of associative memory, *Neural Networks, 1*, 63–74.

Amari, S. & Takeuchi, M. (1978). Mathematical theory on formation of category detecting nerve cells, *Biological Cybernetics, 29*, 127–136.

Amari, S-I., Yoshida, K. & Kanatani, K. (1977). A mathematical foundation for statistical neurodynamics, *SIAM Journal of Applied Mathematics, 33*, 95–126.

AMC (1987). Air Force looks at neural nets for ADI, *Advanced Military Computing, 3*, 18, 1–8.

Amit, J., Gutfruend, H. & Sompolinksy, H. (1985). Spin-glass models of neural networks, *Physical Review Letters A, 32*, 1007–1018.

Amit, J., Gutfruend, H. & Sompolinksy, H. (1987). Statistical mechanics of neural networks near saturation, *Annals of Physics, 173*, 30–67.

An, Z., Mniszewski, S., Lee, Y., Papain, G. & Poolen, G. (1988). Hiertalker: A default hierarchy of high order neural networks that learns to read English aloud, *Neural Networks Supplement: INNS Abstracts, 1*, 285.

Anastassiou, D. (1988). Nonstandard A/D conversion based on symmetric neural networks, *Proceedings of the IEEE International Conference on Neural Networks: Vol. II*, (pp. 181–188). San Diego: IEEE.

Anderson, C. (1987). Strategy learning with multilayer connectionist representations, GTE Laboratories Technical Report, TR 87-509.3.

Anderson, C. & Abrahams, E. (1986). A Bayesian probability network, In J. Denker (Ed.), *AIP Conference Proceedings 151: Neural Networks for Computing*, (pp. 7–11). New York: American Institute of Physics.

Anderson, D. (1986). Coherent optical eigenstate memory, *Optics Letters, 11*, 56 f.

Anderson, D. (1987). Two-port adaptive optical elements, *Workshop on Neural Networks Devices and Applications*, Jet Propulsion Laboratory, 99–112.

Anderson, D. & Erie, M. (1987). Resonator memories and optical novelty filters, *Optical Engineering, 26*, 434–444.

Anderson, D. & Lininger, D. (1987). Dynamic optical interconnects: Volume holograms as optical two-port operators, *Applied Optics, 26*, 5031–5039.

Anderson, D., Lininger, D., & Feinberg, J. (1987). An optical tracking novelty filter, *Optical Letters, 12*, 123.

Anderson, H. (1987). Why artificial intelligence isn't (yet), *AI Expert, 2*, 7, 36–44.

Anderson, J. (1968). A memory storage model utilizing spatial correlation functions, *Kybernetik, 5*, 113–119.

Anderson, J. (1970). Two models for memory organization using interacting traces, *Mathematical Biosciences, 8*, 137–160.

Anderson, J. (1972). A simple neural network generating an interactive memory, *Mathematical Biosciences, 14*, 197–220.

Anderson, J. (1973). A theory for the recognition of items from short memorized lists, *Psychological Review, 80*, 417–438.

Anderson, J. (1977). Neural models with cognitive implications, In D. LaBerge & S. Samuels (Eds.), *Basic Processes in Reading Perception and Comprehension*, (pp. 413–451). Hillsdale, NJ: Lawrence Erlbaum Associates.

Anderson, J. (1983a). Cognitive and psychological computation with neural models, *IEEE Transactions on Systems, Man, and Cybernetics, SMC-13*, 799–815.

Anderson, J. (1983b). Neural models and a little about language, In D. Caplan (Ed.), *Biological Bases of Language*, Cambridge: MIT Press.

Anderson, J. (1986). Psychological implications of parallel systems, *Optics News, 29*, 29–33.

Anderson, J. (1987). Concept learning in neural networks, *Workshop on Neural Network Devices and Applications*, Jet Propulsion Laboratory, 294–336.

Anderson, J., Golden, M. & Murphy, G. (1986). Concepts in distributed systems, *Proceedings of the SPIE, 634*, 260–276.

Anderson, J. & Mozer, M. (1981). Categorization and selective neurons, In G. Hinton & J. Anderson (Eds.), *Parallel Models of Associative Memory*, (pp. 213–236). Hillsdale, NJ: Lawrence Erlbaum Associates.

Anderson, J. & Murphy, G. (1986a). Psychological concepts in a parallel system, *Physica, 22D*, 318–336.

Anderson, J. & Murphy, G. (1986b). Concepts in connectionist models, In J. Denker (Ed.), *AIP Conference Proceedings 151: Neural Networks for Computing*, (pp. 17–22). New York: American Institute of Physics.

Anderson, J., Penz, P., Gately, T. & Collins, D. (1988). Radar signal categorization using a neural network, *Neural Networks Supplement: INNS Abstracts, 1*, 422.

Anderson, J., Silverstein, J., Ritz, S. & Jones, R. (1977). Distinctive features, categorical perception, and probability learning: Some applications of a neural model, *Psychological Review, 84*, 413–451.

Anderson, S., Merrill, J. & Port, R. (1988). Effects of network topology on speech categorization, *Neural Networks Supplement: INNS Abstracts, 1*, 286.

Angeniol, B., De La Croix Van Brois, G. & Le Texier, J-Y. (1988). Self-organizing maps and the traveling salesman problem, *Neural Networks, 1*, 289–293.

Arbib, M. (1964). *Brains, Machines and Mathematics*, New York: McGraw-Hill.

Arbib, M. (1972). *The Metaphorical Brain*, New York: Wiley-Interscience.

Arbib, M. (1975). Artificial intelligence and brain theory: Unities and diversities, *Annual Biomedical Engineering: Vol. 3*, (pp. 238–274).

Arbib, M. & Caplan, D. (1979). Neurolinguistics must be computational, *Behavioral and Brain Sciences, 2*, 449–483.

Ash, T. (1988). Dynamic node creation in backpropagation networks, University of California at San Diego, Institute for Cognitive Science Technical Report 8901.

Ashby, W. (1952). *Design for a Brain*, New York: Wiley & Sons.

Ashby, W. (1957). *An Introduction to Cybernetics*, New York: Chapman & Hall Ltd.

Atiya, A. (1988). Learning on a general network, In D. Anderson (Ed.), *Proceedings of the 1987 IEEE Conference on Neural Information Processing Systems — Natural and Synthetic*, (pp. 22–30). New York: American Institute of Physics.

Averbukh, D. (1969). Random nets of analog neurons, *Automatic Remote Control, 5*, 116–123.

Axelrod, R. (1976). *Structure of Design*, Princeton: Princeton University Press.

Babcok, K. & Westervelt, R. (1986a). Stability and dynamics of simple electronic neural networks with added inertia, *Physica, 23D*, 464–469.

Babcock, K. & Westervelt, R. (1986b). Complex dynamics in simple neural circuits, In J. Denker (Ed.), *AIP Conference Proceedings 151: Neural Networks for Computing*, (pp. 23–28). New York: American Institute of Physics.

Bagherzadeh, N., Kerola, T., Leddy, B., & Brice, R. (1987). On parallel execution of the traveling salesman problem on a neural network model, *Proceedings of the IEEE First International Conference on Neural Networks: Vol. III*, (pp. 317–324). San Diego: IEEE.

Baird, B. (1986). Bifurcation analysis of oscillating network model of pattern recognition in the rabbit olfactory bulb, In J. Denker (Ed.), *AIP Conference Proceedings 151: Neural Networks for Computing*, (pp. 29–34). New York: American Institute of Physics.

Bak, C. & Little, M. (1988). Memory capacity of artificial neural networks with high order node connections, *Proceedings of the IEEE International Conference on Neural Networks: Vol. I*, (pp. 207–216). San Diego: IEEE.

Baldi, P. & Baum, E. (1986). Caging and exhibiting ultrametric structures, In J. Denker (Ed.), *AIP Conference Proceedings 151: Neural Networks for Computing*, (pp. 35–40). New York: American Institute of Physics.

Baldi, P. & Venkatesh, S. (1987). Number of stable points for spin-glasses and neural networks of higher order, *Physical Review Letters, 58*, 913–916.

Baldi, P. & Venkatesh, S. (1988). On properties of neuron-like networks, In D. Anderson (Ed.), *Proceedings of the 1987 IEEE Conference on Neural Information Processing Systems—Natural and Synthetic*, (pp. 41–51). New York: American Institute of Physics.

Ballard, D. (1981). Parameter networks: Toward a theory of low-level vision, *Proceedings of the 7th International Joint Conference on Artificial Intelligence*, (pp. 1068–1078).

Ballard, D. & Brown, C. (1982). *Computer Vision*, Englewood Cliffs: Prentice-Hall.

Ballard, D. & Hayes, P. (1984). Parallel logical inference, *Proceedings of the 6th Cognitive Science Conference*, Hillsdale, NJ: Lawrence Erlbaum Associates.

Ballard, D. & Hayes, P. (1985). Parallel logical inference and energy minimization, University of Rochester, Computer Science Department Technical Report, TR 142.

Ballard, D., Hinton, G. & Sejnowski, T. (1983). Parallel visual computation, *Nature, 306*, 21–26.

Banquet, J. (1988). Connectionist theories, ART and cognitive potentials, *Neural Networks Supplement: INNS Abstracts, 1*, 159.

Barbosa, V. & Huang, H-K. (1988). Static task allocation in heterogeneous distributed systems, University of Rio de Janeiro Tech Report ES-149/88.

Barhen, J., Toomarian, N. & Protopopsecu, V. (1987). Optimization of the computational load of a hypercube supercomputer onboard a mobile robot, *Applied Optics, 26*, 5007–5014.

Barhen, J., Toomarian, N., Protopopsecu, V. & Clinard, M. (1987). Concurrent neuromorphic algorithms for optimization of the computational load of a hypercube supercomputer, *Proceedings of the IEEE First International Conference on Neural Networks: Vol. IV*, (pp. 687–696). San Diego: IEEE.

Barnard, E. & Casasent, D. (1988). New optical neural system architectures and applications, *Proceedings of the SPIE, 963*, in press.

Barr, A. & Feigenbaum, E. (1981). *The Handbook of Artificial Intelligence: Vol I*, Stanford: Heuris-Tech Press.

Barto, A. (1976). A neural network simulation method using the fast Fourier transform, *IEEE Transactions on Systems, Man, and Cybernetics, SMC-8*, 863–866.

Barto, A. (1984). Simulation experiments with goal-seeking adaptive elements, Air Force Wright Aeronautical Laboratories Technical Report, AFWAL-TR-84-1022.

Barto, A. (1985). Learning by statistical cooperation of self-interested neuron-like computing units, *Human Neurobiology, 4*, 229–256.

Barto, A. (1986). Game-theoretic cooperativity in networks of self-interested units, In J. Denker (Ed.), *AIP Conference Proceedings 151: Neural Networks for Computing*, (pp. 41–46). New York: American Institute of Physics.

Barto, A. & Anandan, P. (1985). Pattern recognizing stochastic learning automata, *IEEE Transactions on Systems, Man, and Cybernetics, SMC-15*, 360–375.

Barto, A., Anandan, P. & Anderson, C. (1986). Cooperativity in networks of pattern recognizing stochastic learning automata, In K. Narendra (Ed.), *Adaptive and Learning Systems: Theory and Applications*, New York: Plenum Press.

Barto, A., Anderson, C. & Sutton, R. (1982). Synthesis of nonlinear control surfaces by a layered associative search network, *Biological Cybernetics, 43*, 175–185.

Barto, A. & Jordan, M. (1987). Gradient following without back-propagation in layered networks, *Proceedings of the IEEE First International Conference on Neural Networks: Vol. II*, (pp. 629–636). San Diego: IEEE.

Barto, A. & Sutton, R. (1981a). Goal seeking components for adaptive intelligence: An initial assessment, Air Force Wright Aeronautical Laboratory Technical Report, AFWAL-TR-81-1070.

Barto, A. & Sutton, R. (1981b). Landmark learning: an illustration of associative search, *Biological Cybernetics, 42*, 1–8.

Barto, A. & Sutton, R. (1982). Simulation of anticipatory responses in classical conditioning by a neuron-like adaptive element, *Behavioral and Brain Research, 4*, 221–235.

Barto, A., Sutton, R. & Anderson, C. (1983). Neuron-like adaptive elements that can solve difficult learning control problems, *IEEE Transactions on Systems, Man, and Cybernetics, SMC-13*, 834–846.

Barto, A., Sutton, R. & Brouwer, P. (1981). Associative search network: A reinforcement learning associative memory, *Biological Cybernetics, 40*, 201–211.

Basenberg, S. & Rossi, L. (1988). Optimization of rotationally invariant object recognition in a neural network, *Neural Networks Supplement: INNS Abstracts, 1*, 483.

Baum, E. (1986a). Generalizing backpropagation to computation, In J. Denker (Ed.), *AIP Conference Proceedings 151: Neural Networks for Computing,* (pp. 47–52). New York: American Institute of Physics.

Baum, E. (1986b). Towards practical "neural" computation for combinatorial optimization problems, In J. Denker (Ed.), *AIP Conference Proceedings 151: Neural Networks for Computing,* (pp. 53–58). New York: American Institute of Physics.

Baum, E. & Wilczek, F. (1988). Supervised learning of probability distributions by neural networks, In D. Anderson (Ed.), *Proceedings of the 1987 IEEE Conference on Neural Information Processing Systems — Natural and Synthetic,* (pp. 52–61). New York: American Institute of Physics.

Bavarian, B. (1988, Apr.). Introduction to neural networks for intelligent control, *IEEE Control Systems Magazine,* 3–7.

Bayley, J., Byrne, C., Fiddy, M., Abbiss, J. & Barnes, B. (1988). Image resolution enhancement on a neural network, *Neural Networks Supplement: INNS Abstracts, 1,* 425.

Bentor, I. & Huang, N. (1988). Bounds on the capacity of multi-threshold networks, *Neural Networks Supplement: INNS Abstracts, 1,* 74.

Bernasconi, J. (1988). Analysis and comparison of different learning algorithms for pattern association problems, In D. Anderson (Ed.), *Proceedings of the 1987 IEEE Conference on Neural Information Processing Systems — Natural and Synthetic,* (pp. 72–81). New York: American Institute of Physics.

Bernstein, J. (1981). Profiles: Marvin Minsky, *The New Yorker,* December 14, 50–126.

Bertalanffy, L. V. (1968). *General Systems Theory: Foundations, Development, and Applications,* New York: George Braziller.

Beurle, R. (1962a). Functional organization in random nets, In H. von Foerster & G. Zopf (Eds.), *Principles of Self-Organization,* (pp. 291 f). New York: Pergamon Press.

Beurle, R. (1962b). Information in random networks, In C. Muses (Ed.), *Aspects of the Theory of Artificial Intelligence,* (pp. 19 f). New York: Plenum Press.

Bienenstock, E., Cooper, E. & Munro, P. (1982). Theory for the development of neural selectivity: Orientation specificity and binocular interaction in visual cortex, *Journal of Neuroscience, 2,* 32–48.

Bilbro, G., White, M. & Snyder, W. (1988). Image segmentation with neurocomputers, In R. Eckmiller & C. v. d. Malsburg (Eds.), *NATO ISI Series, Vol. F41: Neural Computers,* (pp. 71–79). Berlin: Springer-Verlag.

Blellich, G. & Rosenberg, C. (1987). Network learning on the connection machine, *Proceedings of the Tenth Annual IJCAI,* Milan, Italy.

Block, H. (1962). The perceptron: A model for brain functioning I, Analysis of a four-layer series-coupled perceptron II, *Review of Modern Physics, 34,* 123–142.

Block, H. (1970). A review of "Perceptrons," *Information and Control, 17,* 501–522.

Block, H., Nilsson, N. & Duda, R. (1964). Determination and detection of features in patterns, In J. Tou & R. Wilcox (Eds.), *Computer and Information Sciences: Collected Papers in Learning, Adaption, and Control in Information Sciences,* (pp. 75–110). Washington: Spartan Books.

Bookman, L. & Zhang, X. (1988). A data flow analysis of connectionist networks, *Neural Networks Supplement: INNS Abstracts, 1,* 77.

Bounds, D. (1986). Numerical simulations of Boltzmann machines, In J. Denker (Ed.), *AIP Conference Proceedings 151: Neural Networks for Computing,* (pp. 59–64). New York: American Institute of Physics.

Bounds, D., Lloyd, P., Mathew, B. & Waddell, G. (1988). A multilayer perceptron network for the diagnosis of low back pain, *Proceedings of the IEEE International Conference on Neural Networks: Vol. II,* (pp. 481–489). San Diego: IEEE.

Bourlard, H. & Wellekens, C. (1987). Multilayer perceptrons and automatic speech recognition, *Proceedings of the IEEE First International Conference on Neural Networks: Vol. IV,* (pp. 407–416). San Diego: IEEE.

Bourlard, H. & Wellekens, C. (1988). A link between Markov models and multilayer perceptrons, *Neural Networks Supplement: INNS Abstracts, 1,* 290.

Bout, D. v. d. & Miller, T. (1988). A traveling salesman objective function that works, *Proceedings of the IEEE International Conference on Neural Networks: Vol. II,* (pp. 299–303). San Diego: IEEE.

Brady, M. & Ragharan, R. (1988). Gradient descent fails to separate, *Proceedings of the IEEE International Conference on Neural Networks: Vol. I,* (pp. 649–656). San Diego: IEEE.

Brandt, R., Wang, Y., Lamb, A. & Mitra, S. (1988). Alternative networks for solving the traveling salesman problem and the list-matching problem, *Proceedings of the IEEE International Conference on Neural Networks: Vol. II,* (pp. 333–340). San Diego: IEEE.

Breitkopf, P. & Walker, R. (1988). Spectral clustering with neural networks for application to multispectral remote sensing of minerals, *Neural Networks Supplement: INNS Abstracts, 1,* 14.

Brooks, M. (1987, April). Fuzzy chip may solve high-tech problems, *Applied Artificial Intelligence Reporter,* 3.

Brown, N. (1988). Neural network implementation approaches for the connection machine, In D. Anderson (Ed.), *Proceedings of the 1987 IEEE Conference on Neural Information Processing Systems—Natural and Synthetic,* (pp. 127–136). New York: American Institute of Physics.

Bruce, A., Canning, A., Forrest, B., Gardner, E. & Wallace, D. (1986). Learning and memory properties in fully connected networks, In J. Denker (Ed.), *AIP Conference Proceedings 151: Neural Networks for Computing,* (pp. 65–70). New York: American Institute of Physics.

Bryson, A. & Ho, Y.-C. (1969). *Applied Optimal Control,* New York: Blaisdell.

Buhmann, J. & Schulten, K. (1986). Influence of noise on the behavior of an autoassociative neural network, In J. Denker (Ed.), *AIP Conference Proceedings 151: Neural Networks for Computing,* (pp. 71–76). New York: American Institute of Physics.

Buhmann, J. & Schulten, K. (1988). Storing sequences of biased patterns in neural networks with stochastic dynamics, In R. Eckmiller & C. v. d. Malsburg (Eds.), *NATO ISI Series, Vol. F41: Neural Computers,* (pp. 231–242). Berlin: Springer-Verlag.

Bullock, D. & Grossberg, S. (1986). Neural dynamics of planned arm movements: Synergies, invariants, and trajectory formation, *Proceedings of the Symposium on Neural Models of Sensori-Motor Control.*

Burr, D. (1986). A neural network digit recognizer, *Proceedings of the 1986 IEEE International Conference on Systems, Man, and Cybernetics,* (pp. 1621–1625). Atlanta: IEEE.

Burr, D. (1988a). Speech recognition experiments with perceptrons, In D. Anderson (Ed.), *Proceedings of the 1987 IEEE Conference on Neural Information Processing Systems—Natural and Synthetic,* (pp. 144–153). New York: American Institute of Physics.

Burr, D. (1988b). Experiments on neural network recognition of spoken and written speech, *IEEE Transactions on Acoustics, Speech and Signal Processing, 36,* 1162–1168.

Busch, A. & Trainer, L. (1988). Neural network models with higher order neural interactions, *Neural Networks Supplement: INNS Abstracts, 1,* 79.

Caillon, J., Angeniol, B. & Markade, E. (1988). Constrained backpropagation, *Neural Networks Supplement: INNS Abstracts, 1,* 539.

Carpenter, G. (1983). A comparative analysis of structure and chaos in models of single nerve cells and circadian rhythms, In E. Basar, H. Flohr, H. Haken, & A. Mandell (Eds.), *Synergetics of the Brain: Vol. 23,* (pp. 311–329). New York: Springer Series in Synergetics.

Carpenter, G. & Grossberg, S. (1983). A neural theory of circadian rhythms: The gated pacemaker, *Biological Cybernetics, 48,* 35–59.

Carpenter, G. & Grossberg, S. (1984). A neural theory of circadian rhythms: Aschoff's rule in diurnal and nocturnal mammals, *American Journal of Physiology, 247,* 1067–1082.

Carpenter, G. & Grossberg, S. (1985a). Neural dynamics of circadian rhythms: The mammalian hypothalamic pacemaker, In J. Eisenfeld & C. DeLisi (Eds.), *Mathematics and Computers in Biomedical Applications,* (pp. 79–85). Amsterdam: North-Holland.

Carpenter, G. & Grossberg, S. (1985b). A neural theory of circadian rhythms: After-effects and motivational interactions, *Journal of Theoretical Biology, 113,* 163–223.

Carpenter, G. & Grossberg, S. (1986a). Adaptive resonance theory: Stable self-organization of neural recognition codes in response to arbitrary lists of input patterns, *Eighth Annual Conference of the Cognitive Science Society,* (pp. 45–62). Hillsdale, NJ: Lawrence Erlbaum Associates.

Carpenter, G. & Grossberg, S. (1986b). Absolutely stable learning of recognition codes by a self-organizing neural network, In J. Denker (Ed.), *AIP Conference Proceedings 151: Neural Networks for Computing,* (pp. 77–85). New York: American Institute of Physics.

Carpenter, G. & Grossberg, S. (1986c). Associative learning, adaptive pattern recognition, and cooperative decision making by neural networks, *Proceedings of the SPIE, 634,* 218–247.

Carpenter, G. & Grossberg, S. (1987a). Invariant pattern recognition and recall by an attentive self-organizing ART architecture in a nonstationary world, *Proceedings of the IEEE First International Conference on Neural Networks: Vol. II,* (pp. 737–746). San Diego: IEEE.

Carpenter, G. & Grossberg, S. (1987b). A massively parallel architecture for a self-organizing neural pattern recognition machine, *Computer Vision, Graphics and Image Understanding, 37,* 54–115.

Carpenter, G. & Grossberg, S. (1987c). ART 2: Self-organization of stable category recognition codes for analog input patterns, *Proceedings of the IEEE First International Conference on Neural Networks: Vol. II,* (pp. 727–736). San Diego: IEEE.

Carpenter, G. & Grossberg, S. (1987d). ART2: Self-organization of stable category recognition codes for analog input patterns, *Applied Optics, 26,* 4919–4930.

Carpenter, G. & Grossberg, S. (1988, Mar.). The ART of adaptive pattern recognition by a self-organizing neural network, *IEEE Computer,* 77–88.

Castelez, P. (1988). Neural networks in defense applications, *Proceedings of the IEEE International Conference on Neural Networks: Vol. II,* (pp. 473–480). San Diego: IEEE.

Cater, J. (1987). Successfully using peak learning rates of 10 (and greater) in backpropagation networks with the heuristic learning algorithm, *Proceedings of the IEEE First International Conference on Neural Networks: Vol. II,* (pp. 645–651). San Diego: IEEE.

Cattaneo, G. & Casa-Bianchi, N. (1988). Microcanonical annealing on neural networks, *Neural Networks Supplement: INNS Abstracts, 1,* 81.

Caudill, M. (1988). Benchmarking the performance of backpropagation and counterpropagation networks, *Neural Networks Supplement: INNS Abstracts, 1,* 165.

Ceci, L., Lynn, P. & Gardner, P. (1988). Efficient distribution of backpropagation models as parallel architectures, *Neural Networks Supplement: INNS Abstracts, 1,* 427.

Cerf, G., Mokry, R. & Weintraub, J. (1988). Backpropagation parameter analysis on multiprocessors, *Neural Networks Supplement: INNS Abstracts, 1,* 541.

Chande, A., DeCleris, N. & Newcomb, R. (1983). Neural-type robotics — An overview, *Proceedings of the 26th Midwest Symposium on Circuits and Systems,* 68–69.

Charney, M. (1988). Noun compound understanding using neural networks, *Neural Networks Supplement: INNS Abstracts, 1,* 293.

Chen, H., Lee, Y., Sun, G., Maxwell, T. & Giles, C. (1986). Higher order correlation model for associative memory, In J. Denker (Ed.), *AIP Conference Proceedings 151: Neural Networks for Computing,* (pp. 86–99). New York: American Institute of Physics.

Chen, S., Xu, X., Tsai, W. & Huang, N. (1988). A case study of solving optimization problems using neural networks, *Neural Networks Supplement: INNS Abstracts, 1,* 151.

Chetayav, N. (1961). *The Stability of Motion,* New York: Pergamon Press.

Cheung, J. and Omidvar, M. (1988). Mathematical analysis of learning behavior of neuronal models, In D. Anderson (Ed.), *Proceedings of the 1987 IEEE Conference on Neural Information Processing Systems—Natural and Synthetic,* (pp. 165–173). New York: American Institute of Physics.

Chieuh, T-D. & Goodman, R. (1988). A neural network classifier based on coding theory, In D. Anderson (Ed.), *Proceedings of the 1987 IEEE Conference on Neural Information Processing Systems—Natural and Synthetic,* (pp. 174–183). New York: American Institute of Physics.

Chou, P. (1988). The capacity of the Kanerva associative memory is exponential, In D. Anderson (Ed.), *Proceedings of the 1987 IEEE Conference on Neural Information Processing Systems—Natural and Synthetic,* (pp. 184–191). New York: American Institute of Physics.

Churchland, P. (1986). *Neurophilosophy: Toward a Unified Science of Mind-Brain,* Cambridge: MIT Press.

Cohen, M. & Grossberg, S. (1982). Some global properties of binocular resonances: Disparity scaling, filling-in and figure-ground, In T. Caelli & P. Dodwell, *Figural Synthesis,* Hillsdale, NJ: Lawrence Erlbaum Associates.

Cohen, M. & Grossberg, S. (1983). Absolute stability of global pattern formation and parallel memory storage by competitive neural networks, *IEEE Transactions on Systems, Man, and Cybernetics, SMC-13,* 815–825.

Cohen, M. & Grossberg, S. (1986). Neural dynamics of speech and language coding: Developmental programs, perceptual grouping, and competition for short-term memory, *Human Neurobiology, 5,* 1–22.

Cohen, M. & Grossberg, S. (1987). Masking fields: A massively parallel neural architecture for learning, recognizing, and predicting multiple groupings of patterned data, *Applied Optics, 26,* 1866–1891.

Cohen, M., Grossberg, S. & Stork, D. (1987). Recent developments in a neural model of real-time speech analysis and synthesis, *Proceedings of the IEEE First International Conference on Neural Networks: Vol. IV,* (pp. 443–454). San Diego: IEEE.

Collins, J. & Helferty, J. (1988). Adaptive control of a one-legged hopping machine, *Neural Networks Supplement: INNS Abstracts, 1,* 330.

Conwell, P. (1987). Effects of connection delays in two-state model neuron, *Proceedings of the IEEE First International Conference on Neural Networks: Vol. III,* (pp. 95–104). San Diego: IEEE.

Cooper, L. (1973). A possible organizaton of animal memory and learning, In B. Lundquist & S. Lundquist (Eds.), *Proceedings of the Nobel Symposium on Collective Properties of Physical Systems: Vol. 24,* (pp. 252–264). New York: Academic Press.

Cooper, L. & Elbaum, C. (1982). Curve follower, U.S. Patent 4,319,331 (awarded on March 9, 1982).

Cooper, L., Elbaum, C. & Reilly, D. (1982). Self organizing general pattern class separator, U.S. Patent 4,326,259 (awarded on April 20, 1982).

Cooper, L., Liberman, F. & Oja, E. (1979). A theory for the acquisition and loss of neuron specificity in visual cortex, *Biological Cybernetics, 33,* 9–28.

Cottrell, G. (1985). A connectionist approach to word sense disambiguation, University of Rochester, Department of Computer Science Technical Report, TR-154.

Cottrell, G., Munro, P. & Zipser, D. (1987). Image compression by backpropagation, University of California at San Diego Institute for Cognitive Science Technical Report 8702.

Cottrell, G. & Small, S. (1983). A connectionist scheme for modeling word sense disambiguation, *Cognition and Brain Theory, 1,* 89–120.

Cottrell, G. & Small, S. (1984). Viewing parsing as word sense discrimination: A connectionist approach, In B. Bara & G. Guida (Eds.), *Computational Models of Natural Language Processing,* (pp. 91–119). New York: Elsevier Science Publishers.

Cottrell, G. & Willen, J. (1988). Image compression with visual system constraints, *Neural Networks Supplement: INNS Abstracts, 1,* 487.

Cottrell, M. (1988). Stability and attractivity in associative memory neural networks, *Biological Cybernetics, 58,* 129–139.

Crane, H. (1960). Neuristor studies, Stanford Electronics Laboratory, Stanford University, Technical Report 15-6-2, July 11.

Crane, H. (1962). Neuristor: A novel device and system concept, *Proceedings of the IRE, 50,* 2048–2060.

Crick, F. (1979). Thinking about the brain, *Scientific American, 241,* 3, 219–232.

Cruetz, M. (1983). Microcanonical Monte Carlo simulations, *Physical Review Letters, 50,* 1411–1414.

Culhane, A., Peckerar, M. & Marrian, C. (1988a). A neural net approach to discrete Fourier transforms, *Neural Networks Supplement: INNS Abstracts, 1,* 432.

Culhane, A., Peckerar, M. & Marrian, C. (1988b). A neural network approach to discrete Fourier transforms, *IEEE Transactions on Systems, Man, and Cybernetics,* in press.

Czarnul, A., Kiruthi, G. & Newcomb, R. (1979). MOS neural pulse modulator, *Electronics Letters,* December.

Dahl, E. (1987a). Accelerated learning using the generalized delta rule, *Proceedings of the IEEE First International Conference on Neural Networks: Vol. II,* (pp. 523–530). San Diego: IEEE.

Dahl, E. (1987b). Neural network algorithm for an NP-complete problem: Map and graph coloring, *Proceedings of the IEEE First International Conference on Neural Networks: Vol. III,* (pp. 113–120). San Diego: IEEE.

DARPA (1988). *DARPA Neural Network Study,* Washington: AFCEA Press.

Daunicht, W. (1988). Neural networks mediating linearizable dynamic redundant sensorimotor reflexes characterized by minimum of Hermetian norm, *Proceedings of the IEEE International Conference on Neural Networks: Vol. II,* (pp. 611–616). San Diego: IEEE.

Davis, G. and Ansari, A. (1987). Sensitivity analysis of Hopfield net, *Proceedings of the IEEE First International Conference on Neural Networks: Vol. III,* (pp. 325–328). San Diego: IEEE.

Dayhoff, R. & Dayhoff, J. (1988). Segmentation of true color microscopic images using a backpropagation neural network, *Neural Networks Supplement: INNS Abstracts, 1,* 169.

Denker, J., Ed. (1986a). *AIP Conference Proceedings 151: Neural Networks for Computing,* New York: American Institute of Physics.

Denker, J. (1986b). Neural network refinements and extensions, In J. Denker (Ed.), *AIP Conference Proceedings 151: Neural Networks for Computing,* (pp. 121–128). New York: American Institute of Physics.

Denker, J. (1987). The power of generalization in a back-propagation network: A case study, *Workshop on Neural Network Devices and Applications,* Jet Propulsion Laboratory, 202–213.

Derthick, M. (1984). Variations on the Boltzmann machine, Carnegie Mellon University, Department of Computer Science Technical Report, CMU-CS-84-120.

Derthick, M. & Tebelskis, J. (1988). "Ensemble" Boltzmann units have collective computational properties like those of Hopfield and Tank neurons, In D. Anderson (Ed.), *Proceedings of the 1987 IEEE Conference on Neural Information Processing Systems—Natural and Synthetic,* (pp. 223–232). New York: American Institute of Physics.

DeSieno, D. (1988). Adding a conscience to competitive learning, *Proceedings of the IEEE International Conference on Neural Networks: Vol. I,* (pp. 117–124). San Diego: IEEE.

Diaconis, P. & Efron, B. (1983, Mar.). Computer-intensive methods in statistics, *Scientific American,* 116–130.

Dietz, W., Kiech, E. & Ali, M. (1988). Pattern-based fault-diagnosis using neural networks, *First International Conference on Industrial and Engineering Applications of AI and Expert Systems,* June 1–3, University of Tennessee Space Institute, Chattanooga, TN, 13–23.

Dodd, N. (1987). Multi-layer perceptron inversion applied to image neighborhood operations, *Proceedings of the IEEE First International Conference on Neural Networks: Vol. IV,* (pp. 293–300). San Diego: IEEE.

Dreyfus, H. & Dreyfus, S. (1986, Jan.). Why computers may never think like people, *Technology Review,* 43–61.

Dreyfus, S. (1987). Neural nets: An alternative approach to AI, *Applied Artificial Intelligence Reporter, 4,* 9, 6.

Dunning, G., Marom, E., Owechko, Y. & Soffer, B. (1986). Optical holographic associative memory using a phase conjugate resonator, *Proceedings of the SPIE, 625,* 205–213.

Dunning, G., Marom, E., Owechko, Y. & Soffer, B. (1987). All-optical associative memory with shift-invariance and multiple-image recall, *Optics Letters, 12,* 346–348.

Durbin, R. & Willshaw, D. (1988). An analogue approach to the traveling salesman problem using an elastic net method, *Nature, 326,* 689–691.

Dutta, S. & Shekhan, S. (1988). Bond rating: A non-conservative application of neural networks, *Proceedings of the IEEE International Conference on Neural Networks: Vol. II,* (pp. 443–458). San Diego: IEEE.

Earle, G. & Szu, H. (1988). Resource optimization using a constraint optimizing adaptive neural network, *Neural Networks Supplement: INNS Abstracts, 1,* 435.

Eberlein, S. (1988). Decision making net for an autonomous roving vehicle, *Neural Networks Supplement: INNS Abstracts, 1,* 333.

Edson, B., Turner, C., Meyers, M., & Simpson, P. (1988). The adaptive network cognitive processor, *Proceedings of the 1988 Aerospace Applications of Artificial Intelligence (AAAIC 88),* Vol. II, Dayton SIGART, Dayton (pp. 119–133).

Egbert, D. & Rhodes, E. (1988). Preprocessing of biomedical images for neurocomputer analysis, *Proceedings of the IEEE International Conference on Neural Networks: Vol. I,* (pp. 561–568). San Diego: IEEE.

Eggers, M. (1988). The Boltzmann machine: A survey and generalization, MIT Lincoln Laboratory Technical Report 805.

Eich, J. (1982). A composite holographic associative recall model, *Psychological Review, 89,* 627–661.

Elman, J. & McClelland, J. (1984). The interactive activation model of speech perception, In N. Lass (Ed.), *Language and Speech,* (pp. 337–374). New York: Academic Press.

Elman, J. & McClelland, J. (1986). Exploiting the lawful variability in the speech wave, In J. Perkell & D. Klatt (Eds.), *Invariance and Variability of Speech Processes,* (pp. 360–380). Hillsdale, NJ: Lawrence Erlbaum Associates.

Elman, J. and Zipser, D. (1987). Learning the hidden structure of speech, University of California at San Diego, Department of Linguistics and Institute for Cognitive Science, ICS Report 8701.

Elman, J. (1988). Finding the structure in time, University of California at San Diego, Center for Research in Language, Technical Report 8801.

Elsley, R. (1988). A learning architecture for control based on backpropagation neural networks, *Proceedings of the IEEE International Conference on Neural Networks: Vol. II,* (pp. 587–594). San Diego: IEEE.

Fanty, M. (1986a). A connectionist simulator for the BBN butterfly multiprocessor, University of Rochester, Department of Computer Science Technical Report, TR 164.

Fanty, M. (1986b). Context-free parsing with connectionist networks, In J. Denker (Ed.), *AIP Conference Proceedings 151: Neural Networks for Computing,* (pp. 140–145). New York: American Institute of Physics.

Farhat, N. (1987a). Self-programming and learning in neural networks: Optoelectronic implementations, *Workshop on Neural Network Devices and Applications,* Jet Propulsion Laboratory, 170–197.

Farhat, N. (1987b). Optoelectronic analogs of self-programming neural nets: architectures and methodologies for implementing fast stochastic learning by simulated annealing, *Applied Optics, 26,* 5093–5103.

Farhat, N., Miyahara, S. & Lee, K. (1986). Optical implementation of 2-D neural networks and their application in recognition of radar targets, In J. Denker (Ed.), *AIP Conference Proceedings 151: Neural Networks for Computing,* (pp. 146–152). New York: American Institute of Physics.

Farhat, N., Psaltis, D., Prata, A. & Paek, E. (1985). Optical implementation of the Hopfield model, *Applied Optics, 24,* 1469–1475.

Farhat, N. & Shae, Z., (1987). Architectures and methodologies for self-organization and stochastic learning in opto-electronic analogs of neural nets, *Proceedings of the IEEE First International Conference on Neural Networks: Vol. III,* (pp. 565–576). San Diego: IEEE.

Farhat, N. & Shae, Z. (1988). Bimodal stochastic optical learning machine, *Proceedings of the IEEE International Conference on Neural Networks: Vol. II,* (pp. 365–372). San Diego: IEEE.

Farley, B. & Clark, W. (1954). Simulation of a self-organizing system by a digital computer, *Transactions of the IRE Professional Group on Information Theory, PGIT-4,* 76–84.

Feldman, J. (1980). A distributed information processing model of visual memory, University of Rochester, Department of Computer Science Technical Report, TR-52.

Feldman, J. (1981a). Memory and change in connectionist networks, University of Rochester, Department of Computer Science Technical Report, TR-96.

Feldman, J. (1981b). A connectionist model of visual memory, In G. Hinton & J. Anderson (Eds.), *Parallel Models of Associative Memory,* (pp. 49–81). Hillsdale, NJ: Lawrence Erlbaum Associates.

Feldman, J. (1985, Apr.). Connections, *Byte,* 277–284.

Feldman, J. (1986). Neural representation of conceptual knowledge, University of Rochester Department of Computer Science Technical Report, TR-189.

Feldman, J. & Ballard, D. (1982). Connectionist models and their properties, *Cognitive Science, 6,* 205–254.

Feldman, J. & Shastri, L. (1986). Evidential inference in activation networks, In N. Sharkey (Ed.), *Advances in Cognitive Science,* New York: Ellis Horwood Publishing.

Ferrara, E. & Widrow, B. (1981). The time-sequenced adaptive filter, *IEEE Transactions on Circuits and Systems, CAS-28,* 519–523.

Field, W. & Navlakha, J. (1988). Choosing non-random input exemplars to form stable states in a transputer-based Hopfield neural network, Florida International University, School of Computer Science Technical Report.

Fiesler, E., Chandry, A. & Caulfield, H. (1988). Weight descretization in backward error propagation neural networks, *Neural Networks Supplement: INNS Abstracts, 1,* 380.

Fisher, A., Lippincott, W. & Lee, J. (1987). Optical implementations of associative networks with versatile adaptive learning capabilities, *Applied Optics, 26,* 5039–5055.

Fleisher, M. (1988). The Hopfield model with multi-level neurons, In D. Anderson (Ed.), *Proceedings of the 1987 IEEE Conference on Neural Information Processing Systems—Natural and Synthetic,* (pp. 278–289). New York: American Institute of Physics.

Fogelman Soulie, F., Gallinari, P., Le Cunn, Y. & Thiria, S. (1987). Evaluation of network architectures on test learning tasks, *Proceedings of the IEEE First International Conference on Neural Networks: Vol. II,* (pp. 653–660). San Diego: IEEE.

Fogler, R., Williams, R. & Hostetler, L. (1988). A billion connection per second feedforward pipeline for computer vision applications, *Neural Networks Supplement: INNS Abstracts, 1,* 436.

Fong, Y-S. & Jensen, J. (1988). A study of the simultaneous delta rule, *Neural Networks Supplement: INNS Abstracts, 1,* 173.

Foo, Y-P. & Takefuji, T. (1988). Stochastic neural networks for solving job-shop scheduling: Parts I & II, *Proceedings of the IEEE International Conference on Neural Networks: Vol. II,* (pp. 275–291). San Diego: IEEE.

Fort, J. (1988). Solving a combinatorial problem via self-organizing process: An application of the Kohonen algorithm to the traveling salesman problem, *Biological Cybernetics, 59,* 33–40.

Fukushima, K. (1969). Visual feature extraction by a multi-layer network of analog threshold elements, *IEEE Transactions on Systems Science and Cybernetics, SSC-5,* 322–333.

Fukushima, K. (1970). An electronic model of the retina, *Proceedings of the IEEE, 58,* 1950–1951.

Fukushima, K. (1973). A model of associative memory in the brain, *Kybernetik, 12,* 58–63.

Fukushima, K. (1975). Cognitron: A self-organizing multi-layered neural network, *Biological Cybernetics, 20,* 121–136.

Fukushima, K. (1978). Self-organizing neural network with a function of associative memory: Feedback-type cognitron, *Biological Cybernetics, 28,* 201–208.

Fukushima, K. (1979). Self-organization of a neural network which gives position-invariant response,

*Proceedings of the Sixth International Joint Conference on Artificial Intelligence,* (pp. 291–293). Hillsdale, NJ: Lawrence Erlbaum Associates.

Fukushima, K. (1980). Neocognitron: A self-organizing neural network for a mechanism of pattern recognition unaffected by a shift in position, *Biological Cybernetics, 36,* 193–202.

Fukushima, K. (1984). A hierarchical neural network model for associative memory, *Biological Cybernetics, 50,* 105–113.

Fukushima, K. (1986). A neural network model for selective attention in visual pattern recognition, *Biological Cybernetics, 55,* 5–15.

Fukushima, K. (1987). A neural network for selective attention in visual pattern recognition and associative recall, *Applied Optics, 26,* 4985–4992.

Fukushima, K. & Miyake, S. (1982). Neocognitron: A new algorithm for pattern recognition tolerant of deformations and shifts in position, *Pattern Recognition, 15,* 455–469.

Fukushima, K., Miyake, S. & Takayuki, T. (1983). Neocognitron: A neural network model for a mechanism of visual pattern recognition, *IEEE Transactions on Systems, Man, and Cybernetics, SMC-13,* 826–834.

Furman, B., Liang, J. & Szu, H. (1988). Constraint optimization neural network for adaptive early vision, *Neural Networks Supplement: INNS Abstracts, 1,* 94.

Furman, B., White, J. & Abidi, A. (1988). CMOS analog implementation of the backpropagation algorithm, *Neural Networks Supplement: INNS Abstracts, 1,* 381.

Gallagher, N. & Coyle, E. (1987). Stack filters, threshold decomposition, and neural networks, *Asilomar Conference on Signals, Systems and Computing,* Monterey, CA.

Gallant, A. & White, H. (1988). There exists a neural network that does not make unavoidable mistakes, *Proceedings of the IEEE International Conference on Neural Networks: Vol. I,* (pp. 657–664). San Diego: IEEE.

Gallant, S. (1987a). Sequential associative memories, Northeastern University College of Computer Science Technical Report, NU-CCS-87-20.

Gallant, S. (1987b). Automated generation of connectionist expert systems for problems involving noise and redundancy, *AAAI Workshop on Uncertainty,* Seattle.

Gallant, S. & Balachandra, R. (1986). Using automated techniques to generate an expert system for R&D project monitoring, *Proceedings of the 1st International Symposium on Economics and Artificial Intelligence,* France.

Gallinari, P., Thiria, S. & Fogelman Soulie, F. (1988). Multilayer perceptrons and data analysis, *Proceedings of the IEEE International Conference on Neural Networks: Vol. I,* (pp. 391–399). San Diego: IEEE.

Gardner, E., Stroud, N. & Wallace, D. (1988). Training with noise: An application to word and text storage, In R. Eckmiller & C. v. d. Malsburg (Eds.), *NATO ISI Series, Vol. F41: Neural Computers,* (pp. 251–260). Berlin: Springer-Verlag.

Gardner, S. (1986). Application of neural network algorithms and architectures to correlation/tracking and identification, In J. Denker (Ed.), *AIP Conference Proceedings 151: Neural Networks for Computing,* (pp. 153–157). New York: American Institute of Physics.

Gawronski, R. (1971). *Bionics: The nervous system as a control system,* Amsterdam: Elsevier.

Gelbard, P. & Lawton, D. (1988). Perceptual grouping network architecture, *Neural Networks Supplement: INNS Abstracts, 1,* 495.

Geman, S. & Geman, D. (1984). Stochastic relaxation, Gibbs distributions, and the Bayesian restoration of images, *IEEE Transactions on Pattern Analysis and Machine Intelligence, PAMI-6,* 721–741.

Getz, W. (1988). An associative memory network for identifying mingling odors, *Neural Networks Supplement: INNS Abstracts, 1,* 251.

Giles, C., Griffin, R. & Maxwell, T. (1988). Encoding geometric invariances in higher-order neural networks, In D. Anderson (Ed.), *Proceedings of the 1987 IEEE Conference on Neural Information Processing Systems—Natural and Synthetic,* (pp. 301–309). New York: American Institute of Physics.

Giles, C. & Maxwell, T. (1987). Learning, invariances, and generalization in high-order neural networks, *Applied Optics, 26,* 4972–4978.

Gilstrap, L. & Lee, R. (1960). Learning machines, Proceedings of the Bionics Symposium, WADD Technical Report 60-600, 437–450.

Gindi, G., Gmitro, A. & Parthasarathay, K. (1988). Hopfield model associative memory with nonzero-diagonal terms in memory matrix, *Applied Optics, 27,* 129–134.

Glover, D. (1988a). Automated process control based on an optical Fourier/electronic neurocomputer, *Neural Networks Supplement: INNS Abstracts, 1,* 498.

Glover, D. (1988b). An optical Fourier/electronic neurocomputer automated inspection system, *Proceedings of the IEEE International Conference on Neural Networks: Vol. I,* (pp. 569–576). San Diego: IEEE.

Gluck, M. & Bower, G. (1988). Evaluating an adaptive network model of human learning, *Journal of Memory and Language, 27,* 166–195.

Gluck, M., Parker, D. & Reifsnider, E. (1988). Some biological implications of the differential-Hebbian learning rule, *Psychobiology, 16,* 298–302.

Godbeer, G., Lipscomb, J. & Luby, M. (1988). On the computational complexity of finding stable state vectors in connectionist models (Hopfield nets), University of Toronto, Department of Computer Science Technical Report 208/88.

Goel, A., Ramanujam, J. & Sadayappan, P. (1988). Towards a 'neural' architecture for abductive reasoning, *Proceedings of the IEEE International Conference on Neural Networks: Vol. I,* (pp. 681–688). San Diego: IEEE.

Gold, B. (1986). Hopfield model applied to vowel and consonant discrimination, In J. Denker (Ed.), *AIP Conference Proceedings 151: Neural Networks for Computing,* (pp. 158–164). New York: American Institute of Physics.

Golden, R. (1986a). The "brain-state-in-a-box" neural model is a gradient descent algorithm, *Journal of Mathematical Psychology, 30,* 73–80.

Golden, R. (1986b). A developmental model of visual word perception, *Cognitive Science, 10,* 241–276.

Goldstein, M., Toomarian, N. & Barhen, J. (1988). A comparison study of optimization methods for the bipartite matching problem (BMP), *Proceedings of the IEEE International Conference on Neural Networks: Vol. II,* (pp. 267–273). San Deigo: IEEE.

Goles, E., Griffin, R. & Maxwell, T. (1988). Encoding geometric invariances in higher-order neural networks, In D. Anderson (Ed.), *Proceedings of the 1987 IEEE Conference on Neural Information Processing Systems — Natural and Synthetic,* (pp. 301–309). New York: American Institute of Physics.

Goles, E. & Vichniac, G. (1986). Lyapunov function for parallel neural networks, In J. Denker (Ed.), *AIP Conference Proceedings 151: Neural Networks for Computing,* (pp. 165–181). New York: American Institute of Physics.

Goodwin, J., Rosen, B. & Vidal, J. (1988a). Exploration of learning in an associative magnetic processor, *Proceedings of the IEEE International Conference on Neural Networks: Vol. II,* (pp. 197–204). San Diego: IEEE.

Goodwin, J., Rosen, B. & Vidal, J. (1988b). Progress on the spin chip associative processor, *Neural Networks Supplement: INNS Abstracts, 1,* 382.

Gorman, P. & Sejnowski, T. (1988a). Analysis of hidden units in a layered network trained to classify sonar targets, *Neural Networks, 1,* 75–90.

Gorman, P. & Sejnowski, T. (1988b). Learned classification of sonar targets using a massively parallel network, *IEEE Transactions on Acoustics, Speech, and Signal Processing, 36,* 1135–1140.

Graf, H., Jackel, L., Howard, R., Straughn, B., Denker, J., Hubbard W., Tennant, D. & Schwartz, D. (1986). VLSI implementation of a neural network memory with several hundreds of neurons, In J. Denker (Ed.), *AIP Conference Proceedings 151: Neural Networks for Computing,* (pp. 182–187). New York: American Institute of Physics.

Grajski, K. (1988). Tactile information processing: A backpropagation model of pattern recognition in the human somatosensory systems, *Neural Networks Supplement: INNS Abstracts, 1,* 253.

Grant, P. & Sage, J. (1986). A comparison of neural network and matched filter processing for detecting lines in images, In J. Denker (Ed.), *AIP Conference Proceedings 151: Neural Networks for Computing,* (pp. 194–199). New York: American Institute of Physics.

Graupe, D. & Uth, J. (1988). Neural networks for adaptive internal correlations in associative memory, *Neural Networks Supplement: INNS Abstracts, 1,* 181.

Greenburg, H. (1988). Equilibria of the Brain-State-in-a-Box (BSB) neural network, *Neural Networks, 1,* 323–324.

Greville, T. (1960). Some applications of the pseudoinverse of a matrix, *SIAM Review, 2,* 15–22.

Grossberg, S. (1964). The theory of embedding fields with applications to psychology and neurophysiology, New York: Rockefeller Institute of Medical Research.

Grossberg, S. (1968a). A prediction theory for some nonlinear functional-differential equations: I. Learning of lists, *Journal of Mathematical Analysis and Applications, 21,* 643–694.

Grossberg, S. (1968b). A prediction theory for some nonlinear functional-differential equations: II. Learning of patterns, *Journal of Mathematical Analysis and Applications, 22,* 490–522.

Grossberg, S. (1968c). Some nonlinear networks capable of learning a spatial pattern of arbitrary complexity, *Proceedings of the National Academy of Sciences, 59,* 368–372.

Grossberg, S. (1969a). On learning, information, lateral inhibition, and transmitters, *Mathematical Biosciences, 4,* 255–310.

Grossberg, S. (1969b). On learning and energy-entropy dependence in recurrent and nonrecurrent signed networks, *Journal of Statistical Physics, 1,* 319–350.

Grossberg, S. (1969c). On the serial learning of lists, *Mathematical Biosciences, 4,* 201–253.

Grossberg, S. (1969d). Some networks that can learn, remember, and reproduce any number of space-time patterns I, *Journal of Mathematics and Mechanics, 19,* 53–91.

Grossberg, S. (1970a). Neural pattern discrimination, *Journal of Theoretical Biology, 27,* 291–337.

Grossberg, S. (1970b). Some networks that can learn, remember, and reproduce any number of space-time patterns II, *Studies in Applied Mathematics, 49,* 135–166.

Grossberg, S. (1972a). A neural theory of punishment and avoidance. II, Qualitative theory, *Mathematical Biosciences, 15,* 253–285.

Grossberg, S. (1972b). Neural expectation: Cerebellar and retinal analogues of cells fired by unlearnable and learnable pattern classes, *Kybernetik, 10,* 49–57.

Grossberg, S. (1973). Contour enhancement, short-term memory, and constancies in reverberating networks, *Studies in Applied Mathematics, 52,* 217–257.

Grossberg, S. (1976a). Adaptive pattern classification and universal recoding: I. Parallel development and coding of neural detectors, *Biological Cybernetics, 23,* 121–134.

Grossberg, S. (1976b). Adaptive pattern classification and universal recoding: II. Feedback, oscillation, olfaction, and illusions, *Biological Cybernetics, 23,* 187–207.

Grossberg, S. (1976c). On the development of feature detectors in the visual cortex with applications to learning and reaction-diffusion systems, *Biological Cybernetics, 21,* 145–159.

Grossberg, S. (1978a). Competition, decision, and consensus, *Journal of Analytic Applications, 66,* 470–493.

Grossberg, S. (1987b). Communication, memory, and development, In R. Rosen & F. Snell (Eds.), *Progress in Theoretical Biology: Vol. 5,* (pp. 183–232). New York: Academic Press.

Grossberg, S. (1980). How does the brain build a cognitive code?, *Psychological Review, 87,* 1–51.

Grossberg, S. (1982a). *Studies of Mind and Brain: Neural Principles of Learning, Perception, Cognition, and Motor Control,* Boston: Reidel Press.

Grossberg, S. (1982b). Processing of expected and unexpected events during conditioning and attention: A psychological theory, *Psychological Review, 89,* 529–572.

Grossberg, S. (1986a). Conditioning, expectancy, attention, and rhythm: The role of gated dipoles, In R. Campan & R. Zayan (Eds.), *Relevance of Models and Theories in Ethology,* (pp. 109–123). Boston: Private I.E.C.

Grossberg, S. (1986b). *The Adaptive Brain: Vols. I and II,* New York: Elsevier Science Publishers.

Grossberg, S. (1986c). The adaptive self-organization of serial order in behavior: Speech, language, and motor control, In E. Schwab & H. Nusbaum (Eds.), *Pattern Recognition by Humans and Machines,* (pp. 187–294). Boston: Academic Press.

Grossberg, S. (1987a). Competitive learning: From interactive activation to adaptive resonance, *Cognitive Science, 11,* 23–63.

Grossberg, S. (1987b). Cortical dynamics of three-dimensional form, color and brightness: Parts I and II, *Perception and Psychophysics, 41,* 87–158.

Grossberg, S. (1988a). Nonlinear neural networks: Principles, mechanisms, and architectures, *Neural Networks, 1,* 17–61.

Grossberg, S. (1988b). *Neural Networks and Natural Intelligence,* Cambridge: MIT Press.

Grossberg, S. & Gutowski, W. (1987). Neural dynamics of decision making under risk: Affective balance and cognitive-emotional interactions, *Psychological Reiew, 94,* 300.

Grossberg, S. & Kuperstein, M. (1986). *Neural Dynamics of Adapative Sensory-Motor Control: Ballistic Eye Movements,* Amsterdam: Elsevier/North-Holland.

Grossberg, S. & Kuperstein, M. (1989). *Neural Dynamics of Adaptive Sensory-Motor Control: Expanded Edition,* Elmsford, NY: Pergamon Press.

Grossberg, S. & Levine, D. (1975). Some developmental and attentional biases in the contrast enhancement and short term memory or recurrent neural networks, *Journal of Theoretical Biology, 53,* 341–380.

Grossberg, S. & Levine, D. (1987). Neural dynamics and attentionally modulated Pavlovian conditioning: Blocking, interstimulus interval, and secondary reinforcement, *Applied Optics, 26,* 5015–5030.

Grossberg, S. & Mingolla, E. (1985). Neural dynamics of perceptual grouping: Textures, boundaries, and emergent segmentations, *Perception and Psychophysics, 38,* 141–171.

Grossberg, S. & Mingolla, E. (1986a). Neural dynamics of surface perception: Boundary webs, illuminants, and shape-from-shading, *Computer Vision, Graphics, and Image Processing, 37,* 116–165.

Grossberg, S. & Mingolla, E. (1986b). The role of illusory contours in visual segmentation, In G. Meyer & S. Petry (Eds.), *Proceedings of the International Conference on Illusory Contours.* Elmsford, NY: Pergamon Press.

Grossberg, S. & Pepe, J. (1971). Spiking threshold and over-arousal effects in serial learning, *Journal of Statistical Physics, 3,* 95–125.

Grossberg, S. & Schmajuk, N. (1987). Neural dynamics and attentionally modulated Pavlovian conditioning: Conditioned reinforcement, inhibition, and opponent processing, *Psychobiology, 15,* 195.

Grossberg, S. & Stone, G. (1986a). Neural dynamics of attention switching and temporal-order information in short-term memory, *Memory and Cognition, 14,* 451–468.

Grossberg, S. & Stone, G. (1986b). Neural dynamics of word recognition and recall: Attentional priming, learning, and resonance, *Psychological Review, 93,* 46–74.

Guha, A. (1988). Using small multilayer networks to search real hyperspaces, *Neural Networks Supplement: INNS Abstracts, 1,* 442.

Guez, A. & Ahmad, Z. (1988). Solution to the inverse kinematics problem in robotics by neural networks, *Neural Networks Supplement: INNS Abstracts, 1,* 337.

Guez, A., Eilbert, J. & Kam, M. (1988, April). Neural network architecture for control, *IEEE Control Systems Magazine,* 22–25.

Guez, A., Protopopsecu, V. & Barhen, J. (1988). On the stability, storage capacity, and design of nonlinear continuous neural networks, *IEEE Transactions on Systems, Man, and Cybernetics, SMC-18,* 80–87.

Guez, A. & Selinsky, J. (1988). A trainable controller based on neural networks, *Neural Networks Supplement: INNS Abstracts, 1,* 336.

Gulati, S. & Iyengar, S. (1987). Nonlinear neural networks for deterministic scheduling, *Proceedings of the IEEE First International Conference on Neural Networks: Vol. IV,* (pp. 745–752). San Diego: IEEE.

Gutzmann, K. (1987). Combinatorial optimization using a continuous state Boltzmann machine, *Proceedings of the IEEE First International Conference on Neural Networks: Vol. III,* (pp. 721–734). San Diego: IEEE.

Guyon, I., Personnaz, L. & Dreyfus, G. (1988). Of points and loops, In R. Eckmiller & C. v. d. Malsburg (Eds.), *NATO ISI Series, Vol. F41: Neural Computers,* (pp. 261–269). Berlin: Springer-Verlag.

Guyon, I., Personnaz, L., Nadal, J. & Dreyfus, G. (1988). High order neural networks for efficient associative memory design, In D. Anderson (Ed.), *Proceedings of the 1987 IEEE Conference on Neural Information Processing Systems—Natural and Synthetic,* (pp. 233–241). New York: American Institute of Physics.

Haines, K. & Hecht-Nielsen, R. (1988). A BAM with increased information storage capacity, *Proceedings of the IEEE International Conference on Neural Networks: Vol. I,* (pp. 181–190). San Diego: IEEE.

Haltsonen, S., Jalanko, M., Bry, K. & Kohonen, T. (1978). Application of novelty filter to segmentation of speech, *Proceedings of the 1978 IEEE International Conference on Acoustics, Speech, and Signal Processing,* (pp. 565–568). New York: IEEE.

Hanson, S. (1987). Knowledge representation in connectionist networks, Bell Communications Research Technical Report.

Hanson, S. & Burr, D. (1988). Minkowski-r back-propagation: Learning in connectionist models with non-Euclidian error signals, In D. Anderson (Ed.), *Proceedings of the 1987 IEEE Conference on Neural Information Processing Systems—Natural and Synthetic,* (pp. 348–357). New York: American Institute of Physics.

Haring, D. (1966). Multithreshold threshold elements, *IEEE Transactions on Electronic Computers, EC-15,* 45–65.

Hassoun, M. & Spitzer, A. (1988). Neural network identification and extraction of repetitive superimposed pulses in noisy 1-D signals, *Neural Networks Supplement: INNS Abstracts, 1,* 443.

Hawkins, J. (1960). A magnetic integrator for the perceptron program, *IRE International Convention Record: Part 2*, (pp. 88–95). New York: IRE.

Hay, J., Martin, F. & Wightman, C. (1960). The mark I perceptron, design and performance, *IRE International Convention Record: Part 2*, (pp. 78–87). New York: IRE.

Hebb, D. (1949). *Organization of Behavior*, New York: John Wiley & Sons.

Hecht-Nielsen, R. (1981). Neural analog information processing, *Proceedings of the SPIE, 298*, 138–141.

Hecht-Nielsen, R. (1982). Neural analog processing, *Proceedings of the SPIE, 360*, 180–189.

Hecht-Nielsen, R. (1983). Book Review of Grossberg's "Studies of Mind and Brain," *Journal of Mathematical Psychology, 27*, 335–340.

Hecht-Nielsen, R. (1985). Artificial neural system design (course notes), University of California at San Diego.

Hecht-Nielsen, R. (1986a). Performance of Optical, Electro-Optical, and Electronic Neurocomputers, *Proceedings of the SPIE, 634*, 277–306.

Hecht-Nielsen, R. (1986b). Artificial neural system design (course notes), University of California at San Diego.

Hecht-Nielsen, R. (1987a). Artificial neural system design (course notes), University of California at San Diego.

Hecht-Nielsen, R. (1987b). Neural network nearest matched-filter classification of spatiotemporal patterns, *Applied Optics, 26*, 1892–1899.

Hecht-Nielsen, R. (1987c). Combinatorial hypercompression, *Proceedings of the IEEE First International Conference on Neural Networks: Vol. II*, (pp. 455–462). San Diego: IEEE.

Hecht-Nielsen, R. (1987d). Kolmogorov's mapping neural network existence theorem, *Proceedings of the IEEE First International Conference on Neural Networks: Vol. III*, (pp. 11–14). San Diego: IEEE.

Hecht-Nielsen, R. (1987e). Counterpropagation networks, *Proceedings of the IEEE First International Conference on Neural Networks: Vol. II*, (pp. 19–32). San Diego: IEEE.

Hecht-Nielsen, R. (1987f). Counterpropagation networks, *Applied Optics, 26*, 4979–4985.

Hecht-Nielsen, R. (1988a). Neurocomputer applications, In R. Eckmiller & C. v. d. Malsburg (Eds.), *NATO ISI Series, Vol. F41: Neural Computers*, (pp. 445–453). Berlin: Springer-Verlag.

Hecht-Nielsen, R. (1988b). Applications of counterpropagation networks, *Neural Networks, 1*, 131–140.

Hecht-Nielsen, R. (1988c). The theory of the backpropagation neural network, in review.

Hegde, S., Sweet, J. & Levy, W. (1988). Determination of parameters in a Hopfield/Tank computational network, *Proceedings of the IEEE International Conference on Neural Networks: Vol. II*, (pp. 291–298). San Diego: IEEE.

Herault, J. & Jutten, C. (1986). Space or time signal processing by neural network models, In J. Denker (Ed.), *AIP Conference Proceedings 151: Neural Networks for Computing*, (pp. 206–211). New York: American Institute of Physics.

Hertz, J., Grinstein, G. & Solla, S. (1986). Memory networks with asymmetric bonds, In J. Denker (Ed.), *AIP Conference Proceedings 151: Neural Networks for Computing*, (pp. 212–218). New York: American Institute of Physics.

Hestenes, D. (1986). How the brain works: The next great scientific revolution, In C. Smith (Ed.), *Maximum Entropy and Bayesian Spectral Analysis and Estimation Problems*, Boston: Reidel Press.

Heuter, G. (1988). Solution of the traveling salesman problem with an adaptive ring, *Proceedings of the IEEE International Conference on Neural Networks: Vol. I*, (pp. 85–92). San Diego: IEEE.

Hinton, G. (1981). A parallel computation that assigns canonical object-based frames of reference, *Proceedings of the 7th International Joint Conference on Artificial Intelligence: Vol. 2*, (pp. 683–685). Hillsdale, NJ: Lawrence Erlbaum Associates.

Hinton, G. (1986). Learning distributed representations of concepts, *Proceedings of the Eighth Annual Conference of the Cognitive Science Society*, (pp. 1–12). Hillsdale, NJ: Lawrence Erlbaum Associates.

Hinton, G., Ackley, D., & Sejnowski, T. (1984). Boltzmann machines: Constraint satisfaction networks that learn, Carnegie-Mellon University, Department of Computer Science Technical Report, CMU-CS-84-119.

Hinton, G. & Anderson, J., Eds., (1981). *Parallel Models of Associative Memory*, Hillsdale, NJ: Lawrence Erlbaum Associates.

Hinton, G. & McClelland, J. (1988). Learning representations by recirculating, In D. Anderson (Ed.), *Proceedings of the 1987 IEEE Conference on Neural Information Processing Systems—Natural and Synthetic*, (pp. 358–366). New York: American Institute of Physics.

Hirsch, M. (1982). Systems of differential equations that are competitive or cooperative, I: Limit sets, *SIAM Journal of Mathematical Analysis, 13*, 423–439.

Hirsch, M. (1985). On systems of differential equations that are competitive or cooperative, II: Convergence almost everywhere, *SIAM Journal of Mathematical Analysis, 16*, 423–439.

Hirsch, M. & Smale, S. (1974). *Differential Equations, Dynamical Systems, and Linear Algebra,* Orlando: Academic Press.

HNC (1987a). Advanced neurocomputer applications course, company literature.

HNC (1987b). Neurocomputing today . . . ANZA, product literature.

HNC (1988). HNC in process control, company literature.

Hodgkin, A. (1964). *The Conduction of the Nervous Impulse,* Liverpool: Liverpool University Press.

Hodgkin, A. & Huxley, A. (1952). A quantittive description of membrane current and its application to conduction and excitation in nerve, *Journal of Physiology, 117*, 500–544.

Homma, T., Atlas, L. & Marks, R. (1988). An artificial neural network for spatio-temporal bipolar patterns: Application to phoneme classification, In D. Anderson (Ed.), *Proceedings of the 1987 IEEE Conference on Neural Information Processing Systems—Natural and Synthetic,* (pp. 31–40). New York: American Institute of Physics.

Hopfield, J. (1982). Neural networks and physical systems with emergent collective computational abilities, *Proceedings of the National Academy of Sciences, 79*, 2554–2558.

Hopfield, J. (1984). Neurons with graded response have collective computational properties like those of two-state neurons, *Proceedings of the National Academy of Sciences, 81*, 3088–3092.

Hopfield, J. (1986a). Collective computation, content-addressable memory, and optimization problems, In Y. Abu-Mostafa (Ed.), *Complexity in Information Theory.* New York: Springer-Verlag.

Hopfield, J. (1986b). Collective computation with continuous variables, In E. Bienenstock (Ed.), *NATO ASI Series Vol. F20: Disordered Systems and Biological Organization,* (pp. 155 f). Berlin: Springer-Verlag.

Hopfield, J., Feinstein, D. & Palmer, R. (1983). "Unlearning" has a stabilizing effect in collective memories, *Nature, 304*, 158–159.

Hopfield, J. & Tank, D. (1985). "Neural" computation of decisions in optimization problems, *Biological Cybernetics, 52*, 141–152.

Hopfield, J. & Tank, D. (1986). Computing with neural circuits: A model, *Science, 233*, 625–633.

Horn, D. (1988). Shift-invariant multiconnected neural networks, Tel Aviv University, School of Physics and Astronomy Technical Report TAUP 1686–88.

Hornick, K., Stinchcombe, M. & White, H. (1988). Multilayer feedforward networks are universal approximators, University of California at San Diego, Department of Economics, Discussion Paper 88-45.

Hotense, W. (1988). Neural network techniques used to create an adaptive spatial input system for the motor-impaired, *Neural Networks Supplement: INNS Abstracts, 1*, 338.

Hsu, K., Brady, D. & Psaltis, D. (1988). Experimental demonstrations of optical neural computers, In D. Anderson (Ed.), *Proceedings of the 1987 IEEE Conference on Neural Information Processing Systems—Natural and Synthetic,* (pp. 377–386). New York: American Institute of Physics.

Huang, W. & Lippman, R. (1988). Neural networks and traditional classifiers, In D. Anderson (Ed.), *Proceedings of the 1987 IEEE Conference on Neural Information Processing Systems—Natural and Synthetic,* (pp. 387–396). New York: American Institute of Physics.

Hubbard, W., Schwartz, D., Denker, J., Graf, H., Howard, R., Jackel, L., Straughn, B. & Tennant, D. (1986). Electronic neural networks, In J. Denker (Ed.), *AIP Conference Proceedings 151: Neural Networks for Computing,* (pp. 227–234). New York: American Institute of Physics.

Hudak, M. (1988). Phonetic descrimination experiments with a spatiotemporal recognition network, *Neural Networks Supplement: INNS Abstracts, 1*, 298.

Hurlbert, A. (1988). Network for learning lightness algorithms, *Neural Networks Supplement: INNS Abstracts, 1*, 502.

Hush, D. & Salas, J. (1988). Improving the learning rate of back-propagation with the gradient reuse algorithm, *Proceedings of the IEEE International Conference on Neural Networks: Vol. I,* (pp. 441–447). San Diego: IEEE.

Irie, B. & Miyake, S. (1988). Capabilities of three-layered perceptrons, *Proceedings of the IEEE International Conference on Neural Networks: Vol. I,* (pp. 641–648). San Diego: IEEE.

Jablon, N. (1986). Steady state analysis of the generalized sidelobe canceller by adaptive noise cancelling techniques, *IEEE Transactions on Antennas and Propagation, AP-34*, 330–337.

Jacobs, R. (1988). Increased rates of convergence through learning rate adaptation, *Neural Networks, 1*, 295–307.

Jacyna, G. & Malaret, E. (1987). Classifiction performance of an auto-associative memory based on neural networks, *Proceedings of the IEEE First International Conference on Neural Networks: Vol. III*, (pp. 329–338). San Diego: IEEE.

Jalanko, M., Haltsonen, S., Bry, K. & Kohonen, T. (1978). Application of orthogonal projection principles to simultaneous phonemic segmentation and labeling of continuous speech, *Proceedings of the 4th International Joint Conference on Pattern Recognition*, (pp. 1006–1008), Kyoto, Japan.

Jang, J., Lee, S. & Shin, S. (1988). An optimization network for matrix inversion, In D. Anderson (Ed.), *Proceedings of the 1987 IEEE Conference on Neural Information Processing Systems— Natural and Synthetic*, (pp. 397–401). New York: American Institute of Physics.

Jeffrey, W. & Rosner, R. (1986). Neural network processing as a tool for function optimization, In J. Denker (Ed.), *AIP Conference Proceedings 151: Neural Networks for Computing*, (pp. 241–246). New York: American Institute of Physics.

Jenkins, B. & Wang, C. (1988). Model for an incoherent optical neuron that subtracts, *Optics Letters, 13*, 892–894.

Jogklekar, U. (1988). Learning to read aloud, *Neural Networks Supplement: INNS Abstracts, 1*, 301.

Johnson, J. (1988). Optical implementation of a shunting network, *Neural Networks Supplement: INNS Abstracts, 1*, 386.

Jong, J., Lee, S. & Shin, S. (1988). An optimization network for matrix inversion, In D. Anderson (Ed.), *Proceedings of the 1987 IEEE Conference on Neural Information Processing Systems— Natural and Synthetic*, (pp. 397–401). New York: American Institute of Physics.

Jordan, M. (1986a). Attractor dynamics and parallelism in a connectionist sequential machine, *Proceedings of the Eighth Annual Conference of the Cognitive Science Society*, (pp. 531–546). Hillsdale, NJ: Lawrence Erlbaum Associates.

Jordan, M. (1986b). Serial order: A parallel, distributed processing approach, University of California at San Diego, Institute for Cognitive Science Technical Report 8604.

Joseph, R. (1960a). On predicting perceptron performance, *IRE International Convention Record: Part 2*, (pp. 71–77). New York: IRE.

Joseph, R. (1960b). Contributions of perceptron theory, Cornell Aeronautical Laboratory Report, VG-1196-G-7.

Josin, G. (1977). Self-control in neural nets, *Biological Cybernetics, 27*, 185–187.

Josin, G. (1988). Neural-space generalization of a topological transformation, *Biological Cybernetics, 59*, 283–290.

Josin, G., Charney, D. & White, D. (1988). Robot control using neural networks, *Proceedings of the IEEE International Conference on Neural Networks: Vol. II*, (pp. 625–631). San Diego: IEEE.

Kadar, I. (1987). Robust tracking novelty filters based on linear models, *Proceedings of the IEEE First International Conference on Neural Networks: Vol. IV*, (pp. 611–618). San Diego: IEEE.

Kadar, I., Wagner, S., Wu, Y. & Hastings, H. (1988). An approach to restoration and recovery problems using parallel hierarchical neural networks, *Neural Networks Supplement: INNS Abstracts, 1*, 449.

Kam, M., Naim, A. & Alteson, K. (1988). The symmetric adaptive resonance theoretic model (SMART), *Neural Networks Supplement: INNS Abstracts, 1*, 103.

Kamgar-Parsi, B. & Kamgar-Parsi, B. (1988). Simultaneous fitting of several curves to point sets using neural networks, *Neural Networks Supplement: INNS Abstracts, 1*, 105.

Kammerer, B. & Kuppu, W. (1988). Experiments for isolated-word recognition with single- and multi-layer perceptrons, *Neural Networks Supplement: INNS Abstracts, 1*, 302.

Kandel, E. (1979). Small systems of neurons, *Scientific American, 241*, 3, 66–87.

Kandel, E. & Schwartz, J. (1985). *Principles of Neuroscience*, New York: Elsevier Publishing.

Kanerva, P. (1984). Self-propagating search: A unified theory of memory, Stanford Center for the Study of Language and Information, Technical Report CSLI-84-7.

Kanerva, P. (1986). Parallel structures in human and computer memory, In J. Denker (Ed.), *AIP Conference Proceedings 151: Neural Networks for Computing*, (pp. 247–258). New York: American Institute of Physics.

Kanerva, P. (1988a). Adjusting to variations in tempo in sequence recognition, *Neural Networks Supplement: INNS Abstracts, 1*, 106.

Kanerva, P. (1988b). *Sparse Distributed Memory*, Cambridge: MIT Press.

Kaplan, D. & Johnson, D. (1988). HNETTER: A heuristically driven neural reasoning system, *Proceedings of the IEEE International Conference on Neural Networks: Vol. II*, (pp. 507–514). San Diego: IEEE.

Karayiannis, N. & Venetsanopoulos, A. (1988). The correlation associative memory realizes Hebbian learning, *Neural Networks Supplement: INNS Abstracts, 1,* 187.

Karsai, G., Anderson, K., Ramaswamy, K. & Cook, G. (1988). Gas tungsten arc welding using a mapping network, *Neural Networks Supplement: INNS Abstracts, 1,* 341.

Katz, B. (1966). *Nerve, Muscle, and Synapse,* New York: McGraw-Hill.

Kawamoto, A. & Anderson, J. (1984). Lexical access using a neural network, *Proceedings of the Sixth Annual Conference of the Cognitive Science Society,* (pp. 204–213). Hillsdale, NJ: Lawrence Erlbaum Associates.

Kawamoto, A. & Anderson, J. (1985). A neural network model of multistable perception, *Acta Psychologica, 59,* 35–65.

Kazmierczak, H. & Steinbuch, K. (1963). Adaptive systems in pattern recognition, *IEEE Transactions on Electronic Computers, EC-12,* 822–835.

Keeler, J. (1986). Basins of attraction of neural network models, In J. Denker (Ed.), *AIP Conference Proceedings 151: Neural Networks for Computing,* (pp. 259–264). New York: American Institute of Physics.

Keeler, J. (1987). Comparison of information capacity of Hebbian neural network models, *Proceedings of the IEEE First International Conference on Neural Networks: Vol. III,* (pp. 253–260). San Diego: IEEE.

Keeler, J. (1988a). Capacity for patterns and sequences in Kanerva's SDM as compared to other associative memory models, In D. Anderson (Ed.), *Proceedings of the 1987 IEEE Conference on Neural Information Processing Systems—Natural and Synthetic,* (pp. 412–421). New York: American Institute of Physics.

Keeler, J. (1988b). Comparison between Kanerva's SDM and Hopfield-type neural network models, *Cognitive Science, 12,* 299–329.

Keller, J. & Hunt, D. (1985). Incorporating fuzzy membership functions into the perceptron algorithm, *IEEE Transactions on Pattern Analysis and Machine Intelligence, PAMI-7,* 693–699.

Kemlos, J. & Paturi, R. (1988). Convergence results in an associative memory model, *Neural Networks, 1,* 239–250.

Khotanzad, A. & Lu, J. (1988). Distortion invariant character recognition by a multi-layer perceptron and backpropagation learning, *Proceedings of the IEEE International Conference on Neural Networks: Vol. I,* (pp. 625–632). San Diego: IEEE.

Kienker, P., Sejnowski, T., Hinton, G. & Schumacher, L. (1986). Separating figure from ground with a parallel network, *Perception, 15,* 197–216.

Kinser, J., Caulfield, H., & Shamir, J. (1988a). All optical big BAM, *Proceedings of the SPIE, 881.*

Kinser, J., Caulfield, H., & Shamir, J. (1988b). Design for a massively parallel all-optical associative memory: The big BAM, *Applied Optics, 27,* 3442–3444.

Kirkpatrick, S., Gelatt, C. & Vecchi, M. (1983). Optimization by simulated annealing, *Science, 220,* 671–680.

Kishimoto, K. & Amari, S. (1979). Existence and stability of local excitations in homogeneous neural fields, *Journal of Mathematical Biology, 7,* 303–318.

Klassen, M., Pao, Y-H. & Chen, V. (1988). Characteristics of the functional link net: A higher order delta rule net, *Proceedings of the IEEE International Conference on Neural Networks: Vol. I,* (pp. 507–512). San Diego: IEEE.

Klopf, A. (1972). Brain function and adaptive systems: A heterostatic theory, Air Force Research Laboratories Research Report, AFCRL-72-0164.

Klopf, A. (1975). A comparison of natural and artificial intelligence, *ACM Special Interest Group on Artificial Intelligence (SIGART) Newsletter,* 52.

Klopf, A. (1979). Goal-seeking systems from goal-seeking components, *Cognition and Brain Theory Newsletter, 3,* 2.

Klopf, A. (1982). *The Hedonistic Neuron: A theory of memory, learning, and intelligence,* Washington: Hemisphere Publishing Corporation.

Klopf, A. (1986). Drive-reinforcement model of single neuron function: An alternative to the Hebbian neuronal model, In J. Denker (Ed.), *AIP Conference Proceedings 151: Neural Networks for Computing,* (pp. 265–270). New York: American Institute of Physics.

Klopf, A. (1987a). Drive-reinforcement learning: A real-time learning mechanism for unsupervised learning, *Proceedings of the IEEE First International Conference on Neural Networks: Vol. II,* (pp. 441–446). San Diego: IEEE.

Klopf, A. (1987b). A neuronal model of classical conditioning, AFWAL Technical Report, AFWAL-TR-97-1139.

Klopf, A. (1987c). Classical conditioning phenomena predicted by a drive-reinforcement model of neuronal function, In J. Byrne & W. Berry (Eds.), *Neural Models of Plasticity: Theoretical and Empirical Approaches,* New York: Academic Press.

Klopf, A. & Gose, E. (1969). An evolutionary pattern recognition network, *IEEE Transactions on Systems, Science, and Cybernetics, SSC-5,* 247–250.

Koch, C. (1987). Analog neuronal networks for real-time vision systems, *Workshop on Neural Network Devices and Applications,* Jet Propulsion Laboratory, 337–359.

Koch, C. (1988). Computing motion in the presence of discontinuities: Algorithm and analog networks, In R. Eckmiller & C. v. d. Malsburg (Eds.), *NATO ISI Series, Vol. F41: Neural Computers,* (pp. 101–110). Berlin: Springer-Verlag.

Koch, C., Luo, J., Mead, C. & Hutchinson, J. (1988). Computing motion using resistive networks, In D. Anderson (Ed.), *Proceedings of the 1987 IEEE Conference on Neural Information Processing Systems—Natural and Synthetic,* (pp. 422–431). New York: American Institute of Physics.

Koch, C., Marroquin, J. & Yuille, A. (1986). Analog "neuronal" networks in early vision, *Proceedings of the National Academy of Sciences, 83,* 4263–4267.

Kohonen, T. (1971a). A class of randomly organized associative memories, *Acta Polytechnic Scandanavica,* El 25.

Kohonen, T. (1971b). Introduction of the principle of virtual images in associative memories, *Acta Polytechnic Scandanavica,* El 29.

Kohonen, T. (1972a). Correlation matrix memories, Helsinki University of Technology Technical Report, TKK-F-A130.

Kohonen, T. (1972b). Correlation associactive memory, *IEEE Transactions on Computers, C-21,* 353–359.

Kohonen, T. (1973). A new model for randomly organized associative memory, *International Journal of Neuroscience, 5,* 27–29.

Kohonen, T. (1974). An adaptive associative memory principle, *IEEE Transactions on Computers, C-23,* 444–445.

Kohonen, T. (1977). *Associative Memory—A System Theoretical Approach,* New York: Springer-Verlag.

Kohonen, T. (1980). *Content-Addressable Memories,* Heidelberg: Springer-Verlag.

Kohonen, T. (1981). Automatic formation of topological maps in a self-organizing system, In E. Oja & O. Simula (Eds.), *Proceedings of the 2nd Scandinavian Conference on Image Analysis,* (pp. 214–220). Espoo: Suomen Hahmontunnistustutkimuksen Seuro.

Kohonen, T. (1982). A simple paradigm for the self-organized formation of structured feature maps, In M. Arbib & S. Amari (Eds.), *Lecture Notes in Biomathematics 45: Competition and Cooperation in Neural Nets,* (pp. 248–266). Berlin: Springer-Verlag.

Kohonen, T. (1984). *Self-Organization and Associative Memory,* Berlin: Springer-Verlag.

Kohonen, T. (1986a). Representation of sensory information in self-organizing feature maps, and relation of these maps to distributed memory networks, *Proceedings of the SPIE, 634,* 248–259.

Kohonen, T. (1986b). Learning vector quantization for pattern recognition, Helsinki University of Technology, Department of Technical Physics Technical Report, TKK-F-A601.

Kohonen, T. (1988a). Learning vector quantization, *Neural Networks Supplement: INNS Abstracts, 1,* 303.

Kohonen, T. (1988b, Mar.). The "neural" phonetic typewriter, *IEEE Computer Magazine,* 11–22.

Kohonen, T., Barnes, G. & Chrisley, R. (1988). Statistical pattern recognition with neural networks: Benchmarking, *Proceedings of the IEEE International Conference on Neural Networks: Vol. I,* (pp. 61–68). San Diego: IEEE.

Kohonen, T., Lehtio, P. & Oja, E. (1981). Storage and processing of information in distributed associative memory systems, In G. Hinton & J. Anderson (Eds.), *Parallel Models of Associative Memory,* (pp. 105–143), Hillsdale, NJ: Lawrence Erlbaum Associates.

Kohonen, T. & Makisara, K. (1986). Representation of sensory information in self-organizing feature maps, In J. Denker (Ed.), *AIP Conference Proceedings 151: Neural Networks for Computing,* (pp. 271–276). New York: American Institute of Physics.

Kohonen, T., Makisara, K. & Saramaki, T. (1984). Phonotopic maps—insightful representation of phonological features for speech recognition, *Proceedings of the 7th International Conference on Pattern Recognition,* (pp. 182–185), Montréal.

Kohonen, T. & Riittinen, H. (1977). A preprocessing transformation for the recognition of two-dimensional patterns shown in different perspectives, Helsinki University of Technology Technical Report, TKK-F-A320.

Kohonen, T., Riittinen, H., Reuhkala, E. & Haltsonen, S. (1984). On-line recognition of spoken words from a large vocabulary, *Information Sciences, 33,* 3–30.

Kohonen, T. & Ruohonen, M. (1973). Representation of associated data by matrix operators, *IEEE Transactions on Computer, C-22,* 701–702.

Koikalainen, P. & Oja, E. (1988). Specification and implementation environment for neural networks using communicating sequential processes, *Proceedings of the IEEE International Conference on Neural Networks: Vol. I,* (pp. 533–540). San Diego: IEEE.

Kollias, S. & Anastassiou, D. (1988a). Digital halftoning of images using feedforward neural networks, *Neural Networks Supplement: INNS Abstracts, 1,* 507.

Kollias, S. & Anastassiou, D. (1988b). Adaptive training of multi-layer neural networks using a least squares estimation technique, *Proceedings of the IEEE International Conference on Neural Networks: Vol. I,* (pp. 383–390). San Diego: IEEE.

Kolodzy, P. & Menon, M. (1988). Simulation and implementation considerations with classification networks, *Neural Networks Supplement: INNS Abstracts, 1,* 545.

Kong, S-G. & Kosko, B. (1989). Adaptive BAM with competition layer, University of Southern California, SIPI Technical Report, in review.

Kosko, B. (1985). Adaptive inference, Verac, Inc. Technical Report.

Kosko, B. (1986a). Fuzzy entropy and conditioning, *Information Sciences, 40,* 165–174.

Kosko, B. (1986b). Fuzzy knowledge combination, *International Journal for Intelligent Systems, 1,* 293–320.

Kosko, B. (1986c). Fuzzy cognitive maps, *International Journal of Man-Machine Studies, 24,* 65–75.

Kosko, B. (1986d). Differential Hebbian learning, In J. Denker (Ed.), *AIP Conference Proceedings 151: Neural Networks for Computing,* (pp. 277–282). New York: American Institute of Physics.

Kosko, B. (1987a). Fuzzy associative memories, In A. Kandel (Ed.), *Fuzzy Expert Systems,* Reading, MA: Addison-Wesley.

Kosko, B. (1987b). Adaptive inference in fuzzy knowledge networks, *Proceedings of the IEEE First International Conference on Neural Networks: Vol. II,* (pp. 261–268). San Diego: IEEE.

Kosko, B. (1987c). Adaptive bidirectional associative memories, *Applied Optics, 26,* 4947–4960.

Kosko, B. (1987d). Competitive adaptive bidirectional associative memories, *Proceedings of the IEEE First International Conference on Neural Networks: Vol. II,* (pp. 759–766). San Diego: IEEE.

Kosko, B. (1987e). Sampling adaptive bidirectional associative memories, *Proceedings of the 21st Annual Asilomar Conference on Signals, Systems, and Computers,* Monterey, CA.

Kosko, B. (1988a). Hidden patterns in combined and adaptive knowledge networks, *International Journal of Approximate Reasoning, 2,* 377–393.

Kosko, B. (1988b). Bidirectional associative memories, *IEEE Transactions on Systems, Man, and Cybernetics, SMC-18,* 42–60.

Kosko, B. (1988c). Feedback stability and unsupervised learning, *Proceedings of the IEEE International Conference on Neural Networks: Vol. I,* (pp. 141–152). San Diego: IEEE.

Kosko, B. & Guest, C. (1987). Optical bidirectional associative memories, *Proceedings of the SPIE, 758.*

Kosko, B. & Limm, J. (1985). Vision as causal activation and association, *Proceedings of the SPIE, 579,* 104–109.

Kuczewski, R. (1987). Neural network approaches to multi-target tracking, *Proceedings of the IEEE First International Conference on Neural Networks: Vol. IV,* (pp. 619–634). San Diego: IEEE.

Kuczewski, R., Myers, M. & Crawford, W. (1987). Exploration of backward error propagation as a self-organized structure, *Proceedings of the IEEE First International Conference on Neural Networks: Vol. II,* (pp. 89–96). San Diego: IEEE.

Kuh, A. (1988). Analysis of feedforward networks that dynamically learn, *Neural Networks Supplement: INNS Abstracts, 1,* 191.

Kukich, K. (1988). Backpropagation topologies for sequence generation, *Proceedings of the IEEE International Conference on Neural Networks: Vol. I,* (pp. 310–308). San Diego: IEEE.

Kung, S. & Huang, J. (1988a). Parallel architectures for artificial neural nets, *Proceedings of the IEEE International Conference on Neural Networks: Vol. II,* (pp. 165–172). San Diego: IEEE.

Kung, S. & Huang, J. (1988b). An algebraic projection analysis for backpropagation learning, *Neural Networks Supplement: INNS Abstracts, 1,* 547.

Kwasny, S. (1988). A PDP approach to deterministic natural language parsing, *Neural Networks Supplement: INNS Abstracts, 1,* 305.

Landauer, T., Kamm, C. & Singhal, S. (1987). Teaching a minimally structured backpropagation network to recognize speech sounds, *Proceedings of the Ninth Annual Conference of the Cognitive Science Society,* (pp. 531–536). Hillsdale, NJ: Lawrence Erlbaum Associates.

Lapedes, A. & Farber, R. (1986a). A self-optimizing, nonsymmetrical neural net for content address-able memory and pattern recognition, *Physica, 22D,* 247–259.

Lapedes, A. & Farber, R. (1986b). Programming a massively parallel, computation universal system: Static behavior, In J. Denker (Ed.), *AIP Conference Proceedings 151: Neural Networks for Computing,* (pp. 283–298). New York: American Institute of Physics.

Lapedes, A. & Farber, R. (1988a). How neural nets work, In D. Anderson (Ed.), *Proceedings of the 1987 IEEE Conference on Neural Information Processing Systems—Natural and Synthetic,* (pp. 442–456). New York: American Institute of Physics.

Lapedes, A. & Farber, R. (1988b). Nonlinear signal processing using neural networks: Prediction and modeling, *Proceedings of the IEEE,* in review.

Le Cunn, Y. (1987). Models connexiannistes de l'apprentissage, Ph.D. Thesis, Universitat P. et M. Curie, Paris 6, Paris.

Le Cunn, Y. (1988). Using curvature information to improve backpropagation, *Neural Networks Supplement: INNS Abstracts, 1,* 168.

Lee, B. & Sheu, B. (1988). An investigation on local minima of Hopfield networks for optimization circuits, *Proceedings of the IEEE International Conference on Neural Networks: Vol. I,* (pp. 45–51). San Diego: IEEE.

Lee, J., Nguyen, D. & Lin, C. (1988). Adaptive object tracking integrating neural networks and intelligent processing, *Neural Networks Supplement: INNS Abstracts, 1,* 509.

Lee, W. (1988). Simulated annealing applied to shipbuilding design, *Neural Networks Supplement: INNS Abstracts, 1,* 453.

Lee, Y., Doolen, G., Chen, H., Sun, G., Maxwell, T., Lee, H. & Giles, C. (1986). Machine learning using a higher order correlation network, *Physica, 22D,* 276–306.

Lehar, S. (1988a). Application of back propagation to long wave infra-red signature analysis, *Neural Networks Supplement: INNS Abstracts, 1,* 454.

Lehar, S. (1988b). Analysis of backpropagation dynamics using a graphical network representation scheme, *Neural Networks Supplement: INNS Abstracts, 1,* 549.

Lehman, A. v., Park, E., Liao, P., Marrakchi, A. & Patel, J. (1988). Factors influencing learning in backpropagation, *Proceedings of the IEEE International Conference on Neural Networks: Vol. I,* (pp. 335–341). San Diego: IEEE.

Lemmon, M. & Kumar, B. (1988). Input output characteristics for a class of laterally inhibited graded neural networks, *Neural Networks Supplement: INNS Abstracts, 1,* 107.

Lendaris, G. (1988). A neural-network approach to implementing conceptual graphs, In S. Foo & J. Sowa (Eds.), *Conceptual Graphs for Knowledge Systems,* in review.

Leung, C. (1988). Structural matching using neural networks, *Neural Networks Supplement: INNS Abstracts, 1,* 31.

Leven, S. (1988). SAM: A triune extension to the ART model, *Third Annual Symposium on Networks in Brain and Computer Architectures,* 1988.

Leven, S. & Yoon, Y. (1988). Dynamic schemas, expert systems, and ART, *Neural Networks Supplement: INNS Abstracts, 1,* 455.

Levine, D. (1983). Neural population modeling and psychology: A review, *Mathematical Biosciences, 66,* 1–86.

Levine, R. (1988). Neural network performance on the stochastic exclusive-or problem, MIT Lincoln Lab Technical Report 808.

Levy, J. & Stenning, K. (1988). A PDP implementation of a psychological model of memory, *Neural Networks Supplement: INNS Abstracts, 1,* 195.

Levy, W. (1982, Aug.). Associative encoding at the synapses, Proceedings of the Fourth Annual Conference of the Cognitive Science Society, Ann Arbor, MI.

Lewis, J. (1988). Creation by refinement: A creativity paradigm for gradient descent learning networks, *Proceedings of the IEEE International Conference on Neural Networks: Vol. II,* (pp. 229–233). San Diego: IEEE.

Lin, J-K., Mei, G-G., Lin, W. & Chen, S-S. (1988). Hierarchical neural network architectures for vision systems, *Neural Networks Supplement: INNS Abstracts, 1,* 511.

Lindsay, P. & Norman, D. (1977). *Human Information Processing: An Introduction to Psychology,* Orlando: Academic Press.

Lippmann, R. (1987). An introduction to computing with neural nets, *IEEE ASSP Magazine, 4,* 4–22.

Lippmann, R. (1988). Neural network classifiers for speech recognition, *The Lincoln Laboratory Journal, 1,* 107–124.

Lippmann, R. & Gold, B. (1987). Neural net classifiers useful for speech recognition, *Proceedings of the IEEE First International Conference on Neural Networks: Vol. IV,* (pp. 417–426). San Diego: IEEE.

Lippmann, R., Gold, R. & Malpass, M. (1986). A comparison of Hamming and Hopfield neural nets for pattern classification, Massachusetts Institute of Technology Lincoln Laboratory Technical Report, TR-769.

Little, M. & Bak, C. (1988). Enhanced memory capacity of a Hopfield neural network, *Proceedings of the SPIE, 698,* 150–156.

Little, W. (1974). The existence of persistent states in the brain, *Mathematical Biosciences, 19,* 101–120.

Little, W. & Shaw, G. (1975). A statistical theory of short and long term memory, *Behavioral Biology, 14,* 115–133.

Little, W. & Shaw, G. (1978). Analytical study of the memory storage capacity of a neural network, *Mathematical Biosciences, 39,* 281–290.

Liu, H., Iberall, T. & Bekey, G. (1988). Building a generic architecture for robot hand control, *Proceedings of the IEEE International Conference on Neural Networks: Vol. II,* (pp. 567–574). San Diego: IEEE.

Longstaff, I. & Cross, J. (1987). A pattern recognition approach to understanding the multilayer perceptron, *Pattern Recognition Letters, 5,* 315–319.

Longuet-Higgins, H. (1968). Holographic model of temporal recall, *Nature,* 217, 104.

Loos, H. (1988). Reflexive associative memories, In D. Anderson (Ed.), *Proceedings of the 1987 IEEE Conference on Neural Information Processing Systems—Natural and Synthetic,* (pp. 495–504). New York: American Institute of Physics.

Lopez, L. (1988). Feedforward shunting: The role of 3rd order correlations in neural synchroneity, *Neural Networks Supplement: INNS Abstracts, 1,* 512.

Lui, H. (1988). Perceptron learning on Hopfield nets, *Neural Networks Supplement: INNS Abstracts, 1,* 198.

Luse, S. (1987). Neural networks for speech applications, *Speech Technology, 4,* 1, 68–72.

Luse, S., Martin, D., Nunn, S. & Waters, J. (1988). Exploring the backpropagation network for speech applications, Naval Ocean Systems Center Technical Document, in review.

Lutterell, S. (1985). The implication of Boltzmann-type machines for SAR data processing: A preliminary survey, Royal Signals and Radar Establishment, Technical Report 3815.

Lutterell, S. (1988a). The use of Bayesian and entropic methods in neural network theory, *Proceedings of the MAXENT Conference,* Cambridge.

Lutterell, S. (1988b). Cluster decomposition of probability density functions, *Neural Networks Supplement: INNS Abstracts, 1,* 109.

Lutterell, S. (1988c). Image compression using a multilayer neural network, *Pattern Recognition Letters,* in review.

Macukow, B. & Arsenault, H. (1987). Optical associative memory model based on neural networks having variable interconnection weights, *Applied Optics, 26,* 924–928.

Madey, G. & Denton, J. (1988). Credit evaluation with missing data fields, *Neural Networks Supplement: INNS Abstracts, 1,* 456.

Malsburg, C. (1973). Self-organization of orientation sensitive cells in the striate cortex, *Kybernetik, 14,* 85–100.

Mann, J., Lippman, R., Berger, B. & Raffel, J. (1988). A self-organizing neural net chip, *IEEE 1988 Custom Integrated Circuits Conference,* 10.3.1–10.3.5.

Marcus, C. & Westervelt, R. (1988a). Basins of attraction for electronic neural nets, In D. Anderson (Ed.), *Proceedings of the 1987 IEEE Conference on Neural Information Processing Systems—Natural and Synthetic,* (pp. 524–533). New York: American Institute of Physics.

Marcus, C. & Westervelt, R. (1988b). Stability of neural networks with time delay, *Neural Networks Supplement: INNS Abstracts, 1,* 111.

Marcus, C. & Westervelt, R. (1988c). Stability of analog neural networks with time delay, *Physical Review A,* in press.

Marcus, R. (1987). A connectionist algorithm for minimum cost network flows, *Proceedings of the IEEE First International Conference on Neural Networks: Vol. III,* (pp. 735–739). San Diego: IEEE.

Marrian, C. & Peckerar, M. (1987). Electronic "neural" net algorithm for maximum entropy decon-volution, *Proceedings of the IEEE First International Conference on Neural Networks: Vol. III,* (pp. 749–757). San Diego: IEEE.

Matsuo, K. (1987). Self-organizations of cooperative and competitive networks in ecological para-digms, *Proceedings of the IEEE First International Conference on Neural Networks: Vol. III,* (pp. 277–280). San Diego: IEEE.

Maxwell, T., Giles, C. & Lee, Y. (1986). Nonlinear dynamics of artificial neural systems, In J. Denker (Ed.), *AIP Conference Proceedings 151: Neural Networks for Computing,* (pp. 299–304). New York: American Institute of Physics.

Maxwell, T., Giles, C. & Lee, Y. (1987). Generalization in neural networks: The contiguity problem, *Proceedings of the IEEE First International Conference on Neural Networks: Vol. II,* (pp. 41–46). San Diego: IEEE.

Maxwell, T., Giles, C., Lee, Y. & Chen, H. (1986). Transformation invariances using higher-order correlations in neural network architectures, *Proceedings of the IEEE International Conference on Systems, Man, and Cybernetics,* 627–632. Atlanta: IEEE.

Mazaika, P. (1987). A mathematical model of the Boltzmann machine, *Proceedings of the IEEE First International Conference on Neural Networks: Vol. III,* (pp. 157–164). San Diego: IEEE.

McAulay, A. (1988). Adaptive 2-D tracking with neural networks, *Neural Networks Supplement: INNS Abstracts, 1,* 457.

McClelland, J. (1979). On the time-relationships of mental processes: An examination of systems of processes in cascade, *Psychological Review, 86,* 287–330.

McClelland, J. & Elman, J. (1986). The TRACE model of speech perception, *Cognitive Psychology, 18,* 1–86.

McClelland, J. & Rumelhart, D. (1981). An interactive activation model of context effects in letter perception: Part 1. An account of basic findings, *Psychological Review, 88,* 375–407.

McCulloch, W. (1965). *Embodiments of Mind,* Cambridge: MIT Press.

McCulloch, W. & Pitts, W. (1943). A logical calculus of the ideas immanent in nervous activity, *Bulletin of Mathematical Biophysics, 7,* 115–133.

McDuff, R. & Simpson, P. (1989). An adaptive resonating diagnostics system, *AUTOTESTCON '89,* in review.

McEliece, R., Posner, E., Rodemich, E. & Venkatesh, S. (1987). The capacity of the Hopfield as-sociative memory, *IEEE Transactions on Information Theory, IT-33,* 461–482.

McInerny, J., Haines, K., Biafore, S. & Hecht-Nielsen, R. (1989). Can error surfaces traversed by backpropagation have local error minima?, *Proceedings of the IEEE/INNS International Joint Con-ference on Neural Networks,* in review.

Mead, C. (1985, Mar.). A sensitive electronic photoreceptor, *1985 Chapel Hill Conference on Very Large Scale Integration,* (pp. 463–471).

Mead, C. (1989). *Analog VLSI and Neural Systems,* Reading, MA: Addison-Wesley.

Mead, C. & Conway, L. (1980). *Introduction to VLSI Systems,* Reading, MA: Addison-Wesley.

Mead, C. & Mahowald, M. (1988). A silicon model of early visual processing, *Neural Networks, 1,* 91–97.

Means, R. & Caid, B. (1988). A backpropagation network error correcting decoder for convolution and block codes, *Neural Networks Supplement: INNS Abstracts, 1,* 461.

Mei, G. & Liu, W. (1988). Design graph search problems with learning: A neural network approach, *Neural Networks Supplement: INNS Abstracts, 1,* 200.

Menon, M. & Kolodzy, P. (1988). A comparative study of neural network classifiers, *Neural Networks Supplement: INNS Abstracts, 1,* 114.

Mentazemi, A. & Conrath, D. (1986, Mar.). The use of cognitive mapping for information requirement analysis, *Management Information Systems Quarterly.*

Michael, A., Farrell, J. & Porod, W. (1988). Stability results for neural networks, In D. Anderson (Ed.), *Proceedings of the 1987 IEEE Conference on Neural Information Processing Systems—Natural and Synthetic,* (pp. 554–563). New York: American Institute of Physics.

Midorikawa, H. (1988). The face pattern identification by backpropagation learning procedure, *Neural Networks Supplement: INNS Abstracts, 1,* 515.

Miikkulainen, R. & Dyer, M. (1987). Building distributed representations without microfeatures, Uni-versity of California at Los Angeles, Department of Computer Science Technical Report, UCLA-AI-87-17.

Miller, R. (1987). *Neural Networks,* Atlanta: SEAI Technical Publications.

Minsky, M. (1954). Neural-analog networks and the brain model problem, Princeton University, Ph.D. Thesis.

Minsky, M. (1961). Steps toward artificial intelligence, *Proceedings of the IRE, 49*, 5–30.

Minsky, M. & Papert, S. (1969). *Perceptrons*, Cambridge: MIT Press.

Minsky, M. & Selfridge, O. (1961). Learning in random nets, In C. Cherry (Ed.), *Information Theory: Fourth London Symposium*, London: Butterworths.

Miyata, Y. (1987). Organization of action sequences in a hierarchical sequential network, University of California at San Diego, Institute for Cognitive Science Report 8707.

Mjolsness, E. (1987). Control of attention in neural networks, *Proceedings of the IEEE International Conference on Neural Networks: Vol. II*, (pp. 567–574). San Diego: IEEE.

Mjolsness, E., Gindi, G. & Anandan, P. (1988). Optimization in model matching and perceptual organization: A first look, Yale University, Department of Computer Science Technical Report YALU/DSC/RR-634.

Montgomery, B. & Vijaya Kumar, B. (1986). Evaluation of the use of the Hopfield neural network model as a nearest-neighbor algorithm, *Applied Optics, 25*, 3759–3766.

Moody, J. (1987). Internal representations for associative memory, *Workshop on Neural Network Devices and Applications*, Jet Propulsion Laboratory, 214–223.

Moody, J. & Denker, J. (1988). Speedy alternatives to back propagation, *Neural Networks Supplement: INNS Abstracts, 1*, 202.

Moopen, A., Langenbacher, H., Thakoor, A. & Khanna, S. (1988). Programmable synaptic chip for electronic neural networks, In D. Anderson (Ed.), *Proceedings of the 1987 IEEE Conference on Neural Information Processing Systems — Natural and Synthetic*, (pp. 564–572). New York: American Institute of Physics.

Moopen, A., Thakoor, A. & Duong, T. (1988). A neural network for Euclidian distance minimization, *Proceedings of the IEEE International Conference on Neural Networks: Vol. II*, (pp. 349–356). San Diego: IEEE.

Moore, B. (1988). ART1 and pattern clustering algorithms, *Neural Networks Supplement: INNS Abstracts, 1*, 116.

Moore, B. & Poggio, T. (1988). Representation properties of multilayer feedfoward networks, *Neural Networks Supplement: INNS Abstracts, 1*, 203.

Morgan, J., Patterson, E., & Klopf, A. (1988). A network of two drive-reinforcement neurons that learns a solution to a real-time dynamic control problem, *Neural Networks Supplement: INNS Abstracts, 1*, 117.

Moya, M., Fogler, R. & Hostetler, L. (1988). Back-propagation for perspective-invariant pattern recognition in SAR imagery, *Neural Networks Supplement: INNS Abstracts, 1*, 204.

Munro, P. (1988). A dual back-propagation scheme for concept structures, *Proceedings of the Ninth Annual Conference of the Cognitive Science Society*, (pp. 165–176). Hillsdale, NJ: Lawrence Erlbaum Associates.

Murdock, B. (1982). A theory for the storage and retrieval of item and associative information, *Psychological Review, 89*, 609–626.

Musari, M., Rajavelu, A., Sahai, S. & Zhao, J. (1988). Analysis and generalization of back propagation in neural networks, *Neural Networks Supplement: INNS Abstracts, 1*, 118.

Myers, M. (1986). Some speculation on artificial neural system technology, *Proceedings of the National Aerospace and Electronics Conference — NAECON*, (pp. 1298–1302). Dayton, OH: IEEE.

Myers, M. (1987). Spatiotemporal image processing using neural networks, *Workshop on Neural Network Devices and Applications*, Jet Propulsion Laboratory, 366–376.

Myers, M., Turner, C., Kuczewski, R., & Simpson, P. (1988). ANCP Adaptive Network Cognitive Processor: Vols. I & II, TRW MEAD, Final Report prepared for Air Force Wright Aeronautical Laboratories.

Nabet, B. & Darling, R. (1988). Implementation of optical sensory neural networks by simple discrete and monolithic circuits, *Neural Networks Supplement: INNS Abstracts, 1*, 396.

Narendra, K. & Thathachar, M. (1974). Learning automata — a survey, *IEEE Transactions on Systems, Man, and Cybernetics, SMC-4*, 323–334.

Nasrabadi, N. & Feng, Y. (1988a). Vector quantization of images based upon the Kohonen self-organizing feature map, *Proceedings of the IEEE International Conference on Neural Networks: Vol. I*, (pp. 101–105). San Diego: IEEE.

Nasrabadi, N. & Feng, Y. (1988b). Vector quantization based upon the Kohonen self-organization feature maps, *Neural Networks Supplement: INNS Abstracts, 1*, 518.

Naylor, J. & Li, K. (1988a). Analysis of a neural network algorithm for vector quantization of speech parameters, *Neural Networks Supplement: INNS Abstracts, 1,* 310.

Naylor, J. & Li, K. (1988b). Speaker recognition using Kohonen's self-organizing feature map algorithm, *Neural Networks Supplement: INNS Abstracts, 1,* 311.

Nestor, Inc. (1987a). Nestor and the Nestor system (company literature).

Nestor, Inc. (1987b). Learning systems based upon multiple neural networks (company literature).

Nestor, Inc. (1988). The Nestor Development System (company literature).

Neuman, J. v. (1958). *The Computer and the Brain,* New York: W. W. Norton & Co.

Newman, C. (1988). Memory capacity in neural network models: Rigorous lower bounds, *Neural Networks, 1,* 223–238.

Nguyen, D. & Lee, J. (1988). A new LMS-based algorithm for rapid adaptive classification in dynamic environments: Theory and preliminary results, *Proceedings of the IEEE International Conference on Neural Networks: Vol. I,* (pp. 455–463). San Diego: IEEE.

Nilsson, N. (1965). *Learning Machines,* New York: McGraw-Hill.

Noetzel, A. & Grazinni, M. (1988). Global combinatorial optimization by neural networks, *Neural Networks Supplement: INNS Abstracts, 1,* 119.

O'Callaghan, M. & Anderson, D. (1988). Optical implementations of neural network interconnects and learning, *Neural Networks Supplement: INNS Abstracts, 1,* 397.

Oja, E. & Kohonen, T. (1988). The subspace learning algorithm as a formalization for pattern recognition and neural networks, *Proceedings of the IEEE International Conference on Neural Networks: Vol. I,* (pp. 277–284). San Diego: IEEE.

Olafson, S. & Abu-Mostafa, Y. (1988). The capacity of multilevel threshold functions, *IEEE Transactions on Pattern Analysis and Machine Intelligence, PAMI-10,* 277–281.

Omidvar, M. (1987). Analysis of neuronal plasticity, Ph.D. Dissertation, School of Electrical Engineering, University of Oklahoma.

Owechko, Y. (1987). Optoelectronic resonator neural networks, *Applied Optics, 26,* 5104–5111.

Owechko, Y., Soffer, B. & Dunning, G. (1988). Optoelectronic neural networks based on holographically interconnected image processors, *Proceedings of the SPIE, 882,* 143–153.

Palm, G. (1980). On associative memory, *Biological Cybernetics, 36,* 19–31.

Papert, S. (1961). Some mathematical models of learning, In C. Cherry (Ed.), *Proceedings of the Fourth London Symposium of Information Theory,* New York: Academic Press.

Papoulis, A. (1965). *Probability, Random Variables, and Stochastic Processes,* New York: McGraw-Hill.

Parker, D. (1982). Learning logic, Invention report, S81-64, File 1, Office of Technology Licensing, Stanford University.

Parker, D. (1987a). Optimal algorithms for adaptive networks: Second order back propagation, second order direct propagation, and second order Hebbian learning, *Proceedings of the IEEE First International Conference on Neural Networks: Vol. II,* (pp. 593–600). San Diego: IEEE.

Parker, D. (1987b). Second order LMS: Newton's method in O(n) operations, *IEEE ASSP Magazine,* in review.

Parker, D. (1987c). Second order back propagation: Implementing an optimal O(n) approximation to Newton's method as an artificial neural network, *Computer,* in review.

Parks, M. (1987). Characterization of the Boltzmann machine learning rate, *Proceedings of the IEEE First International Conference on Neural Networks: Vol. III,* (pp. 715–720). San Diego: IEEE.

Parey, C. & Bonnemay, A. (1988). Three-valued logic and neural networks: Applications to reliability analysis, *Neural Networks Supplement: INNS Abstracts, 1,* 458.

Pati, Y., Krishnaprasad, P., Peckerrar, M. & Marrian, C. (1988). Neural networks and tactile imaging, *Neural Networks Supplement: INNS Abstracts, 1,* 459.

Paulos, J. & Hollis, P. (1988). A VLSI architecture for feedforward networks with integral back-propagation, *Neural Networks Supplement: INNS Abstracts, 1,* 399.

Pawlicki, T., Lee, D-S., Hull, J., & Srihari, S. (1988). Neural networks and their application to handwritten digit recognition, *Proceedings of the IEEE International Conference on Neural Networks: Vol. II,* (pp. 63–70). San Diego: IEEE.

Pearson, R. (1988). Ultrametrics, pseudo-ultrametrics, fuzzy sets, and pattern classification, *Neural Networks Supplement: INNS Abstracts, 1,* 120.

Pemberton, J. & Vidal, J. (1988a). Noise immunity of generalized delta rule learning, *Neural Networks Supplement: INNS Abstracts, 1,* 209.

Pemberton, J. & Vidal, J. (1988b). When is the generalized delta rule a learning rule?, *Proceedings of the IEEE International Conference on Neural Networks: Vol. I*, (pp. 309–316). San Diego: IEEE.

Peretto, P. (1984). Collective properties of neural networks: A statistical physics approach, *Biological Cybernetics, 50,* 51–62.

Peretto, P. (1988). On learning rules and memory storage abilities of asymmetric neural networks, *Journal of Physics—France, 49,* 711–726.

Peretto, P. & Niez, J. (1986b). Stochastic dynamics of neural networks, *IEEE Transactions on Systems, Man, and Cybernetics, SMC-16,* 73–83.

Peretto, P. & Niez, J. (1986b). Stochastic dynamics of neural networks, *IEEE Transactions on Systems, Man and Cybernetics, SMC-16,* 73–83.

Peterson, C. (1988). Track finding with neural networks, *Nuclear Instruments,* in review.

Peterson, C. & Anderson, J. (1987). Neural networks and NP-complete optimization problems: A performance study on the graph bisection problem, MCC Technical Report MCC-EI-287-87.

Petsche, T. & Dickson, B. (1988). A trellis-structured neural network, In D. Anderson (Ed.), *Proceedings of the 1987 IEEE Conference on Neural Information Processing Systems—Natural and Synthetic,* (pp. 592–601). New York: American Institute of Physics.

Pineda, F. (1987). Generalization of backpropagation to recurrent neural networks, *Physical Review Letters, 18,* 2229–2232.

Pineda, F. (1988). Generalization of backpropagation to recurrent and high-order neural networks, In D. Anderson (Ed.), *Proceedings of the 1987 IEEE Conference on Neural Information Processing Systems—Natural and Synthetic,* (pp. 602–611). New York: American Institute of Physics.

Platt, J. & Barr, A. (1988). Constrained differential optimization, In D. Anderson (Ed.), *Proceedings of the 1987 IEEE Conference on Neural Information Processing Systems—Natural and Synthetic,* (pp. 612–621). New York: American Institute of Physics.

Platt, J. & Hopfield, J. (1986). Analog decoding using neural networks, In J. Denker (Ed.), *AIP Conference Proceedings 151: Neural Networks for Computing,* (pp. 364–369). New York: American Institute of Physics.

Plaut, D., Nowlan, S. & Hinton, G. (1986). Experiments on learning by back propagation, Carnegie-Mellon University, Department of Computer Science Technical Report, CMU-CS-86-126.

Plonsey, R. & Fleming, D. (1969). *Bioelectric Phenomena,* New York: McGraw-Hill.

Pollack, J. (1988). Recursive auto-associative memory, *Neural Networks Supplement: INNS Abstracts, 1,* 122.

Pomerleau, D., Gusciora, G., Touretzky, D. & King, H. (1988). Neural networks simulation at warp speed: How we got 17 million connections per second, *Proceedings of the IEEE International Conference on Neural Networks: Vol. II,* (pp. 143–150). San Diego: IEEE.

Pourboghrat, F. & Sayeh, M. (1988a). Neural network learning controller for manipulators, *Neural Networks Supplement: INNS Abstracts, 1,* 356.

Pourboghrat, F. & Sayeh, M. (1988b). Neural path planning and motion control of mobile robots, *Neural Networks Supplement: INNS Abstracts, 1,* 460.

Prager, R., Harrison, T. & Fallside, F. (1986). Boltzmann machines for speech recognition, *Computer Speech and Language, 1,* 3–27.

Provence, J. (1987). Neural network implementation for maximum-likelihood sequence estimation of binary signals in Gaussian noise, *Proceedings of the IEEE First International Conference on Neural Networks: Vol. III,* (pp. 703–714). San Diego: IEEE.

Psaltis, D. & Farhat, N. (1984). A new approach to optical information processing based on the Hopfield model, *Digest of the 13th Congress of the International Commission on Optics: Vol. ICO-13,* (pp. 24). Sapporo, Japan.

Psaltis, D. & Farhat, N. (1985). Optical information processing based on an associative-memory model of neural nets with thresholding and feedback, *Optics Letters, 10,* 98–100.

Psaltis, D. & Hong, J. (1986). Shift invariant optical associative memories, *Optical Engineering, 26,* 10–15.

Psaltis, D. & Neifield, M. (1988). The emergence of generalization in networks with constrained representation, *Proceedings of the IEEE International Conference on Neural Networks: Vol. I,* (pp. 371–381). San Diego: IEEE.

Psaltis, D., Park, C-H. & Hong, J. (1988). Higher order associative memories and their optical implementations, *Neural Networks, 1,* 149–164.

Psaltis, D., Sideris, A. & Yamamura, A. (1988, Apr.). A multilayered neural network controller, *IEEE Control Systems Magazine,* 17–21.

Quian, N. & Sejnowski, T. (1988). Predicting the secondary structure of globular proteins using neural network models, *Journal of Molecular Biology,* in review.

Raibert, M. (1988). Hopping in legged systems—modeling and simulation for the two-dimensional one-legged case, *IEEE Transaction on Systems, Man, and Cybernetics, SMC-14*, 451–463.

Rak, S. & Kolodzy, P. (1988). Invariant object recognition with the adaptive resonance (ART) network, *Neural Networks Supplement: INNS Abstracts, 1*, 43.

Ramamoorthy, P., Gouird, G. & Iyer, V. (1988). Signal modeling and prediction using neural networks, *Neural Networks Supplement: INNS Abstracts, 1*, 461.

Ramanujam, J. & Sadayappan, P. (1988). Optimization by neural networks, *Proceedings of the IEEE International Conference on Neural Networks: Vol. II*, (pp. 325–332). San Diego: IEEE.

Randall, A. & Caelli, T. (1988). Stochastic relaxation and correspondence problems in object recognition, *Neural Networks Supplement: INNS Abstracts, 1*, 522.

Ransil, P. & Siegel, K. (1988). Control of a deformable mirror using an adaptive network, *Neural Networks Supplement: INNS Abstracts, 1*, 462.

Rashevsky, N. (1948). *Mathematical Biophysics*, Chicago: University of Chicago Press.

Rasure, J. & Salas, J. (1988). A VLSI three-layer perceptron for binary image classification, *Neural Networks Supplement: INNS Abstracts, 1*, 402.

Reilly, D., Cooper, L. & Elbaum, C. (1982). A neural model for category learning, *Biological Cybernetics, 45*, 35–41.

Reuhkala, E., Jalanko, M. & Kohonen, T. (1979). A redundant hash addressing method adapted for the postprocessing and error-correction of computer recognized speech, *Proceedings of the 1979 IEEE International Conference on Acoustics, Speech, and Signal Processing*, (pp. 591–594). Washington: IEEE.

Riccotti, L., Ragazzini, S. & Martinelli, G. (1988). Learning of word stress in a sub-optimal second order backpropagation neural network, *Proceedings of the IEEE International Conference on Neural Networks: Vol. I*, (pp. 355–361). San Diego: IEEE.

Richards, G. (1988). Investigation of a layered network as an associative memory, *Neural Networks Supplement: INNS Abstracts, 1*, 213.

Ridgeway, W. (1962). An adaptive logic system with generalizing properties, Stanford University, Stanford Electronics Lab Technical Report No. 1556-1.

Rimey, R., Gouin, P., Scofield, C. & Reilly, D. (1986). Real time 3-D classification using a learning system, *Proceedings of the SPIE, 726*, 552–557.

Ritter, H. & Schulten, K. (1986a). Topology conserving mappings for learning motor tasks, In J. Denker (Ed.), *AIP Conference Proceedings 151: Neural Networks for Computing*, (pp. 376–380). New York: American Institute of Physics.

Ritter, H. & Schulten, K. (1986b). On the stationary state of Kohonen's self-organizing sensory mapping, *Biological Cybernetics, 54*, 99–106.

Ritter, H. & Schulten, K. (1988a). Kohonen's self-organizing feature maps: Exploring their computational capabilities, *Proceedings of the IEEE International Conference on Neural Networks: Vol. I*, (pp. 109–116). San Diego: IEEE.

Ritter, H. & Schulten, K. (1988b). Extending Kohonen's self-organizing mapping algorithm to learn ballistic movements, In R. Eckmiller & C. v. d. Malsburg (Eds.), *NATO ISI Series, Vol. F41: Neural Computers*, (pp. 393–4406). Berlin: Springer-Verlag.

Ritter, H. & Schulten, K. (1988c). Convergence properties of Kohonen's topology conserving maps: Fluctuations, stability, and dimension selection, *Biological Cybernetics, 60*, 59–71.

Ritter, H. & Schulten, K. (1988d). Topology conserving maps for motor control, *Neural Networks Supplement: INNS Abstracts, 1*, 357.

Roberts, I. (1988). Neural network for radar terrain image recognition, *Neural Networks Supplement: INNS Abstracts, 1*, 463.

Roberts, L. (1960). Pattern recognition with an adaptive network, *IRE International Convention Record: Part 2*, (pp. 66–70). New York: IRE.

Robinson, A. & Fallside, F. (1988). Static and dynamic error propagation networks with application to speech coding, In D. Anderson (Ed.), *Proceedings of the 1987 IEEE Conference on Neural Information Processing Systems—Natural and Synthetic*, (pp. 632–641). New York: American Institute of Physics.

Rock, A., Xu, X., King, K., Jones, J. & Vanderbilt, H. (1988). Study of real-time weld seam tracking visual image analysis using a neural network, *Neural Networks Supplement: INNS Abstracts, 1*, 464.

Rogers, D. (1988). Using data tagging to improve the performance of Kanerva's SDM, RIACS Technical Report, 88.5.

Rogers, D. (1989a). Kanerva's sparse distributed associative memory: An associative memory algorithm well suited to the Connection Machine, *International Journal of High Speed Computing*, in press.

Rogers, D. (1989b). Statistical prediction with Kanerva's sparse distributed memory, *Proceedings of the 1988 Neural Information Processing Systems Conference*, in press.

Rohwer, R. & Forrest, B. (1987). Training time-dependence in neural networks, *Proceedings of the IEEE International Conference on Neural Networks: Vol. II*, (pp. 701–708). San Diego: IEEE.

Roney, K. & Shaw, G. (1980). Analytical study of assemblies of neurons in memory science, *Mathematical Biosciences, 51*, 25–41.

Rosen, B., Goodwin, J. & Vidal, J. (1988). State recurrence learning, *Neural Networks Supplement: INNS Abstracts, 1*, 48.

Rosenberg, C. & Sejnowski, T. (1986). The spacing effect on NETtalk, a massively parallel network, *The Eighth Annual Conference of the Cognitive Science Society*, (pp. 72–89). Hillsdale, NJ: Lawrence Erlbaum Associates.

Rosenblatt, F. (1957). The perceptron: A perceiving and recognizing automation (project PARA), Cornell Aeronautical Laboratory Report, 85-460-1.

Rosenblatt, F. (1958a). The perceptron: A theory of statistical separability in cognitive systems, Cornell Aeronautical Laboratory Report, VG-1196-G-1.

Rosenblatt, F. (1958b). The perceptron; A probabilistic model for information storage and organization in the brain, *Psychological Review, 65*, 386–408.

Rosenblatt, F. (1959). Two theorems of statistical separability in the perceptron, *Mechanization of Thought Processes: Vol. I*, London: Her Majesty's Stationery Office.

Rosenblatt, F. (1960). Perceptron simulation experiments, *Proceedings of the IRE, 48*, 301–309.

Rosenblatt, F. (1962). *Principles of Neurodynamics*, Washington: Spartan Books.

Rosenblatt, F. (1964). A model for experiential storage in neural networks, In J. Tou & R. Wilcox (Eds.), *Computer and Information Sciences*, (pp. 16–66). Washington: Spartan Books.

Rosenfeld, E. (1987). Neurocomputing — A new industry, *Proceedings of the IEEE First International Conference on Neural Networks: Vol. IV*, (pp. 831–838). San Diego: IEEE.

Rozonoer, L. (1969a). Random logic nets I, *Automatic Remote Control, 5*, 137–147.

Rozonoer, L. (1969b). Random logic nets II, *Automatic Remote Control, 6*, 99–109.

Rozonoer, L. (1969c). Random logic nets III, *Automatic Remote Control, 7*, 129–136.

Rumelhart, D. (1977). Toward an interactive model of reading, In S. Dornic (Rd.), *Attention and Performance VI*, Hillsdale, NJ: Lawrence Erlbaum Associates.

Rumelhart, D. (1988). Tutorial 12: Parallel distributed processing, *IEEE International Conference on Neural Networks*. San Diego: IEEE.

Rumelhart, D., Hinton, G. & Williams, R. (1986). Learning representations by backpropagating errors, *Nature, 323*, 533–536.

Rumelhart, D. & McClelland, J. (1982). An interactive activation model of context effects in letter perception: Part 2. The contextual enhancement effect and some tests and extensions of the model, *Psychological Review, 89*, 60–94.

Rumelhart, D. & McClelland, J. (1986). *Parallel Distributed Processing: Explorations in the Microstructure of Cognition: Vols. 1 and 2*, Cambridge: Bradford Books/MIT Press.

Rumelhart, D. & Zipser, D. (1985). Feature discovery by competitive learning, *Cognitive Science, 9*, 75–112.

Russell, S. (1913). A practical device to simulate the working of nervous discharges, *Journal of Animal Behaviour, 3*, 15 f.

Ryan, T. (1988). The resonance correlation network, *Proceedings of the IEEE International Conference on Neural Networks: Vol. I*, (pp. 673–680). San Diego: IEEE.

Ryan, T. & Winter, C. (1987). Variations on adaptive resonance, *Proceedings of the IEEE First International Conference on Neural Networks: Vol. II*, (pp. 767–776). San Diego: IEEE.

Ryan, T., Winter, C. & Turner, C. (1987). Dynamic control of an artificial neural system: The property inheritance network, *Applied Optics, 26*, 4961–4971.

Sage, J. (1987). Artificial neural system implementations using CCD and NMOS technologies, *Workshop on Neural Network Devices and Applications*, Jet Propulsion Laboratory, 72–84.

Sage, J., Thompson, K. & Withers, R. (1986). An artificial neural network integrated circuit based on NMOS/CCD principles, In J. Denker (Ed.), *AIP Conference Proceedings 151: Neural Networks for Computing*, (pp. 381–385). New York: American Institute of Physics.

SAIC (1988). Sigma-1 neurocomputer workstation, product literature.

Samad, T. (1988). Back-propagaton is significantly faster if the expected value of the source unit is used for update, *Neural Networks Supplement: INNS Abstracts, 1*, 216.

Samad, T. & Harper, P. (1987). Associative memory storage using a variant of the generalized delta rule, *Proceedings of the IEEE First International Conference in Neural Networks: Vol. III*, (pp. 173–184). San Diego: IEEE.

Sandon, P. & Uhr, L. (1988). A local interaction heuristic for adaptive networks, *Proceedings of the IEEE International Conference on Neural Networks: Vol. I*, (pp. 317–324). San Diego: IEEE.

Sasiela, R. (1986). Forgetting as a way to improve neural-net behavior, In J. Denker (Ed.), *AIP Conference Proceedings 151: Neural Networks for Computing*, (386–391). New York: American Institute of Physics.

Savely, R. (1987). The implementation of neural network technology, *Proceedings of the IEEE First International Conference on Neural Networks: Vol. IV*, (pp. 477–484). San Diego: IEEE.

Saylor, J. & Stork, D. (1986). Parallel analog neural networks for tree searching, In J. Denker (Ed.), *AIP Conference Proceedings 151: Neural Networks for Computing*, (pp. 392–397). New York: American Institute of Physics.

Scalettar, R. & Zee, A. (1988). Perception of left and right by a feedforward net, *Biological Cybernetics, 58*, 193–201.

Scheff, K. & Szu, H. (1987). 1-D optical Cauchy machine infinite film spectrum search, *Proceedings of the IEEE First International Conference on Neural Networks: Vol. III*, (pp. 673–680). San Diego: IEEE.

Sejnowski, T. (1976). On global properties of neuronal interaction, *Biological Cybernetics, 22*, 85–95.

Sejnowski, T. (1977a). Statistical constraints on synaptic plasticity, *Journal of Mathematical Biology, 64*, 385–389.

Sejnowski, T. (1977b). Storing covariance with nonlinearly interacting neurons, *Journal of Mathematical Biology 4*, 303–321.

Sejnowski, T. (1981). Skeleton filters in the brain, In G. Hinton & J. Anderson (Eds.), *Parallel Models of Associative Memory*, (pp. 189–212). Hillsdale, NJ: Lawrence Erlbaum Associates.

Sejnowski, T. (1986). Higher-order Boltzmann machines, In J. Denker (Ed.), *AIP Conference Proceedings 151: Neural Networks for Computing*, (pp. 398–403). New York: American Institute of Physics.

Sejnowski, T. (1987). Learned classification of sonar targets using a massively parallel network, *Workshop on Neural Network Devices and Applications*, Jet Propulsion Laboratory, 224–237.

Sejnowski, T. & Hinton, G. (1986). Separating figure from ground with a Boltzmann machine, In M. Arbib & A. Hanson (Eds.), *Vision, Brain and Cooperative Computation*, Cambridge: MIT Press/Bradford Books.

Sejnowski, T., Kienker, P. & Hinton, G. (1986). Learning symmetry groups with hidden units: Beyond the perceptron, *Physica, 22D*, 260–275.

Sejnowski, T. & Rosenberg, C. (1986). NETtalk: A parallel network that learns to read aloud, Johns Hopkins University, Department of Electrical Engineering and Computer Science Technical Report JHU/EECS-86/01.

Sejnowski, T. and Rosenberg, C. (1987). Parallel networks that learn to pronounce English text, *Complex Systems, 1*, 145–168.

Sethares, W. (1988). A convergence theorem for the modified delta rule, *Neural Networks Supplement: INNS Abstracts, 1*, 130.

Shannon, C. (1951). Presentation of a maze-solving machine, *Transactions of the Eighth Conference on Cybernetics*, (pp. 173–180). New York: Josiah Macy Foundation.

Shannon, C. & McCarthy, J., Eds., (1956). *Automata Studies*, Princeton: Princeton University Press.

Shastri, L. (1987). Evidential reasoning in semantic networks: A formal theory and its parallel implementation, University of Rochester Department of Computer Science Technical Report, TR-166.

Shaw, G. (1978). Space-time correlation of neuronal firing related to memory storage capacity, *Brain Research Bulletin, 3*, 107–113.

Shaw, G. & Roney, K. (1979). Analytical solution of a neural network theory based on an Ising spin system, *Physics Letters, 74A*, 1 & 2.

Shaw, G. & Vasudevan, R. (1974). Persistent states of neural networks and the random nature of synaptic transmission, *Mathematical Biosciences, 21*, 207 f.

Shepanski, J. (1988). Fast learning in artificial neural networks: Multilayer perceptron training using optimal estimation, *Proceedings of the IEEE International Conference on Neural Networks: Vol. I*, (pp. 465–472). San Diego: IEEE.

Shimohara, K., Tokunuga, Y., Uchiyama, T. & Kimura, Y. (1988). A neural network system with an automatic generation mechanism for distorted patterns, *Neural Networks Supplement: INNS Abstracts, 1*, 52.

Shimohara, K., Uchiyama, T. & Tokunuga, Y. (1988). Backpropagation networks for event-driven temporal sequence processing, *Proceedings of the IEEE International Conference on Neural Networks: Vol. I*, (pp. 665–672). San Diego: IEEE.

Shirvaiker, M. & Musari, M. (1988). A neural network classifier for character recognition, *Neural Networks Supplement: INNS Abstracts, 1,* 524.

Sietsma, J. & Dow, R. (1988). Neural net pruning—why and how, *Proceedings of the IEEE International Conference on Neural Networks: Vol. I*, (pp. 325–333). San Diego: IEEE.

Simmes, S. (1987). Programming parallel computers using energy minimization algorithms, *Proceedings of the IEEE First International Conference on Neural Networks: Vol. II*, (pp. 205–212). San Diego: IEEE.

Simpson, P. (1987). A survey of artificial neural systems, Naval Ocean Systems Center Technical Document, TD-1106.

Simpson, P. (1988a). Bidirectional associative memory systems, *Applied Optics*, in review. Also, General Dynamics Electronics Division, Intelligent Systems Group Technical Report GDE-ISG-PKS-02.

Simpson, P. (1988b). An algorithm for encoding an arbitrary number of patterns in a system of discrete bidirectional associative memories, *Neural Networks Supplement: INNS Abstracts, 1,* 220.

Simpson, P. (1988c). Higher-ordered and intraconnected bidirectional associative memories, *IEEE Transactions on Systems, Man, and Cybernetics*, in review. Also, General Dynamics Electronics Division, Intelligent Systems Group Technical Report GDE-ISG-PKS-03.

Simpson, P. & Deich, R. (1988). Neural networks, fuzzy logic, and acoustic signal processing, *Proceedings of the 1988 Aerospace Applications of Artificial Intelligence (AAAIC 88)*, Vol. II, Dayton SIGART, Dayton (pp. 119–133).

Singh, J., Hong, S. & Bhattacharya, P. (1988). Implementation of neural networks using quantum well based excitonic devices—device requirement studies, *Proceedings of the IEEE International Conference on Neural Networks: Vol. II*, (pp. 411–419). San Diego: IEEE.

Singleton, R. (1962). A test for linear separability as applied to self-organizing machines, In M. Yovits, G. Jacobi, & G. Goldstein (Eds.), *Self-Organizing Systems—1962*, (pp. 503–524). Washington: Spartan Books.

Sitte, J. (1988). Basins of attraction and spurious states in neural networks, *Neural Networks Supplement: INNS Abstracts, 1,* 132.

Sivilotti, M., Emerling, M. & Mead, C. (1986). VLSI architectures for implementation of neural networks, In J. Denker (Ed.), *AIP Conference Proceedings 151: Neural Networks for Computing*, (pp. 408–413). New York: American Institute of Physics.

Smieju, F. (1988). The significance of underlying correlations in the training of a layered net, *Neural Networks Supplement: INNS Abstracts, 1,* 221.

Smith, M. (1988). Loan underwriting using a neural network, *Neural Networks Supplement: INNS Abstracts, 1,* 468.

Sobajic, S., Lu, J-J. & Pao, Y-H. (1988). Intelligent control of the intelledex 605T robot manipulator, *Proceedings of the IEEE International Conference on Neural Networks: Vol. II*, (pp. 633–640). San Diego: IEEE.

Soffer, B. (1987). Holographic associative memories, *Workshop on Neural Network Devices and Applications*, Jet Propulsion Laboratory, 125–146.

Soffer, B., Marom, E. , Owechko, Y. & Dunning, G. (1986a). Holographic associative memory employing phase conjugation, *Proceedings of the SPIE, 684,* 2–6.

Soffer, B., Dunning, G., Owechko, Y. & Marom, E. (1986b). Associative holographic memory with feedback using phase-conjugate mirrors, *Optics Letters, 11,* 118–120.

Solomon, J. (1987). Neural networks, spectral pattern recognition, and spectral mixing decomposition. *Workshop on Neural Network Devices and Applications*, Jet Propulsion Laboratory, 408–422.

Standley, D. & Wyatt, J. (1988). Design method for a lateral inhibition network that is provably stable in the presence of parasites, *Neural Networks Supplement: INNS Abstracts, 1,* 135.

Steinbuch, K. (1961). Die lernmatrix, *Kybernetik, 1,* 36–45.

Steinbuch, K. & Piske, U. (1963). Learning matrices and their applications, *IEEE Transactions on Electronic Computers, EC-12,* 846–862.

Steinbuch, K. & Widrow, B. (1965). A critical comparison of two kinds of adaptive classification networks, *IEEE Transactions on Electronic Computers, EC-14,* 737–740.

Steinbuch, K. & Zendeh, F. (1963). Self-correcting translator circuits, *Information Processing*, (pp. 359–365). Amsterdam: North-Holland.

Stirk, C. (1987). Effects of noise on an optical implementation of an additive lateral inhibitory network,

*Proceedings of the IEEE First International Conference on Neural Networks: Vol. III*, (pp. 615–624). San Diego: IEEE.

Stoll, H. & Lee, L-S. (1988). A continuous-time optical neural network, *Proceedings of the IEEE International Conference on Neural Networks: Vol. II*, (pp. 373–384). San Diego: IEEE.

Stone, G. (1986). An analysis of the delta rule and the learning of statistical associations, In D. Rumelhart & J. McClelland (Eds.), *Parallel Distributed Processing: Vol. I*, (pp. 444–459). Cambridge: MIT Press.

Stornetta, W. & Huberman, B. (1987). An improved three-layer backpropagation algorithm, *Proceedings of the IEEE First International Conference on Neural Networks: Vol. II*, (pp. 637–644). San Diego: IEEE.

Strachey, J. (1966). *The Standard Edition of the Complete Psychological Works of Sigmund Freud: Vol. I, Pre-Psycho-Analytic Publications and Unpublished Drafts*, London: The Hogarth Press.

Stubbs, D. & Good, P. (1976). Connectivity in random networks, *Bulletin of Mathematical Biology, 38*, 295–304.

Styblinski, M. & Meyer, B. (1988). Fuzzy cognitive maps, signal flow graphs, and qualitative circuit analysis, *Proceedings of the IEEE International Conference on Neural Networks: Vol. II*, (pp. 549–556). San Diego: IEEE.

Suddarth, S., Sutton, S. & Holden, A. (1988). A symbolic-neural method of solving control problems, *Proceedings of the IEEE International Conference on Neural Networks: Vol. I*, (pp. 515–523). San Diego: IEEE.

Sung, C.-H., Priebe, C. & Marchette, D. (1988). Temporal knowledge: Recognition and learning of time-based patterns, *Neural Networks Supplement: INNS Abstracts, 1*, 317.

Surkan, A. & Chen, M-L. (1988). APL implementation of a neural network with dynamically generated middle layers of arbitrary number and length, *Neural Networks Supplement: INNS Abstracts, 1*, 555.

Sutton, G., Maisog, J. & Reggia, J. (1988). Implementing competitive learning using competitive activation, *Neural Networks Supplement: INNS Abstracts, 1*, 140.

Sutton, R. (1978). Single channel theory: A neuronal theory of learning, *Brain Theory Newsletter, 3*, 72–75.

Sutton, R. (1984). Temporal credit assignment in reinforcement learning, University of Massachusetts, Computer and Information Systems Technical Report, COINS-TR-84-02.

Sutton, R. (1986). Two problems with backpropagation and other steepest-descent learning procedures for networks, *Proceedings of the Eighth Annual Conference of the Cognitive Science Society*, (pp. 823–831). Hillsdale, NJ: Lawrence Erlbaum Associates.

Sutton, R. (1987). Learning to predict by the methods of temporal differences, GTE Laboratories Technical Report, TR87-509.1.

Sutton, R. & Barto, A. (1981a). Toward a modern theory of adaptive networks: Expectation and prediction, *Psychological Review, 88*, 135–171.

Sutton, R. & Barto, A. (1981b). An adaptive network that constructs and uses an internal model of its environment, *Cognition and Brain Theory Quarterly, 4*, 217–246.

Symon, J., Rajgopal, S., Miller, T. & v. d. Bount, D. (1988). STONN: A neural network IC using stochastic techniques, *Neural Networks Supplement: INNS Abstracts, 1*, 412.

Syntonics (1988a). DENDROS-1G, patent pending, company literature.

Syntonics (1988b). DENDROS-2, patent pending, company literature.

Szu, H. (1986a). Fast simulated annealing, In J. Denker (Ed.), *AIP Conference Proceedings 151: Neural Networks for Computing*, (pp. 420–425). New York: American Institute of Physics.

Szu, H. (1986b). Non-convex optimization, *Proceedings of the SPIE, 698*, 59–65.

Szu, H. (1986c). Panel discussion, *Proceedings of the SPIE, 634*, 331–348.

Szu, H. & Messner, R. (1987). Adaptive invariant novelty filters, *Proceedings of the IEEE, 74*, 518–519.

Szu, H. (1987). Applications of fast simulated annealing, *Workshop on Neural Network Devices and Applications*, Jet Propulsion Laboratory, 377–407.

Szu, H. (1988). Fast TSP algorithm based on binary neuron output and analog neuron input using the zero-diagonal interconnect matrix and necessary and sufficient constraints on the permutation matrix, *Proceedings of the IEEE International Conference on Neural Networks: Vol. II*, (pp. 259–266). San Diego: IEEE.

Szu, H. & Hartley, R. (1987). Nonconvex optimization by fast simulated annealing, *Proceedings of the IEEE, 75*, 1538–1540.

Taber, W. & Deich, R. (1988). A comparison of feedforward neural networks: Fuzzy operators and acoustic ship signatures, *International Journal of Intelligent Systems,* in review.

Taber, W., Deich, R., Simpson, P. & Fagg, A. (1988). The recognition of orca calls with a neural network, *International Workshop on Fuzzy Systems Applications,* Iizuka City, Japan, August 21–24.

Taber, W. & Siegel, M. (1987). Estimation of expert weights using fuzzy cognitive maps, *Proceedings of the IEEE First International Conference on Neural Networks: Vol. II,* (pp. 319–326). San Diego: IEEE.

Taber, W., Siegel, M. & Deich, R. (1988). Fuzzy sets and neural networks, *Proceedings of the First Joint Technology Workshop on Neural Networks and Fuzzy Logic,* NASA/University of Houston, Houston, TX.

Tagliarini, G. & Page, E. (1987). Solving constraint satisfaction problems with neural networks, *Proceedings of the IEEE First International Conference on Neural Networks: Vol. III,* (pp. 741–747). San Diego: IEEE.

Tagliarini, G. & Page, E. (1988). A neural-network solution to the concentrator assignment problem, In D. Anderson (Ed.), *Proceedings of the 1987 IEEE Conference on Neural Information Processing Systems—Natural and Synthetic,* (pp. 775–782). New York: American Institute of Physics.

Tai, H-M. & Jang, T-L. (1988). Extended Hopfield neural network: A complementary approach, *Neural Networks Supplement: INNS Abstracts, 1,* 225.

Takeda, M. & Goodman, J. (1986). Neural networks for computation: Number representations and programming complexity, *Applied Optics, 25,* 3033–3046.

Takeuchi, A. & Amari, S. (1979). Formation of topographic maps and columnar microstructures in nerve fields, *Biological Cybernetics, 35,* 63–72.

Takiyama, R. (1978). Multithreshold perceptron, *Pattern Recognition, 10,* 27–30.

Takiyama, R. (1985). The separating capacity of multithreshold threshold elements, *IEEE Transactions on Pattern Analysis and Machine Intelligence, PAMI-7,* 112–116.

Tam, D., Perkell, D. & Tucker, W. (1988). Correlation of multiple neuronal spike trains using the backpropagation error correction algorithm, *Neural Networks Supplement: INNS Abstracts, 1,* 277.

Tanaka, H., Matsuda, S., Ogi, H., Izui, Y., Taoka, H. & Sakeguchi, T. (1988). Redundant encoding for fault tolerant computing on a Hopfield network, *Neural Networks Supplement: INNS Abstracts, 1,* 141.

Tank, D. & Hopfield, J. (1986). Simple "neural" optimization networks: An A/D converter, signal decision circuit, and a linear programming circuit, *IEEE Transactions on Circuits and Systems, CAS-33,* 533–541.

Tank, D. & Hopfield, J. (1987a). Neural computation by concentrating information in time, *Proceedings of the National Academy of Sciences, 84,* 1896–1900.

Tank, D. & Hopfield, J. (1987b). Concentrating information in time: Analog neural networks with possible applications to speech recognition, *Proceedings of the IEEE First International Conference on Neural Networks: Vol. IV,* (pp. 455–468). San Diego: IEEE.

Tank, D. & Hopfield, J. (1987c). Collective computation in neuronlike circuits, *Scientific American, 257,* 6, 104–114.

Tarvel, R. & Thakoor, A. (1988). Neural networks for robotic control, *Neural Networks Supplement: INNS Abstracts, 1,* 361.

TeKolste, R. & Guest, C. (1987). Designs and devices for optical bidirectional associative memory, *Applied Optics, 26,* 5055–5061.

Tenorio, M., Tom, M. & Schwartz, R. (1988). Adaptive networks as a model for human speech development, *Proceedings of the IEEE International Conference on Neural Networks: Vol. II,* (pp. 235–242). San Diego: IEEE.

Tesauro, G. (1986). Simple neural models of classical conditioning, *Biological Cybernetics, 55,* 187–200.

Tesauro, G. (1987). Scaling relationships in backpropagation learning: Dependence on training set size, *Complex Systems, 1,* 367–372.

Tesauro, G. & Sejnowski, T. (1988). A "neural" network that learns to play backgammon, In D. Anderson (Ed.), *Proceedings of the 1987 IEEE Conference on Neural Information Processing Systems—Natural and Synthetic,* (pp. 794–803). New York: American Institute of Physics.

Thakoor, A. (1986, Nov.). Electronic neural networks, *Amplifier,* 4–10.

Thakoor, A. (1987). Electronic neural networks, *Workshop on Neural Network Devices and Applications,* Jet Propulsion Laboratory, 16–42.

Thakoor, A., Lamb, J., Moopen, A. & Lambe, J. (1986). Binary synaptic connections based on memory switching in a-Si:H, In J. Denker (Ed.), *AIP Conference Proceedings 151: Neural Networks for Computing*, (pp. 426–431). New York: American Institute of Physics.

Tickner, A. & Barrett, H. (1988). Optical implementations of Boltzmann machines, *Optical Engineering, 26,* 16–21.

Tillery, S. & Combs, N. (1987). The problem of internal representations in neural nets: Concepts, implications, and a proposed metric, *Proceedings of the IEEE First International Conference on Neural Networks: Vol. II,* (pp. 585–592). San Diego: IEEE.

Tishby, N. (1988). Nonlinear dynamical modeling of speech using neural networks, *Neural Networks Supplement: INNS Abstracts, 1,* 279.

Togai, M. & Watanabe, H. (1985). A VLSI implementation of a fuzzy inference engine: Toward an expert system on a chip, *Proceedings of the Second IEEE CAIA.*

Togai, M. & Watanabe, H. (1986). Expert system on a chip: An engine for realtime approximate reasoning, *IEEE Expert, 1,* 55–62.

Tolat, V. (1988). An adaptive "broom-balancer" with visual inputs, *Proceedings of the IEEE International Conference on Neural Networks: Vol. II,* (pp. 641–647). San Diego: IEEE.

Tolat, V. & Widrow, B. (1988). An adaptive neural net controller with visual inputs, *Neural Networks Supplement: INNS Abstracts, 1,* 362.

Toomarian, N. (1988). A concurrent neural network algorithm for the traveling salesman problem, *Third Conference on Hypercube Concurrent Computers and Applications,* Pasadena.

Torioka, T. (1979). Pattern separability in a random neural network with inhibitory connections, *Biological Cybernetics, 34,* 53–62.

Touretzky, D. (1986a). BoltzCONS: Reconciling connectionism with the recursive nature of stacks and trees, *Proceedings of the Eighth Annual Conference of the Cognitive Science Society,* (pp. 522–530). Hillsdale, NJ: Lawrence Erlbaum Associates.

Touretzky, D. (1986b). Representing and transforming recursive objects in a neural network, or "trees do grow on Boltzmann machines," *Proceedings of the 1986 IEEE International Conference on Systems, Man, and Cybernetics,* (pp. 12–16). New York: IEEE.

Touretzky, D. & Derthick, M. (1987). Symbol structures in connectionist networks: Five properties and five architectures, *Proceedings of the IEEE COMPCON,* San Francisco: IEEE.

Touretzky, D. & Hinton, G. (1988). A distributed connectionist production system, *Cognitive Science, 12,* 423–466.

Treurniet, W., Hunt, M., Lefebyre, C. & Jackson, Z. (1988). Phoneme recognition with a neural network: Comparison of acoustic representation including those produced by an auditory model, *Neural Networks Supplement: INNS Abstracts, 1,* 320.

Troudel, T. & Tabatabai, A. (1988). An adaptive neural net approach to the segmentation of mixed gray-level and binary pictures, *Proceedings of the IEEE International Conference on Neural Networks: Vol. I,* (pp. 585–592). San Diego: IEEE.

Troxel, S., Rogers, S. & Kabrisky, M. (1988). The use of neural networks in PSRI target recognition, *Proceedings of the IEEE International Conference on Neural Networks: Vol. I,* (pp. 593–600). San Diego: IEEE.

TRW (1987). TRW MEAD AI Center, The TRW Mark III-1 artificial neural system processor, product literature.

Tsetlin, M. (1973). *Automaton Theory and Modeling of Biological Systems,* New York: Academic Press.

Tsutsumi, K. & Matsumoto, H. (1987). Neural computation and learning strategy for manipulating motor control, *Proceedings of the IEEE First International Conference on Neural Networks: Vol. IV,* (pp. 525–534). San Diego: IEEE.

Tsutsumi, K., Katayama, K. & Matsumoto, H. (1988). Neural computation for controlling the configuration of 2-dimensional truss structure, *Proceedings of the IEEE International Conference on Neural Networks: Vol. II,* (pp. 575–586). San Diego: IEEE.

Ullman, J. (1962). A consistency technique for pattern association, *IRE Transactions on Information Theory, IT-8,* S74–S81.

Uttley, A. (1956a). Conditional probability machines and conditioned reflexes, In C. Shannon & J. McCarthy (Eds.), Automata Studies, (pp. 253–276). Princeton: Princeton University Press.

Uttley, A. (1956b). Temporal and spatial patterns in a conditional probability machine, In C. Shannon & J. McCarthy (Eds.), Automata Studies, (pp. 277–285). Princeton: Princeteon University Press.

Uttley, A. (1966). The transmission of information and the effect of local feedback in theoretical and neural networks, *Brain Research, 2,* 21–50.

Uttley, A. (1975). The informon: A network for adaptive pattern recognition, *Journal of Theoretical Biology, 49,* 355–376.

Uttley, A. (1976a). A two-pathway informon theory of conditioning and adaptive pattern recognition, *Brain Research, 102,* 23–35.

Uttley, A. (1976b). Simulation studies of learning in an informon network, *Brain Research, 102,* 35–53.

Uttley, A. (1976c). Neurophysiological predictions of a two-pathway informon theory of neural conditioning, *Brain Research, 102,* 55–70.

Uttley, A. (1979). *Information Transmission in the Nervous System.* London: Academic Press.

Vecchi, M. & Salehi, J. (1988). Neuromorphic networks based upon sparse optical orthogonal codes, In D. Anderson (Ed.), *Proceedings of the 1987 IEEE Conference on Neural Information Processing Systems—Natural and Synthetic,* (pp. 814–823). New York: American Institute of Physics.

Venkatesh, S. (1986). Epsilon capacity of neural networks, In J. Denker (Ed.). *AIP Conference Proceedings 151: Neural Networks for Computing,* (pp. 440–445). New York: American Institute of Physics.

Venkatesh, S. & Psaltis, D. (1987). Information storage and retrieval in two associative nets, *IEEE Transactions on Information Theory,* in review.

Verleyson, M., Sirletti, B. & Jespers, P. (1988). A large VLSI Hopfield network for pattern recognition problems, *Neural Networks Supplement: INNS Abstracts, 1,* 414.

Vichniac, G., Lepp, M. & Steenstrup, M. (1988). A neural network for the optimizaton of communications network design, *Neural Networks Supplement: INNS Abstracts, 1,* 144.

Vogl, T., Mangis, J., Rigler, A., Zink, W. & Alkon, D. (1988). Accelerating the convergence of the back-propagation method, *Biological Cybernetics, 59,* 257–263.

Wacholder, E., Han, J. & Mann, R. (1988a). An extension of the Hopfield-Tank model for solution of the multiple traveling salesman problem, *Proceedings of the IEEE International Conference on Neural Networks: Vol. II,* (pp. 305–323). San Diego: IEEE.

Wacholder, E., Han, J. & Mann, R. (1988b). A neural network algorithm for the target-weapon assignment problem, *Neural Networks Supplement: INNS Abstracts, 1,* 147.

WADD (1960). *Bionics Symposium,* USAF Wright Air Development Division (WADD) Technical Report 60-600.

Wagner, K. (1987). Multilayer optical learning networks, *Workshop on Neural Network Devices and Applications,* Jet Propulsion Laboratory, 147–169.

Wagner, K. and Psaltis, D. (1987a). Multilayer optical learning networks, *Applied Optics, 26,* 5061–5077.

Wagner, K. & Psaltis, D. (1987b). Nonlinear etalons in competitive optical learning networks, *Proceedings of the First IEEE International Conference on Neural Networks: Vol. III,* (pp. 585–594). San Diego: IEEE.

Waibel, A., Hanazawa, T., Hinton, G., Shikano, K. & Lang, K. (1987). Phoneme recognition using time-delay neural networks, ATR Interpreting Telephony Research Laboratories Technical Report, TR-1-0006.

Walter, W. (1950, May). An imitation of life, *Scientific American,* 42–45.

Walter, W. (1952, Aug.). A machine that learns, *Scientific American,* 60–63.

Wang, C. & Jenkins, B. (1988a). Implementation considerations of a subtracting incoherent optical neuron, *Proceedings of the IEEE International Conference on Neural Networks: Vol. II,* (pp. 403–410). San Diego: IEEE.

Wang, C. & Jenkins, B. (1988b). Potential difference learning and its optical architecture, *Proceedings of the SPIE, 882,* in press.

Wang, S. (1988). Training multi-layered neural networks with trust region based algorithms, *Neural Networks Supplement: INNS Abstracts, 1,* 228.

Wasserman, P. (1988). Combined backpropagation/Cauchy machine, *Neural Networks Supplement: INNS Abstracts, 1,* 556.

Watson, M. (1987). A neural networks model for phoneme recognition using the generalized delta rule for connection strength modification, *Proceedings of the IEEE First International Conference on Neural Networks: Vol. IV,* (pp. 389–396). San Diego: IEEE.

Watrous, R. (1987). Learning algorithms for connectionist networks: Applied gradient methods of nonlinear optimization, *Proceedings of the IEEE First International Conference on Neural Networks: Vol. II,* (pp. 619–628). San Diego: IEEE.

Waxman, A., Wong, W-L., Goldenberg, R., Bayle, S. & Baloch, A. (1988). Robotic eye-head-neck motion and visual-navigation reflex learning using adaptive linear neurons, *Neural Networks Supplement: INNS Abstracts, 1,* 365.

Wechsler, H. & Zimmerman, L. (1988). Distributed associated memories and data fusion, *Neural Networks Supplement: INNS Abstracts, 1,* 59.

Wee, W. (1968). Generalized inverse approach to adaptive multiclass pattern classification, *IEEE Transactions on Computers, C-17,* 1157–1164.

Wee, W. (1970). On feature selection in a class of distribution-free pattern classifiers, *IEEE Transactions on Information Theory, IT-16,* 47–55.

Wee, W. (1971). Generalized inverse approach to clustering, feature selection, and classification, *IEEE Transactions on Information Theory, IT-17,* 262–269.

Weiland, A. & Leighton, R. (1988). Shaping schedules as a method for accelerating learning, *Neural Networks Supplement: INNS Abstracts, 1,* 231.

Weiland, A., Leighton, R. & Jacyna, G. (1988). An analysis of noise tolerance for a neural network recognition system, MITRE Technical Report, MP-88W00021.

Weiner, N. (1948). *Cybernetics,* New York: J. Wiley & Sons.

Werbos, P. (1974). Beyond regression: New tools for prediction and analysis in the behavioral sciences, Ph.D. Dissertation, Harvard University.

Werbos, P. (1987a). Learning how the world works: Specifications for predictive networks in robots and brains, *Proceedings of the IEEE International Conference on Systems, Man, and Cybernetics* (pp. 302–310). New York: IEEE.

Werbos, P. (1987b). Building and understanding adaptive systems: A statistical/numerical approach to factory automation and brain research, *Transactions on Systems, Man, and Cybernetics, SMC-17,* 7–20.

Werbos, P. (1987c). Backpropagation versus content-addressable memory: Applications, evaluation and synthesis, in review.

Werbos, P. (1988). Generalization of backpropagation with application to a recurrent gas market model, *Neural Networks, 1,* 339–356.

White, H. (1987). Some asymptotic results for learning in single hidden layer feedforward network models, University of California at San Diego, Department of Economics Technical Report, 87-13.

White, H. (1988). Some asymptotic results for learning in single hidden layer feedforward network models, University of California at San Diego, Department of Economics, Discussion Paper 87-13.

White, H., Aldridge, N. & Lindsay, I. (1988). Digital and analogue holographic associative memories, *Optical Engineering, 27,* 30–37.

Widrow, B. (1959). Adaptive sampled-data systems — A statistical theory of adaptation, *1959 WESCON Convention Record: Part 4,* 74–85.

Widrow, B. (1960). An adaptive "adaline" neuron using chemical "memistors," Stanford Electronics Laboratory Technical Report, 1553-2.

Widrow, B. (1962). Generalization and information storage in networks of adaline "neurons," In M. Yovits, G. Jacobi & G. Goldstein (Eds.), *Self-Organizing Systems — 1962,* (pp. 435–461). Washington: Spartan Books.

Widrow, B. (1970). Adaptive filters, In R. Kalman & N. Claris (Eds.), *Aspects of Networks and System Theory,* (pp. 563–587). New York: Holt, Rinehart and Winston.

Widrow, B. (1987). Learning phenomena in layered neural networks, *Proceedings of the IEEE First International Conference on Neural Networks: Vol. II,* (pp. 411–430). San Diego: IEEE.

Widrow, B. (1988). The original adaptive neural network broom balancer, *International Symposium on Circuits and Systems,* 351–357.

Widrow, B., Glover, J., Kaunitz, J., Williams, C. & Hearn, R. (1975). Adaptive noise cancelling: Principles and applications, *Proceedings of the IEEE, 63,* 1692–1716.

Widrow, B., Groner, G., Hu, M., Smith, F., Specht, D. & Talbert, L. (1963). Practical applications for adaptive data-processing systems, *1963 WESCON Convention Record,* Section 11.4.

Widrow, B., Gupta, N. & Maitra, S. (1973). Punish/reward: Learning with a critic in adaptive threshold systems, *IEEE Transactions on Systems, Man, and Cybernetics, SMC-5,* 455–465.

Widrow, B. & Hoff, M. (1960). Adaptive switching circuits, *1960 WESCON Convention Record: Part 4,* 96–104.

Widrow, B., Mantey, P. & Griffiths, L. (1967). Adaptive antenna systems, *Proceedings of the IEEE, 55,* 2143–2159.

Widrow, B. & McCool, J. (1976). A comparison of adaptive algorithms based upon the methods of steepest descent and random search, *IEEE Transactions on Antennas and Propagation, AP-24*, 615–637.

Widrow, B. & Smith, F. (1964). Pattern-recognizing control systems, In J. Tow & R. Wilcox (Eds.), *Computer and Information Sciences*, (pp. 288–317). Washington: Spartan Books.

Widrow, B. & Stearns, S. (1985). *Adaptive Signal Processing*, Englewood Cliffs: Prentice-Hall.

Widrow, B. & Winter R. (1988, Mar.). Neural nets for adaptive filtering and adaptive pattern recognition, *IEEE Computer*, 25–39.

Widrow, B., Winter, R. & Baxter, R. (1988). Layered neural networks for pattern recognition, *IEEE Transactions on Acoustics, Speech and Signal Processing, ASSP-36*, 1109–1118.

Williams, R. (1983). Unit activation rules for cognitive networks, University of California at San Diego, Institute for Cognitive Science Technical Report 8303.

Williams, R. (1985a). Feature discovery through error-correction learning, University of California at San Diego, Institute for Cognitive Science Technical Report 8501.

Williams, R. (1985b). Inference of spatial relations by self-organizing networks, University of California at San Diego, Institute for Cognitive Science Technical Report 8502.

Williams, R. (1986). Reinforcement learning in connectionist networks: A mathematical analysis, University of California at San Diego, Institute for Cognitive Science Technical Report 8605.

Williams, R. (1987). Reinforcement-learning connectionist systems, Northeastern University, College of Computer Science Technical Report, NU-CCS-87-3.

Williams, R. & Zipser, D. (1988). A learning algorithm for continually running fully recurrent neural networks, University of California at San Diego, Institute for Cognitive Science Technical Report 8805.

Willshaw, D. (1971). Models of distributed associative memory, Ph.D. Thesis, University of Edinburgh.

Willshaw, D. (1972). A simple network capable of inductive generalization, *Proceedings of the Royal Society of London, 182*, 233–247.

Willshaw, D., Buneman, O. & Longuet-Higgins, H. (1969). Non-holographic associative memory, *Nature, 222*, 960–962.

Willshaw, D. & Longuet-Higgins, H. (1969). The holophone — Recent developments, In B. Meltzer & D. Michie (Eds.), *Machine Intelligence: Vol. 4*, (pp. 349–357). Edinburgh: Edinburgh University Press.

Willshaw, D. & Longuet-Higgins, H. (1970). Associative memory models, In B. Meltzer & D. Michie (Eds.), *Machine Intelligence: Vol. 5*, Edinburgh: Edinburgh University Press.

Willshaw, D. & Malsburg, C. v. d. (1976). How patterned neural connections can be set up by self-organization, *Proceedings of the Royal Society of London, B194*, 431–445.

Wilson, G. & Pawley, G. (1988). On the stability of the traveling salesman problem algorithm of Hopfield and Tank, *Biological Cybernetics, 58*, 63–70.

Winder, R. (1963). Bounds on threshold gate realizability, *IEEE Transactions on Electronic Computers, EC-12*, 561–564.

Winter, C. (1988). An adaptive network that flees pursuit, *Neural Networks Supplement: INNS Abstracts, 1*, 367.

Winter, C., Ryan, T. & Turner, C. (1987). TIN: A trainable inference network, *Proceedings of the IEEE First International Conference on Neural Networks: Vol. II*, (pp. 777–786). San Diego: IEEE.

Winter, R. & Widrow, B. (1988). Madaline Rule II: A training algorithm for neural networks, *Proceedings of the IEEE International Conference on Neural Networks: Vol. I*, (pp. 401–408). San Diego: IEEE.

Winters, J. (1988). Super-resolution in air using neural networks, *Proceedings of the IEEE International Conference on Neural Networks: Vol. I*, (pp. 609–616). San Diego: IEEE.

Wittner, B. & Denker, J. (1988). Strategies for teaching layered networks classification tasks, In D. Anderson (Ed.), *Proceedings of the 1987 IEEE Conference on Neural Information Processing Systems — Natural and Synthetic*, (pp. 850–859). New York: American Institute of Physics.

Wood, C. (1978). Variations on a theme by Lashley: Lesion experiments on the neural model of Anderson, Silverstein, Ritz and Jones, *Psychological Review, 85*, 582–591.

Woods, D. (1988). Back and counter propagation abberations, *Proceedings of the IEEE International Conference on Neural Networks: Vol. I*, (pp. 473–479). San Diego: IEEE.

Wolf, L. (1988). Recurrent nets for the storage of cyclic sequences, *Proceedings of the IEEE International Conference on Neural Networks: Vol. I*, (pp. 53–60). San Diego: IEEE.

Wong, A. (1988). Recognition of general patterns using neural networks, *Biological Cybernetics, 58*, 361–372.

Wong, Y., Banik, J. & Bower, J. (1988). Neural networks for template matching: Application to real-time classification of real neurons, In D. Anderson (Ed.), *Proceedings of the 1987 IEEE Conference on Neural Information Processing Systems — Natural and Synthetic,* (pp. 103–113). New York: American Institute of Physics.

Works, G. (1988). The creation of Delta: A new concept in ANS programming, *Proceedings of the IEEE International Conference on Neural Networks: Vol. II,* (pp. 159–164). San Diego: IEEE.

Wright, W. (1988). Contextual image segmentation with a neural network, *Neural Networks Supplement: INNS Abstracts, 1,* 531.

Wyatt, J. & Standley, D. (1988). A method for the design of stable lateral inhibition networks that are robust in the presence of circuit parasites, In D. Anderson (Ed.), *Proceedings of the 1987 IEEE Conference on Neural Information Processing Systems — Natural and Synthetic,* (pp. 860–867). New York: American Institute of Physics.

Xu, X., Tsai, W. & Huang, N. (1988a). Information capacity of McCulloch-Pitts model, *Neural Networks Supplement: INNS Abstracts, 1,* 149.

Xu, X., Tsai, W. & Huang, N. (1988b). A generalized neural network model, *Neural Networks Supplement: INNS Abstracts, 1,* 150.

Yanai, H., Hayakawa, Y. & Sawada, Y. (1988). An electrical hardware neural network of an optimization-problem solver, *Neural Networks Supplement: INNS Abstracts, 1,* 475.

Yang, H. & Guest, C. (1987). Performance of backpropagation for rotation invariant pattern recognition, *Proceedings of the IEEE First International Conference on Neural Networks: Vol. IV,* (pp. 365–370). San Diego: IEEE.

Yeates, M. (1988). Neural-like architectures can implement complex signal processing algorithms, *Neural Networks Supplement: INNS Abstracts, 1,* 476.

Yeung, D. & Bekey, G. (1988). Game-theoretic interaction among stochastic learning networks for adaptive load balancing, *Neural Networks Supplement: INNS Abstracts, 1,* 368.

Yovitz, M. & Cameron, S. (1960). *Self-Organizing Systems,* New York: Pergamon Press.

Yovitz, M., Jacobi, G. & Goldstein, G. (1962). *Self-Organizing Systems,* Washington: Spartan Books.

Yu, W. & Teh, H-H. (1988). An error-tolerant environment of multilayer perceptrons with controlled learning, *Neural Networks Supplement: INNS Abstracts, 1,* 323.

Zador, T., Gindi, G., Mjolsness, E. & Anandan, P. (1988). Neural network for model based recognition: Simulation results, *Neural Networks Supplement: INNS Abstracts, 1,* 532.

Zhang, W., Bezdek, J. & Pettus, R. (1988). NPN relations and cognitive map development, *Proceedings of the International Symposium on Methodologies for Intelligent Systems,* (pp. 271–281). Charlotte, NC, October 13–17.

Zhang, W. & Chen, S. (1988). A logical calculus for cognitive maps, *Proceedings of the IEEE International Conference on Neural Networks: Vol. I,* (pp. 231–238). San Diego: IEEE.

Zhao, Y. & Mendel, J. (1988). An artificial neural minimum-variance estimator, *Proceedings of the IEEE International Conference on Neural Networks: Vol. II,* (pp. 499–506). San Diego: IEEE.

Zhou, Y., Chellappa, R. & Jenkins, B. (1987). A novel approach to image restoration based on a neural network, *Proceedings of the IEEE First International Conference on Neural Networks: Vol. IV,* (pp. 269–276). San Diego: IEEE.

Zhou, Y. & Chellappa, R. (1988a). Computation of optical flow using a neural network, *Proceedings of the IEEE International Conference on Neural Networks: Vol. II,* (pp. 71–78). San Diego: IEEE.

Zhou, Y. & Chellappa, R. (1988b). A neural network approach to computation of optical flow, *Neural Networks Supplement: INNS Abstracts, 1,* 532.

Zhou, Y., Chellappa, R., Vaid, A. & Jenkins, B. (1988). Image restoration using a neural network, *IEEE Transactions on Acoustics, Speech and Signal Processing, ASSP-36,* 1141–1151.

Zipser, D. (1983a). The representation of location, University of California at San Diego, Institute for Cognitive Science Technical Report 8301.

Zipser, D. (1983b). The representation of maps, University of California at San Diego, Institute for Cognitive Science Technical Report 8304.

Zipser, D. (1984a). A computational model of hippocampus place-fields, University of California at San Diego, Institute for Cognitive Science Technical Report 8405.

Zipser, D. (1984b). A theoretical model of hippocampal learning during classical conditioning, University of California at San Diego, Institute for Cognitive Science Technical Report 8408.

Zipser, D. (1985). A computational model of hippocampal place fields, *Behavioral Neuroscience, 99,* 1006–1018.

Zipser, D. (1986). Programming neural nets to do spatial computations, University of California at San Diego Institute for Cognitive Science Technical Report 8608.

Zmuda, J. (1988). Target recognition using adaptive resonance neural networks, *Neural Networks Supplement: INNS Abstracts, 1,* 478.

# Author Index

# Subject Index

# Applications Index

# Implementations Index

# About the Author

*Patrick K. Simpson* (B.A., Computer Science, University of California at San Diego) is the principal investigator of the neural networks internal research and development project at General Dynamics Electronics Division, specializing in the application of neural networks, fuzzy logic, and artificial intelligence to difficult defense-related problems. Mr. Simpson teaches neural network courses at the University of California at San Diego Extension. He was the Tutorial Chair at the 1988 IEEE International Conference on Neural Networks, has been appointed to the IEEE TAB Neural Network Committee, and is the Local Arrangements Chair of the 1990 International Joint Conference on Neural Networks. Mr. Simpson has published several papers on topics that include associative memory systems, online learning spatiotemporal pattern classifiers, high-ordered heterocorrelation associative memories, Hebbian learning law variants, and the application of neural networks to battlefield surveillance, EW/ECM, and diagnostics.